ONE NIGHT WILDERNESS

PORTLAND

Top Backcountry Getaways Within Three Hours of the City

Becky Ohlsen
& Douglas Lorain

2nd Edition

WILDERNESS PRESS . . . ***on the trail since 1967***

One Night Wilderness: Portland: Top Backcountry Getaways Within Three Hours of the City

Published by Wilderness Press
Distributed by Publishers Group West
Printed in the United States of America
Second edition, first printing

Cataloging-in-Publication Data is available from the Library of Congress.

ISBN 978-0-89997-894-9 (pbk.); ISBN 978-0-89997-895-6 (ebook)

Photos: © 2020 by Becky Ohlsen, unless otherwise noted
Cartography: Scott McGrew and Douglas Lorain
Cover design: Scott McGrew
Interior design: Monica Ahlman
Project editor: Holly Cross
Copy editor: Kate Johnson
Proofreader: Emily Beaumont
Indexer: Rich Carlson

Cover photos: Front: Snowgrass Flat Loop (Trip 11, page 49); *back:* Lower Deschutes River Canyon (Trip 31, page 115); both © 2020 by Becky Ohlsen

WILDERNESS PRESS
An imprint of AdventureKEEN
2204 First Ave. S., Ste. 102
Birmingham, AL 35233
888-443-7227, fax 205-326-1012

Visit wildernesspress.com for a complete listing of our books and for ordering information. Contact us at our website, at facebook.com/wildernesspress1967, or at twitter.com/wilderness1967 with questions or comments. To find out more about who we are and what we're doing, visit blog.wildernesspress.com.

Safety Notice: Although Wilderness Press and the authors have made every attempt to ensure that the information in this book is accurate at press time, they are not responsible for any loss, damage, injury, or inconvenience that may occur to anyone while using this book. You are responsible for your own safety and health while in the wilderness. The fact that a trail is described in this book does not mean that it will be safe for you. Be aware that trail conditions can change from day to day. Always check local conditions, know your own limitations, and consult a map.

"Thousands of tired, nerve-shaken, over-civilized people are beginning to find out that going to the mountains is going home; that wildness is a necessity; and that mountain parks and reservations are useful not only as fountains of timber and irrigating rivers, but as fountains of life."

—*John Muir,* Our National Parks *(1901)*

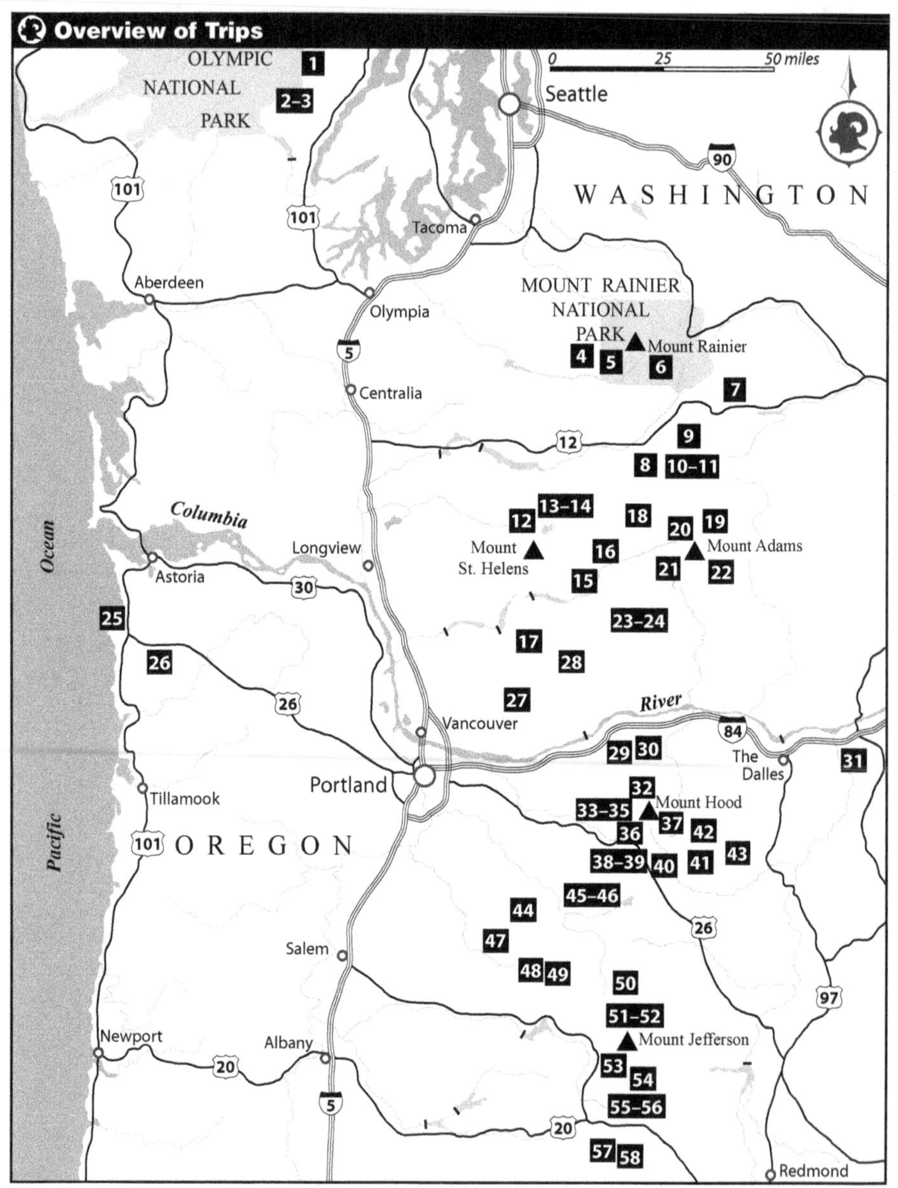
Overview of Trips
OLYMPIC NATIONAL PARK
1
2–3
0
25
50 miles
Seattle
90
WASHINGTON
101
101
Tacoma
Aberdeen
Olympia
5
MOUNT RAINIER NATIONAL PARK
Mount Rainier
4
5
6
7
Centralia
12
9
8
10–11
Columbia
13–14
12
18
20
19
Mount St. Helens
16
Mount Adams
Longview
21
22
Astoria
30
15
Ocean
25
23–24
26
17
28
26
27
River
Vancouver
84
29
30
The Dalles
31
Portland
32
33–35
Mount Hood
37
42
Tillamook
36
Pacific
101
OREGON
38–39
40
41
43
45–46
44
26
47
Salem
48
49
50
97
51–52
Newport
Albany
Mount Jefferson
20
53
54
5
55–56
20
57
58
Redmond

Contents

Acknowledgments

First and foremost, I want to thank Douglas Lorain for putting together the first edition of this book, and the editors at Wilderness Press for commissioning me to update it. Working on *One Night Wilderness: Portland* was probably the most fun I've ever had researching an outdoors guidebook. As always, the editorial, production, and marketing teams at AdventureKEEN do a fantastic job of bringing these books into the world and making sure that people know about them.

Thanks also to my parents for taking us kids on backpacking trips at a very young age, and to all the friends since then who've accompanied me on various wilderness adventures (shout-outs to Paul, Maureen, and Molly). And thanks to everyone who works in the outdoors industry, from my fellow guidebook authors to the volunteers who build and maintain trails, the parks employees and forest rangers who share updates and information online or in person, and the many bloggers and backpackers who post trip reports—a great way to gather intel on trail status and (especially) road conditions before setting out on a hike.

—*Becky Ohlsen*

Preface

Fortune has smiled on outdoors lovers in the Portland metropolitan area. Within a short drive of their homes, hikers face an almost unbelievable array of options. They can choose to walk through massive old-growth forests or to visit any of several hundred waterfalls. They can climb across massive glaciers or traipse through wildflower-covered mountain meadows. They can beachcomb on surf-pounded sand or explore semidesert canyonlands filled with the aroma of sagebrush. Only one or two other cities in the country can boast such a wide assortment of opportunities so close at hand.

Most of these wonders are accessible to day hikers. But as thousands of walkers have discovered over the years, to appreciate fully the charms and wonders of the wilderness, nothing compares to packing in your gear and spending the night. The outdoor experience is infinitely richer, more exhilarating, and certainly more memorable if you extend your stay, enjoying a place where the stars outshine the streetlights; where the hooting of owls and the howling of coyotes replace the honking of horns and the wail of sirens; and where crowded cityscapes, although closer than you'd think, seem to be a million miles away.

This book is designed for two groups of people: those who already know the pleasures and rejuvenating qualities of spending a night in the wilderness and those who hope to join that club. The goal is to provide a guide to the best one-night (and a few two-night) hikes within a 3-hour drive of Portland. There are trips here for all ability levels, from short and easy strolls suitable for backpackers of any age to extended trips of 20 miles or more that will test even the fittest hiker. What they all have in common is a proximity to Portland, terrific scenery, and inviting campsites.

As any hiker knows, nature and our pathways into it are ever-changing; wildfires reshape whole forests and open up views, floods and landslides obliterate long-established routes, and roads and trails constantly change as new routes are built and old trails are abandoned. Your comments on recent developments or changes for future editions are always welcome. Please write to Wilderness Press at info@wildernesspress.com or directly to me at bohlsen@gmail.com.

—*B. O.*

Summary of Featured Trips

EASY HIKES	Scenery (1–10)	Difficulty (1–10)	Solitude (1–10)	Total Length (Miles)	Elevation Gain (feet)	Trail Use
1 Duckabush River Trail (first camp)	5	2	6	4.4	900	kids
3 Lower Lena Lake	6	4	2	6.2	1,350	kids
8 Cispus Point	7	4	9	5.6	1,400	kids, dogs
9 Packwood Lake	6	3	2	9	300	kids
15 Lewis River Trail	5	2	6	5.2	200	kids, dogs
16 Quartz Creek	5	3	8	9.2	750	kids, dogs
17 Siouxon Creek	7	2	4	7.6	700	kids, dogs
23 Lemei and Blue Lakes Loop	7	4	5	12.3	1,800	kids, dogs
25 Tillamook Head (south)	6	4	4	3	820	
26 Soapstone Lake	5	1	9	2.4	250	kids, dogs
28 Soda Peaks Lake	6	5	7	4.6	1,300	kids, dogs
30 Bear Lake	6	2	6	2.6	480	kids, dogs
30 North Lake	6	1	6	1.6	190	kids, dogs
31 Lower Deschutes River Canyon	7	4	4	7.3	820	kids, dogs
33 Ramona Falls	6	4	5	7	1,100	kids, dogs
37 Elk Meadows	7	4	5	6	1,250	kids, dogs
38 Salmon River Trail (lower)	6	1	6	4	250	kids, dogs
39 Veda Lake	5	3	8	2.8	750	kids, dogs
40 Lower Twin Lake	5	2	3	4	700	kids, dogs
41 Boulder Lake	6	1	7	0.6	200	kids, dogs
43 Badger Creek	5	2	7	5.8	450	kids, dogs
45 Shining Lake	7	3	7	8.8	800	kids, dogs
46 Shellrock Lake	7	1	4	1.4	200	kids, dogs
48 Pansy Lake	6	1	5	2.2	400	kids
50 Olallie Lake Scenic Area Loop	7	3	5	9.1	1,200	kids, dogs
51 Firecamp Lakes	6	2	4	2.4	640	kids, dogs
53 Pamelia Lake	6	3	3	4.4	800	kids, dogs
54 Carl Lake	7	4	5	9.8	1,000	dogs
55 Duffy Lake	8	3	5	7	800	kids, dogs
MODERATE HIKES	**Scenery (1–10)**	**Difficulty (1–10)**	**Solitude (1–10)**	**Total Length (Miles)**	**Elevation Gain (feet)**	**Trail Use**
1 Duckabush River Trail (last camp)	5	6	6	13.4	2,800	
4 Goat Lake and Gobblers Knob	8	6	6	9	2,850	dogs
7 Dumbbell and Sand Lakes Loop	6	6	6	11.3	1,550	kids, dogs
10 Heart Lake	8	7	6	13.4	2,400	dogs
11 Snowgrass Flat Loop	10	7	1	14.3	3,000	
12 Dome Camp	9	6	3	14.2	1,950	
14 Mount Margaret Backcountry Lakes	8	6	4	15.8	3,100	
19 Foggy Flat	8	7	5	13.5	1,300	dogs
20 High Camp and Killen Creek	9	6	4	8.4	2,350	kids, dogs
21 Horseshoe Meadow	7	6	7	14	1,400	dogs
24 Lake Wapiki	7	6	6	9.6	2,500	kids, dogs
25 Tillamook Head (north)	6	5	4	8.8	1,200	
27 Silver Star Mountain	8	7	6	12.5	2,600	kids, dogs
29 Herman Creek Trail (Cedar Swamp)	6	5	7	14.6	2,850	kids, dogs

MODERATE HIKES *(continued)*	Scenery (1-10)	Difficulty (1-10)	Solitude (1-10)	Total Length (Miles)	Elevation Gain (feet)	Trail Use
30 Warren Lake	6	6	6	6.8	2,100	dogs
32 Cairn Basin	10	7	4	8.4	2,000	dogs
34 Burnt Lake	7	5	3	5.4	1,500	dogs
35 Cast Lake and Zigzag Mountain Loop	7	6	6	10.6	2,600	dogs
36 Paradise Park	7	6	3	10.1	2,100	dogs
37 Elk Meadows Loop	7	7	5	13.1	2,700	dogs
38 Salmon River Trail (full trail)	6	6	6	14.3	2,700	dogs
40 Twin Lakes Loop	5	5	3	9	1,500	kids, dogs
42 Lookout Mountain and Oval Lake	7	7	6	6.4	2,050	dogs
44 High Lake	6	7	9	6.6	2,300	
46 Serene Lake Loop	7	6	4	12	2,050	kids
48 Twin Lakes	6	6	5	13.8	2,950	
49 Big Slide Lake	7	5	7	10.8	2,325	dogs
52 Jefferson Park (west)	10	5	2	11.8	1,900	
54 Carl Lake Loop	7	6	5	15.6	1,900	dogs
55 Santiam Lake	8	5	5	9.6	1,200	kids, dogs
57 Washington Ponds	7	5	7	12	1,150	dogs
58 Cache Creek	7	5	9	5.5	900	dogs

DIFFICULT HIKES	Scenery (1-10)	Difficulty (1-10)	Solitude (1-10)	Total Length (Miles)	Elevation Gain (feet)	Trail Use
2 Lake of the Angels	8	8	7	7.4	3,400	
3 Upper Lena Lake	9	8	2	14.4	3,900	
5 Indian Henry's Hunting Ground and Pyramid Park	9	9	5	18	4,900	
6 Indian Bar and Cowlitz Park	9	8	2	15	4,000	
9 Coyote Ridge Loop	8	9	8	25.4	4,350	
13 Goat Mountain and Green River Loop	7	8	8	17.9	3,700	
18 Dark Meadow via Jumbo Peak	8	8	8	14	3,100	dogs
19 Avalanche Valley	10	10	5	24.4	4,800	
21 Crystal Lake	7	8	7	20	1,900	dogs
22 Sunrise Camp	9	8	5	8	2,650	
29 Herman Creek Trail (Mud Lake)	6	8	7	19	3,700	dogs
32 Elk Cove	10	8	4	13.6	2,450	dogs
33 Yocum Ridge	9	9	5	18.6	4,500	
47 Pechuck Lookout	6	8	8	7.2	2,200	
52 Jefferson Park (north)	10	8	2	13	2,700	
53 Shale Lake Loop	8	8	3	17.7	3,000	dogs
56 Three Fingered Jack Loop	9	8	5	20.5	3,300	
57 George Lake	7	8	7	17.5	1,600	dogs

Introduction

It's a busy world out there. Ask anyone you meet how they're doing, and chances are that's what they'll say: "Busy!" Little old Portland is growing and changing; the pace of life here is not as mellow as it used to be. Despite being surrounded by natural wonders, most of us spend our days looking at screens, checking tweets and emails around the clock, and then when it's finally time to relax, we're too tired to do much more than sink into the couch and stare at another screen.

Which makes escaping into nature more important than ever. There's a good reason "forest bathing" has become a trend, even if many of us roll our eyes at the term. Studies have shown that just 5 minutes in nature can transform your body and mind, making you more relaxed, more creative, smarter, and happier overall. It's good for the brain, it's good for the soul, and it's even good for our social media profiles, in the long run. We know we need it.

But it can be hard to find the time to get away. That's the beauty of this book: you don't have to find much time at all. A single overnight excursion into the backcountry can have a huge impact, and these trips are all within a few hours' drive of the city. Some are ideal for getting short blasts of nature, a quick booster shot. They involve hikes of just a mile or two, which means you could conceivably pack up on a Friday after work, hustle out to the trailhead, and be sipping hot cocoa and gazing at stars that same night. Imagine waking up on Saturday morning, peeking through the tent flap at mist on a lake, and sipping your morning coffee from a sleeping bag—with no laptop in sight.

And if a quick, one-night trip is good, a longer trip is even better. I say this from experience: nothing realigns your perspective quite like scrambling up the rocky side of a valley scooped out by glaciers and cresting the rim to see glittering Mount Adams, right there, almost close enough to touch. Add to that a picnic lunch beside an iridescent turquoise lake, a campsite that feels like some kind of hover pad floating in a cloud city, and a gentle stroll the next day through some of the most enchanting alpine valleys in the Pacific Northwest. Stress? What stress? You can find all this, by the way, on the Snowgrass Flat Loop hike (page 49).

You could do many of these trips as day hikes, especially if you get to the trailhead early in the day. But there's something about spending the night—maybe because carrying everything you need makes you feel tough and self-reliant—that adds immeasurably to the experience. The Portland area is rich with writers who love the outdoors, so there are dozens of excellent guides to day hikes in the area. There are also several good volumes on extended backpacking trips, the kind you plan and prepare for months to pull off. I've been lucky enough to work on one of those guides too. But this book strikes the perfect balance between the two: a hand-picked range of accessible hikes, often kid-friendly and requiring minimal time commitment, that also gives you backpacker-friendly details like where to find the best campsites and water sources, what permits and regulations apply, and the best way to get to the trailhead.

It's true we're all busy—but there's a good reason we live in this fantastic place, where the outdoors is so easily within reach. I hope you'll take time to enjoy it, and if you're so inclined, send me a note about your trip at bohlsen@gmail.com.

Epic views like this one of Mount Hood, from Trip 42, Lookout Mountain and Oval Lake (page 150), are more accessible than you might think.

Tips on Backpacking in the Pacific Northwest

Although this is more of a where-to than a how-to guide, it may be helpful, especially for those new to our area, to cover a few basic tips and ideas specific to backcountry travel in the Pacific Northwest.

GET THE RIGHT PERMITS Most national forests in our region require that a Northwest Forest Pass be displayed in the window of all vehicles parked within 0.25 mile of any major, developed trailhead. Isolated trailheads with minimal or no facilities are generally exempt. In 2019 daily permits were $5 and an annual pass was $30. The annual passes are available at ranger stations and at many local sporting goods stores, or they can be purchased online at discovernw.org (click on "Store").

CHECK THE SNOWPACK The winter snowpack has a significant effect, not only on when a trail opens, but also on wildflower blooming times, peak stream flows, and how long seasonal water sources will be available. It's a good idea to check the snowpack on or about April 1 (the usual seasonal maximum), and make a note of how it compares to normal. This information is available online at nrcs .usda.gov (click on "State Websites" and navigate to Oregon or Washington). If the snowpack is significantly above or below average, adjust the trip's seasonal recommendations accordingly.

WATCH OUT FOR LOGGING TRUCKS When driving on forest roads in our area, keep an eye out for logging trucks, especially on weekdays. These scary behemoths often barrel along with little regard for those annoying speed bumps known as passenger cars.

CHECK TRAIL CONDITIONS The Northwest's frequently severe winter storms create annual problems for trail crews. Occasionally trails are washed out for years, but at a minimum, early-season hikers should expect to crawl over deadfall and search for routes around slides and flooded riverside trails. Depending on current funding and the trail's popularity, maintenance may not be completed until several weeks after a trail is snow-free and officially open. Unfortunately, this means that trail maintenance is often done well after the optimal time to visit. On the positive side, trails are usually less crowded before the maintenance has been completed.

LEAF IT, DON'T LEAVE IT For environmentally conscious backpackers, one good solution to the old problem of how to dispose of toilet paper is to find a natural alternative. Two excellent options are the large, soft leaves of thimbleberry at lower elevations, and the light-green lichen that hangs from trees at higher elevations. They're not exactly Charmin soft, but they get the job done.

WARN HUNTERS YOU'RE NOT A DEER General deer-hunting season in Oregon and Washington runs from late September to early November. For safety, anyone planning to travel on national or state forest land during these periods (particularly those doing any cross-country travel) should carry and wear a bright red or orange cap, vest, pack, or other conspicuous article of clothing. Hunting is generally not allowed in state or national parks (apart from some very limited and specific exceptions for waterfowl), so this precaution does not apply to those areas.

YOU'RE NOT AN ELK, EITHER Along the same lines as the above, elk-hunting season is generally held in late October or early November. The exact season varies in different parts of each state.

BE CAREFUL WITH FUNGI Mushrooms are a Northwest backcountry delicacy. Although our damp climate makes it possible to find mushrooms in any season, late August–November is usually best. Where and when the mushrooms can be found varies with elevation, precipitation, and other factors. In some places, you're not allowed to take anything out of the forest without a permit; if you do find any fungi, be sure it's OK to collect them for personal use. Also make absolutely sure that you know your fungi. There are several poisonous species of mushrooms in our forests, and every year people become ill or even die when they make a mistake in identification.

BRING THE BEATER Sadly, car break-ins and vandalism are regular occurrences at trailheads. This is especially true at popular trailheads and a particular problem for backpackers who leave their vehicles unattended overnight. Thus, hikers need to take reasonable precautions. Do not encourage the criminals by providing unnecessary temptation. Preferably, leave the new car at home and drive to the trailhead in an older vehicle. Even more important, leave nothing of value inside, especially not in plain sight.

Safety

While backpacking is not an inherently dangerous sport, there are certain risks you take anytime you venture away from the comforts of civilization. The trips in this book go through remote wilderness terrain. In an emergency, medical supplies and facilities will not be immediately available. The fact that a hike is

Spectacular scenery makes the Snowgrass Flat Loop (Trip 11, page 49) extremely popular.

described in this book does not guarantee that it will be safe for you. Hikers must be properly equipped and in adequate physical condition to handle a given trail. Because trail conditions, weather, and hiker ability all vary considerably, the author and the publisher cannot assume responsibility for anyone's safety. Use plenty of common sense and a realistic appraisal of your abilities, and you will be able to enjoy these trips safely.

The following section outlines the common hazards encountered in the Portland area outdoors and discusses how to approach them.

Plant Hazards

POISON OAK If you recognize only one plant in the Pacific Northwest, it should probably be this one, which grows as a low-lying shrub or bush. Its glossy, oaklike leaves grow in clusters of three and turn bright red in the fall before dropping off in the winter. The leaves and stems contain an oil (urushiol) that causes a strong allergic reaction in most people, creating a long-lived, maddeningly itchy rash where the oil contacts the skin. Wash skin thoroughly with soap and water as soon as possible, and clean any clothing and pets that may have come into contact with the plant as well.

Photo by Jane Huber

poison oak

Animal Hazards

BEARS Black bears are found throughout Oregon and Washington. If you encounter one, stay calm, avoid eye contact, and back away slowly. In areas known to have bears, use the food storage boxes provided at campgrounds, and carry your food and any other scented items in bear canisters.

MOUNTAIN LIONS Although these large felines are still rarely seen and pose minimal threat, reported sightings in Oregon and Washington have recently increased as population growth has caused cougar habitat to shift gradually into more urban areas. In 2018 a cougar was suspected of having killed a hiker on Mount Hood, marking the first-ever fatal mountain lion attack in Oregon history. If you do encounter an aggressive mountain lion, stay calm, maintain eye contact, make yourself look as large as possible, and do not run away. If you have children with you, pick them up.

RACCOONS AND MICE While not a threat to humans, these scavengers have learned that campgrounds and trail camps are prime locations for free meals. They are a major hazard for food supplies. Never leave your food unattended, and always store it somewhere safe at night—ideally hanging in a critter-proof bag from a nearby tree. Food lockers are provided at many trail camps.

RATTLESNAKES Common in high-desert environments, these venomous creatures like to bask on hot rocks in the sun and typically begin to emerge from winter hibernation as temperatures warm in spring. They usually flee at the first sight of people and will attack only if threatened. Be wary when hiking off-trail, and don't put your hands where you can't see them when scrambling on rocky slopes. Rattlesnake bites are rarely fatal. If you are bitten, the goal is to reduce the rate at which the poison circulates through your body: Try to remain calm, keep the bite site below the level of your heart, remove any constricting items (rings, watches) from the soon-to-be-swollen extremity, and do not apply ice or chemical cold to the bite, as this can cause further damage to the surrounding tissue. Seek medical attention as quickly as possible.

Northern Pacific rattlesnake

Photo by Jane Huber

TICKS These parasites are common in areas of scrub oak (such as along the Columbia River Gorge and the Rogue River in Oregon) and the forests of western Washington, especially during early spring. Always perform regular body checks when hiking through tick country. If you find a tick attached to you, do not try to pull it out with your fingers or to pinch the body; doing so can increase the risk of infection. Using tweezers, gently pull the tick out by lifting upward from the base of the body where it is attached to your skin. Pull straight out until the tick releases, and do not twist or jerk, as this may break off the mouthparts under your skin. Treat any tick bite by washing the area with soap and water, disinfecting it, and keeping it clean to prevent infection.

Ticks are known for transmitting Lyme disease, but cases of Lyme in Oregon and Washington are relatively uncommon. Even if you are bitten, an infected tick must be attached for 24 hours to transmit the disease. Lyme disease can be life-threatening if not diagnosed in its early phases. Common early symptoms include fatigue, chills and fever, headache, muscle and joint pain, swollen lymph nodes, and a blotchy skin rash that clears centrally to produce a characteristic bull's-eye shape 3–30 days after exposure. If you fear that you have been exposed to Lyme disease, consult a doctor immediately.

Physical Dangers

GIARDIA *Giardia lamblia* is a microscopic organism found in many backcountry water sources. Existing as a dormant cyst while in the water, it develops in the gastrointestinal tract upon consumption and can cause diarrhea, excessive flatulence, foul-smelling excrement, nausea, fatigue, and abdominal cramps. All water taken from the backcountry, even if it looks perfectly clear, should be purified with a filter, with a chemical treatment, or by boiling it for 3 minutes.

HEATSTROKE Heatstroke (hyperthermia) occurs when the body is unable to control its internal temperature and overheats. Usually brought on by excessive exposure to the sun and accompanying dehydration, symptoms include cramping, headache, and mental confusion. Treatment entails rapid, aggressive cooling of the body through whatever means available—cooling the head and torso is most important. Stay hydrated and have some type of sun protection for your head if you expect to travel along a hot, exposed section of trail.

HYPOTHERMIA The opposite of heatstroke, this life-threatening condition occurs when the body is unable to stay adequately warm and its core temperature begins to drop. Initial symptoms include uncontrollable shivering, mental confusion, slurred speech, and weakness. Cold, wet weather poses the greatest hazard as wet clothes conduct heat away from the body much faster than dry layers. Fatigue reduces the body's ability to produce its own heat, and wind poses an increased risk as it can quickly strip away warmth. Immediate treatment is critical. Raise the body's core temperature as fast as possible. Get out of the wind, take off wet clothes, drink warm beverages, eat simple energy foods, and take shelter in a warm tent or sleeping bag. Do not drink alcohol, as this dilates the blood vessels and causes increased heat loss.

Taking Precautions

LEAVE AN ITINERARY Always tell someone where you are hiking and when you expect to return. Friends, family, rangers, and visitor centers are all valuable resources that can save you from a backcountry disaster if you fail to reappear on time.

KNOW YOUR LIMITS Don't undertake a hike that exceeds your physical fitness or outdoor abilities.

AVOID HIKING ALONE A hiking partner can provide the buffer between life and death in the event of a serious backcountry mishap.

BRING THE RIGHT GEAR Packing the proper equipment, especially survival and first aid supplies, increases your margin of safety.

The 10 Essentials

Except when hiking on gentle trails in city parks, hikers should always carry a pack with certain essential items. The standard "10 Essentials" have evolved from a list of individual items to functional systems that will help keep you alive and reasonably comfortable in emergency situations:

1. Emergency shelter: a tent, a bivy sack, or an emergency blanket
2. Fire: a candle or other firestarter and matches in a waterproof container
3. First aid supplies
4. Hydration: extra water and a means to purify more on longer trips
5. Illumination: a flashlight or headlamp
6. Insulation: extra clothing that is both waterproof and warm, including a hat
7. Navigation: a topographic map and compass, in addition to a GPS device
8. Nutrition: enough extra food so you return with a little left over
9. Repair kit: particularly a knife for starting fires, first aid, and countless other uses
10. Sun protection: sunglasses and sunscreen, especially in the mountains

Just carrying these items, however, does not make you prepared. Unless you know things like how to apply basic first aid, how to build an emergency fire, and how to read a topographic map or use a compass, then carrying these items does you no good. These skills are all fairly simple to learn, and at least one member of your group should be familiar with each of them.

More important to your safety and enjoyment than any piece of equipment or clothing is exercising common sense. When you are far from civilization, a simple injury can be life-threatening. Don't take unnecessary chances. Never, for example, jump onto slippery rocks or logs or crawl out onto dangerously steep slopes hoping to get a better view. Fortunately, the vast majority of wilderness injuries are easily avoidable.

Advice for the First-Time Backpacker

There is something enormously liberating about spending a night in the wilderness. Many of the Pacific Northwest's most spectacular attractions are beyond the reach of a comfortable day hike, leaving them for the overnight hiker to enjoy. But there are a few things to keep in mind as you plan your first few backpacking trips.

Differences Between Backpacking and Day Hiking

Many people who regularly take day hikes assume that backpacking is just day hiking plus spending the night. Wrong! The two activities have some very important differences.

PHYSICAL DEMANDS People often assume that since they regularly go on day hikes of 10 miles or more, they can cover the same distance when carrying overnight gear. This is a fundamental error because backpacking is an activity in which gravity displays its most sinister qualities. Your hips, shoulders, feet, knees, and probably a few body parts you had not even thought about in years will feel every extra ounce.

HIKING COMPANIONS Perhaps even more important, backpacking calls for a different mental attitude. It is usually unwise, for example, to travel alone, at least on your first few trips. This advice applies even to people who regularly take solo day hikes. Most people assume that this recommendation is for safety reasons, but while there is some safety in numbers, the main reason not to go backpacking alone is mental. Human

Having good company on the trail (in this case, the Deschutes River Trail) can make your backpacking trip even more enjoyable.

beings are social animals. Most people enjoy backpacking (or any activity) much more if they have along at least one compatible companion with whom they can share the day's events and experiences. Having a hiking partner will also make your journey more comfortable because you can lighten your load by sharing the weight of community items such as a tent, cookstove, and water filter. If you don't have the sales skills to talk reluctant friends or skeptical family members into coming along, consider joining a hiking club, where you will find plenty of people with similar outdoor interests. (See Appendix C, page 217, for the names and addresses of some local organizations.)

SKILLS NEEDED Another thing that distinguishes backpacking from day hiking is that backpackers need a different set of skills. They need to know how to hang their food to keep out bears and other critters. They need to know how to select an appropriate campsite, one where breezes will keep the bugs away, where there aren't dangerous or unstable snags overhead, where the runoff from overnight rains won't create a lake beneath their tent, and a host of other variables. They need to know the optimal way to put things into their packs (where heavy items belong versus lighter ones) to carry a heavier load in the most comfortable way possible. Although the list of skills is long, they are all interesting, relatively easy to learn, and well worth the time and effort to acquire. (Turn to the recommended reading section in Appendix B, page 215, for a list of books that will help.)

IMPACT ON NATURE One final, often-overlooked difference between day hiking and backpacking is that backpackers need to be much more careful to minimize their impact on the land. All hikers should do things like pick up litter, avoid fragile vegetation, avoid cutting switchbacks, and leave wildlife alone. For backpackers, however, there are additional considerations.

Because you'll probably be doing a lot of wandering around near camp, it is crucial that you put your tent in a place that is either compacted from years of use or can easily take the impact without being damaged. A campsite on sand, on rock, or in a densely wooded area is best. Never camp on fragile meadow vegetation or immediately beside a lake or stream. If you see a campsite starting to develop in an inappropriate location, be proactive: place a few limbs or rocks over the area to discourage further use, scatter horse apples, and remove any fire-scarred rocks.

In a designated wilderness area, regulations generally require that you camp at least 100 feet from water. In places with long-established camps that are already heavily impacted, however, land managers usually prefer that you use the established site, even if it is technically too close to water, rather than trampling a new area.

CAMPFIRES Do not build campfires. Although fires were once a staple of camping and backpacking, today few areas can sustain the negative impact of fires. In many wilderness areas and national parks, fires are now officially prohibited, especially at higher elevations. For cooking, use a lightweight stove (they are more reliable, easier to use, and cleaner than fires). For warmth, try adding a layer of clothing or going for an evening stroll.

EQUIPMENT Probably the most obvious difference between day hiking and backpacking is the equipment involved. Like day hikers, all backpackers should carry the "10 Essentials" listed in the previous section. But when you are spending the night, there are numerous other items you will need to remain safe and reasonably comfortable. Important items that every backpacker should carry but that day hikers rarely need include:

- A sleeping bag or backpacking quilt (preferably filled with synthetic material, as down doesn't work as well in our wet climate)
- A tent (with a rain fly, mosquito netting, and a waterproof bottom). And don't forget to run a test by putting the thing up in the backyard first, so you aren't trying to puzzle out how it works and discovering you are three stakes short of accomplishing the task as a rainstorm starts in the backcountry. (Don't ask me how I know this—just take my word for it.)
- A water filter or other water-purification system
- A lightweight sleeping pad for comfort and insulation against the cold ground
- Fifty feet of nylon cord for hanging your food away from critters at night
- Personal hygiene items
- Insect repellent (especially in July and early August in the mountains)
- A lightweight backpacker's stove with fuel, cooking pots, and utensils if you want hot meals

Gear

FOOTWEAR The appropriate hiking footwear provides stability and support for your feet and ankles while protecting them from the abuses of the environment. A pair of lightweight hiking boots or trail-running shoes is generally adequate for most hikes, though hikers with weak ankles may want to opt for heavier, midweight hiking boots. When selecting footwear, keep in mind that the most important feature is a good fit—your toes should not hit the front while going downhill, your heel should be locked in place inside the boot to prevent friction and blisters, and there should be minimal extra space around your foot (although you should be able to wiggle your toes freely). When lacing them, leave the laces over the top of your foot (instep) loose, but tie them tightly across the ankle to lock the heel down. Break in new boots before taking them on an extended hike to minimize the chance of blisters—simply wear them around as much as possible beforehand.

SOCKS After armpits, feet are the sweatiest part of the human body—and wet feet are much more prone to blisters. Good hiking socks wick moisture away from your skin and provide padding for your feet. Avoid cotton socks as these quickly saturate, stay wet inside your shoes, and take forever to dry. Wool provides warmth and padding and, while it does absorb roughly 30 percent of its weight in water, effectively keeps your feet dry. If regular wool makes your feet itch, try softer

Middle Rock Lake, on the Shellrock and Serene Lakes Loop (Trip 46, page 163), makes a good goal for an intermediate-level backpacking trip.

merino wool. Nylon, polyester, acrylic, and polypropylene (also called olefin) are all synthetic fibers that absorb very little water, dry quickly, and add durability.

BLISTER KIT Blisters are usually caused by friction from foot movement (slippage) inside the shoe. Prevent them by buying properly fitting footwear, taking a minimum of one to two weeks to break them in, and wearing appropriate socks. If your heel is slipping and blistering, try tightening the laces across your ankle to keep the heel in place. If you notice a blister or hot spot developing, stop immediately and apply adhesive padding (such as moleskin) over the spot. Bring a lightweight pair of scissors to easily cut the moleskin.

FABRICS Avoid wearing cotton—it absorbs water quickly and takes a long time to dry, leaving a cold, wet layer next to your skin and increasing the risk of hypothermia. In hot, dry environments, however, cotton can be useful as the water it retains helps keep you cool as it evaporates. Polyester and nylon are two commonly used, and recommended, fibers in outdoor clothing. They dry almost instantly, wick moisture effectively, and are more lightweight than natural fibers. Fleece (made from polyester) provides good insulation and will keep you warm even when wet, as will wool and wool blends. Synthetic materials melt quickly, however, if placed in contact with a heat source (campstove, fire, sparks). A lightweight down vest or jacket adds considerable warmth with minimal bulk and weight, though it must be kept dry—wet down loses all of its insulating ability.

RAIN AND WIND GEAR Good raingear is crucial for hikes in the Pacific Northwest. There are three types available: waterproof and breathable, waterproof and nonbreathable, and water-resistant. Waterproof, breathable shells contain Gore-Tex or an equivalent material and effectively keep water out while allowing water vapor (i.e., sweat) to pass through. They keep you more comfortable during heavy exertions in the rain (though you will still get damp from the inside) and are generally bulky and more expensive. Waterproof, nonbreathable shells are typically made from coated nylon or a rubberlike material. They keep water out but hold all your sweat in, but they are cheap and often very lightweight. Water-resistant shells are usually lightweight nylon windbreakers coated with a water-repellent chemical. They will often keep you dry for a short time but will quickly soak through in a heavy rain. All three are good in the wind.

HATS AND GAITERS The three most important parts of the body to insulate are the torso, neck, and head. Your body will strive to keep these a constant temperature at all times. A thin balaclava or warm hat and neck gaiter are small items, weigh almost nothing, and are more effective at keeping you warm than an extra jacket. Add a lightweight pair of gloves in the spring and fall, and in alpine regions.

PACK For most people, an overnight pack with 3,000–4,000 cubic inches of capacity is generally necessary, though many ultralight hikers get away with less. The most important feature is a good fit. A properly fitting backpack allows you to carry the majority of weight on your hips and lower body, sparing the easily fatigued muscles of the shoulders and back. When trying on packs, loosen the shoulder straps, position the waist belt so that the top of your hips (the bony iliac crest) is in the middle of the belt, attach and cinch the waist belt, and then tighten the shoulder straps. The waist belt should fit snugly around your hips, with no gaps. The shoulder straps should rise slightly off your shoulders before dipping back down to attach to the pack about an inch below your shoulders—weight should not rest on top of your shoulders, and you should be able to shrug them freely. Most packs will have load-stabilizer straps that attach to the pack behind your ears and lift the shoulder straps upward, off your shoulders. A sternum strap links the two shoulder straps together across your chest and prevents them from slipping away from your body. Most packs are highly adjustable—a knowledgeable employee at an outdoor-equipment shop can be help you achieve the proper fit. Load your pack to keep its center of gravity as close to your mid- and lower back as possible. The heaviest items should go against your back, and you should pack items from heaviest to lightest outward and upward. Do not place heavy items at or below the level of the hip belt—doing so precludes the ability to carry that weight on the lower body and is one of the main reasons packs feature sleeping bag compartments in that location.

EXTRAS A length of nylon cord is useful for hanging food, stringing clotheslines, and guying out tents. A simple repair kit should include a needle, thread, and duct tape. A plastic trowel is nice for digging catholes. Insect repellent will keep the bugs away; Deet-free versions are increasingly common. A pair of sandals or running shoes for around camp is a great relief from hiking boots. A pen and waterproof notebook allow you to record outdoor epiphanies on the spot. Extra zip-top or garbage bags always come in handy. Compression stuff sacks will reduce the bulk of your sleeping bag and clothes.

Make sure your camera is ready for outdoor abuse, and keep it safe from dirt and moisture. A good protective camera bag costs much less than a new camera. A polarizing filter is good for taking outdoor pictures with lots of sky and water. Also consider a small tripod for low-light photography, binoculars, a Frisbee, and playing cards.

Reintroducing Yourself to Backpacking

Maybe it's been a while since you slept beneath the stars. If your last backpack was bright orange with an industrial-grade external frame and your sleeping bag weighed 25 pounds, you are in for a pleasant surprise. The synthetic clothing and high-tech gear described in previous sections deliver much higher performance at a much lower weight than in the old days, and more so every year. If you're not sure how much backpacking you'll want to do, try renting a pack for your first trip or two; most outdoors stores have rental models they can fit for you.

One more thing to note if you haven't backpacked recently: places that you previously visited on the spur of the moment may now require permits—to park at the trailhead, to spend the night, or even to hike the trail at all. Each hike profiled here lists any permits required; how much they cost, if anything; and where and how to get them.

The first step for anyone contemplating a backpacking trip is to get into some kind of reasonable shape. Blisters while you hike and painfully sore muscles when you return are not badges of honor; they just hurt. Therefore, some simple, regular aerobic exercise and strengthening key muscle groups (such as the calves, thighs, and shoulders) are crucial to having a good time.

Step two is to gather together all the gear you'll need. You remember—it's that pile of musty stuff in the basement that you haven't looked at in years but haven't had the heart to give away since you always told yourself you'd use it again. Pull it all out, clean it up, and check for and repair any damage, such as seams that have torn, places where mice have chewed through the shoulder straps, and tent seams that are no longer waterproof. Make sure things still fit properly (no offense, but that hip belt might need to be let out some). Finally, using the suggested gear list in the previous chapter, decide if you have everything you need and if newer versions of any of your old equipment might be significantly improved.

Introducing Your Kids to Backpacking

Even though it requires considerably more work and planning, few things in life are more gratifying or enjoyable than taking a kid backpacking. One big reason for this is that children have the unique capacity to renew your appreciation of the outdoors. No matter how commonplace and mundane things may be to you, everything is new and interesting to a child. The list of wonders includes all kinds of "little" things—mushrooms, tadpoles, fern fronds, discarded feathers—that many adults no longer appreciate or even notice. In fact, it is downright humbling to see how much a child notices, and the feeling is only slightly reduced by the realization that children possess a natural height advantage when it comes to seeing things that are close to the ground.

Although backpacking with a child may be fun for the adult, it is even better for the kid. A growing body of evidence suggests that regular contact with the outdoors is a natural antidote for attention deficit disorder, depression, and obesity and is crucial for a child's overall mental and physical development. What better way to fill that need than to take them to a place where electronic screens simply aren't an option, and where they can explore a world filled with newts and flowers, pine cones and toads, and countless other real-world wonders?

To ensure that the backpacking experience is a great one (for both young and old), here are a few tips and guidelines to keep in mind:

- When backpacking with young children, leave the teensy, ultralight, supposedly-for-two-people-but-only-if-they-are-on-their-honeymoon tent at home, and pack a nice roomy shelter.
- Don't forget that children, much more than adults, need a few comforts of home. Bringing along that favorite blankie, stuffed animal, or bedtime storybook may be essential to everyone getting a good night's sleep.
- Remember that young bodies are less tolerant of weather extremes than older ones. Precautions such as sun protection, drinking plenty of water, and bundling up for the cold, for example, are all much more important for children than adults.
- Recognize that your kids will get dirty—probably downright filthy, in fact. Live with it. Don't bother to scrub them clean every time you see them. Getting dirty usually means they are having fun.
- If your kids are too young to recognize natural dangers (poison oak, steep drop-offs, anthills, and the like) then you will need to physically block these off or designate an adult to keep watch.
- A little entertainment makes a big difference. In the evening, kids love the idea of having a headlamp, so bring along one for every member of the party. Bring simple games. Playing cards, pick-up sticks, and small board games all work well. Finally, don't forget to brush up on your storytelling. It is still the best way to spend an evening with kids in the outdoors.
- Don't forget to bring snacks—lots of 'em.
- Get the kids involved in the planning. Delegate to older kids tasks like planning the menu and checking the weather, and consider providing each kid with a printed map or a notebook for recording their impressions along the trip.

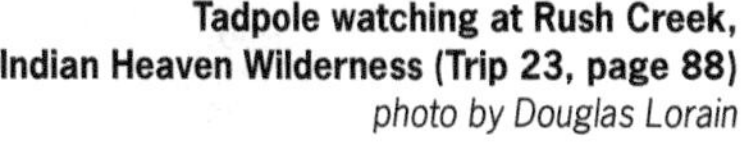

Tadpole watching at Rush Creek, Indian Heaven Wilderness (Trip 23, page 88)
photo by Douglas Lorain

- Be thoroughly familiar with child first aid, and recheck your first aid kit to ensure that it contains children's aspirin, lots of bandages (often great for psychological comfort even when the child isn't really hurt), and tweezers for removing splinters.
- Consider bringing along the child's best friend, or even that friend's whole family. It may not fit with your idea of solitude in the wilderness, but kids usually love having a playmate while exploring the outdoors.
- How much leeway and independence you give your children depends on their ages and ability to follow instructions. But even the most responsible youngsters may at times stray too far from camp when searching for huckleberries, chasing a squirrel, or engaging in some other equally distracting activity. To help combat this problem, all children should carry a whistle, preferably on a necklace, that they have been instructed to blow if (and only if) they become lost.

Your choice of backpacking location is especially crucial when traveling with young hikers. Unlike adults, children are rarely impressed by great views and invariably complain about steep climbs. (To be fair, adults often complain about steep climbs as well.) This book includes dozens of backpacking trips that are especially well suited to children. Identified both in the summary chart on pages x–xi and by icons on the first page of each individual hike, these trips are relatively short, involve less elevation gain, and include plenty of the things that youngsters love—splashing creeks, wildlife, berries, lakes to explore, and the like.

Elk Meadows (Trip 37, page 137) boasts a picture-postcard view of Mount Hood.
photo by Paul Gerald

An excellent time to schedule a backpacking trip with kids, especially into the Cascade Mountains, is late August. This is huckleberry season, when children (and adults) can stuff themselves with handfuls of the delicious berries. In fact, one measure of the success of a hike at this time of year is how purple one's fingers and tongue are by day's end. In addition, the mosquitoes are usually gone by this time, and the mountain lakes remain warm enough for a reasonably comfortable swim. Finally, your trip will take place just before kids go back to school, so they will have impressive stories to tell when the teacher asks the inevitable, "So what did *you* do this summer?"

For further information on backpacking with children, see the recommended reading in Appendix B, page 215.

How to Use This Guide

The trips in this book are broken down by geographic region, starting from the southeastern Olympic Mountains in the north and working down to the Mount Jefferson and Mount Washington area in the south.

Each individual trip begins with a quick overview of the hike's vital statistics, including scenery, solitude, and difficulty ratings, as well as distance, elevation gain, managing agency, best time to visit, and more. This allows you to rapidly narrow your options based on your preferences, your abilities, and the time of year.

Just below the trip title are numerical **RATINGS** (1–10) of the three qualities that traditionally attract or deter hikers the most: scenery, difficulty, and the degree of solitude you can expect.

The **SCENERY** rating is my opinion of the trip's overall scenic quality on a 1 (just OK) to 10 (absolutely gorgeous) scale. Of course, this rating is completely subjective: I happen to swoon over alpine meadows sprinkled with wildflowers, while you might prefer a riverside trail through deep woods. There are no bad choices; every hike in the book has beautiful scenery, it's just that some of them are so spectacular they'll make your wide-angle lens think it died and went to heaven.

The **DIFFICULTY** rating is also subjective and runs from 1 (barely leave the La-Z-Boy) to 10 (the Ironman triathlon). Keep in mind that this book is designed not necessarily for lifelong backpackers but for those of us who don't manage to get out there as often as we'd like. We might be fitter than average, but we're not in the habit of carrying all our food and shelter (and maybe our children's food and shelter) up steep and rocky mountain trails. The difficulty ratings reflect this; the few hikes rated a 1 are either nearly flat or very short, or both. Hikes rated 9 or 10 are extremely challenging (but so rewarding!). I'd prefer to have someone leave the trail thinking, "That was easier than I expected," rather than, "Good grief, if that was a 5, I'm not even going to think about trying a 9!"

Because **SOLITUDE** is one of the things backpackers are seeking, it helps to know roughly how much company you can expect. This rating is also on a 1 (bring stilts to see over the crowds) to 10 (just you and the marmots) scale. Of course, even on a hike rated 10, it is possible that you could unexpectedly run into a pack of unruly Cub Scouts, but generally this rating is pretty accurate. Note that there are trade-offs: extreme solitude usually means the trailhead is hard to reach.

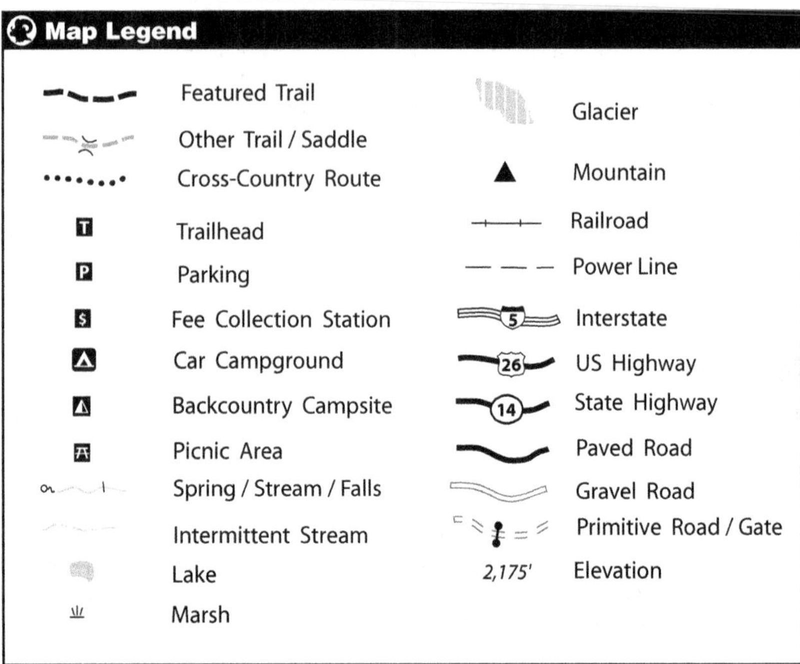

To boost your chances of camping solo in more popular, accessible areas, try to go midweek or in the shoulder seasons.

The next two lines list total **ROUND-TRIP DISTANCE** and **ELEVATION GAIN** for that trip. For many hikers, the difficulty of a trip is determined more by how far up they go than by the mileage they cover, so pay especially close attention to the second number, which includes the total of all ups and downs, not merely the net change in elevation.

Every trip includes a map that is as up-to-date and as accurate as possible. But common sense dictates that you'll also want to carry a topographic map. The **OPTIONAL MAP** entry identifies our recommended map(s) for the described trip.

Next you will find two seasonal entries. **USUALLY OPEN** tells you when a trip is typically snow-free enough for hiking (although this can vary considerably from year to year). **BEST TIME** lists the particular time of year when the trip is at its best, such as when the flowers peak, the huckleberries are ripe, or the mosquitoes have died down.

AGENCY is the local land agency responsible for the area described in the hike; these are the people to call if you need a map or want to double-check road and trail conditions before setting out.

PERMIT tells you if a permit is currently required to enter or camp in the area and how to obtain one. It notes the few instances when permits are not free or advance reservations are required, along with the necessary details. When a Northwest Forest Pass is required to park at the trailhead, this is also indicated. (If you're planning to do a lot of hiking in the area, it's worth buying the $30 annual Northwest Forest Pass to keep in your vehicle; if you're going only once or twice, you can usually buy a day pass at the parking area for $5.)

ICONS AND TRAIL USES:

 This hike is good for children.

 Pets are allowed, and the trail is both safe and suitable for dogs.

HIGHLIGHTS: This quick preview of each hike's main characteristics—epic views, ferns and fir trees, a pretty lake—should give you a sense of whether this particular trail is the kind of thing you're looking for.

GETTING THERE provides driving directions to the trailhead from Portland, including GPS coordinates for the trailhead. As you plan your trip, keep in mind that it can take 3 hours to drive 70 miles if half of those miles are on rough or winding gravel roads. Don't trust the maps app on your smartphone; allow extra time to reach out-of-the-way hikes.

In **HIKING IT,** we describe your hiking route in detail, beginning at the trailhead and on through each trail junction you'll encounter.

Get a healthy dose of moss-covered rocks along the Duckabush River Trail (Trip 1, page 20).

Southeastern Olympic Mountains

Remote enough that many Portlanders probably haven't spent much time hiking there, the Olympic Mountains nevertheless loom large in the conceptual—and actual—landscape of the Pacific Northwest. The mountains fill the center of the Olympic Peninsula, a wild extension of land in western Washington that is separated from the rest of our region by Puget Sound and its numerous tidal arms. This was one of the last areas in the Lower 48 to be explored, and to this day much of the peninsula remains wonderfully undeveloped, thanks largely to the protection provided by Olympic National Park. Although relatively low in elevation (the highest peaks are only around 7,000 feet), the mountains are remarkably "tall" because they begin practically at sea level. They are also exceptionally rugged, having been eroded into sharp ridges and deep valleys by ancient glaciers and the enormous quantities of rain that continue to fall today.

Only a small portion of the far southeastern edge of this range is close enough to Portland to make a reasonable weekend destination, but that sampling is well worthwhile and, with the exception of lush rainforests, includes all of the attributes found elsewhere in these mountains: plenty of wildflowers, abundant wildlife, lovely streams and lakes, and terrific mountain scenery.

Get a taste of the Olympic Peninsula's delights along the Duckabush River Trail (Trip 1, page 20).

1 Duckabush River Trail

RATINGS	Scenery **5** Difficulty **2–6** Solitude **6**
ROUND-TRIP DISTANCE	4.4 miles to first camp; 13.4 miles to park boundary
ELEVATION GAIN	900' to first camp; 2,800' to park boundary
OPTIONAL MAP	Green Trails, *The Brothers (No. 168)*
USUALLY OPEN	April–November
BEST TIME	Late April–June; October
AGENCY	Hood Canal Ranger District (Olympic National Forest), 360-765-2200, fs.usda.gov/recarea/olympic/recreation/recarea/?recid=47691
PERMIT	Self-issued wilderness permit required at national park boundary, 6.7 miles from trailhead; an overnight fee of $8 per person applies if camping within the national park. Northwest Forest Pass required.

Highlights

Although it features some exceptionally nice views along the way, the Duckabush River Trail is primarily a forest hike that follows one of the largest and most important rivers flowing out of the eastern Olympic Mountains. Because the trail is open for most of the year, this is a particularly good choice for a spring or fall adventure, when the higher mountains are still encased in snow.

Getting There

Drive 110 miles north of Portland on I-5 to Olympia and take Exit 104 for US 101. After 6 miles, take Exit 101 to stay on US 101, and then drive 50 miles to a junction with paved Duckabush Road near milepost 310. Turn left (west), drive 6.1 miles on pavement then gravel (with lots of potholes, but OK for passenger cars if you drive slowly) past Collins Campground and to a junction, bear right, and reach the road-end trailhead after another 0.2 mile.

GPS COORDINATES N47° 41.070' W123° 03.570'

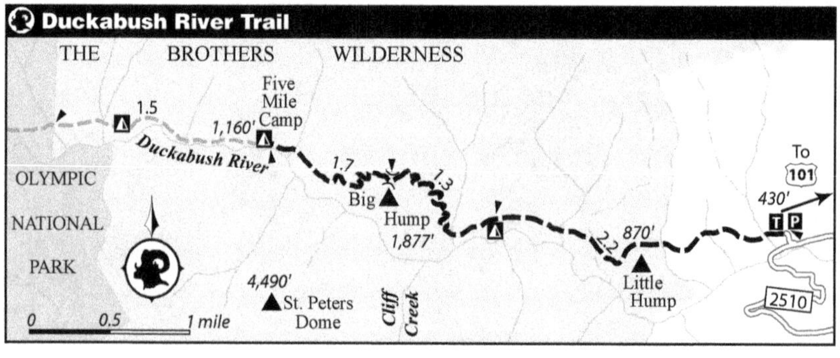

Hiking It

The gravel-strewn trail begins on a hillside well away from the river as it makes a gentle climb through a forest of Douglas firs and western hemlocks. After gaining 450 feet in 1.2 miles, the trail reaches the relatively unimpressive top of a rocky spur called Little Hump. From about the 2-mile mark, you enter an area that was burned in a 2011 fire, which started at Five Mile Camp (farther along the trail). At 2.2 miles is an excellent campsite beside the clear Duckabush River (although be somewhat cautious about camping near snags and dead trees). If you are backpacking with children, this is a good place to spend the night.

Beyond the first camp, you face the trip's biggest obstacle, a 1,000-foot climb over the top of Big Hump. This rocky mass, left behind by ancient glaciers, requires two dozen short, fairly steep, and rather tiring switchbacks to conquer. Fortunately, partway up is a perfect rest stop at an overlook with a superb view of the forested Duckabush Valley. Across the valley to the south rises prominent St. Peters Dome, whose towering sheer sides make it look as if it were transplanted from California's Yosemite Valley. Beyond this viewpoint, more uphill walking takes you past a nice but not as impressive viewpoint before you come to the top of Big Hump.

It is nearly all downhill from here as switchbacks descend 700 feet to the cascading Duckabush River just above where the water cuts a gorge around Big Hump. Not far upstream is Five Mile Camp (actually at 5.2 miles), a popular site for camping and fishing, with room for a few tents. Beyond here the trail stays in valley forests, making many small ups and downs but never straying too far from the water. There are several possible campsites along the way, but if you go beyond 6.7 miles, where the trail enters the national park, you will need a park wilderness permit (self-issued at the park entrance). The park also prohibits firearms and pets, as well as fires above 3,500 feet elevation. Hardy hikers can continue their wilderness adventure, reaching lovely Ten Mile Camp at (you guessed it) a little over 10 miles and eventually climbing to the gorgeous high meadows and lakes around Marmot Lake and O'Neil Pass. Both of these destinations are more than 20 miles into the heart of the glorious Olympic backcountry.

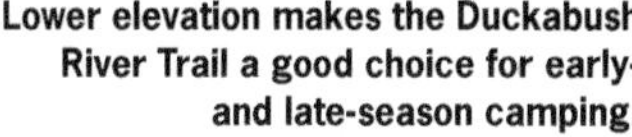

Lower elevation makes the Duckabush River Trail a good choice for early- and late-season camping.

2 Lake of the Angels

RATINGS	Scenery **8** Difficulty **8** Solitude **7**
ROUND-TRIP DISTANCE	7.4 miles
ELEVATION GAIN	3,400'
OPTIONAL MAPS	Green Trails *The Brothers (No. 168)* and *Mount Steel (No. 167)*
USUALLY OPEN	Mid-July–October
BEST TIME	Mid-July–October
AGENCY	Hood Canal Ranger District (Olympic National Forest), 360-765-2200, fs.usda.gov/recarea/olympic/recreation/recarea/?recid=47691; Olympic National Park, Wilderness Information Center, 600 E. Park Ave., Port Angeles, 360-565-3130, nps.gov/olym
PERMIT	National Park Service permit required for camping at the lake (or anywhere within Olympic National Park). You can usually get this at the second trailhead, off the old roadbed; to be safe, contact the park's wilderness information center. Permits are $8 per person per night. No fires allowed above 3,500'. *Note:* The National Park Service periodically closes this area for mountain goat management; check online ahead of time.

Highlights

Although relatively short, this is a steep and challenging hike that takes you to a wonderfully scenic little alpine lake high in the Olympic Mountains. In addition to being a great destination in itself, the lake is a fine place to set up a base camp for explorations of the surrounding mountains. Due to the steepness and exposure of this route, those who are afraid of heights should not attempt this hike. Boots with good traction are a must, especially if conditions are wet.

Getting There

Drive 110 miles north of Portland on I-5 to Olympia and take Exit 104 for US 101. After 6 miles take Exit 101 to stay on US 101, and then drive 43.8 miles to a junction with paved Hamma Hamma Road near milepost 318. Turn left (west), drive 6.5 miles to a T-junction, turn right, and then go 5.7 miles (first on pavement then good gravel) to the signed Putvin Trailhead immediately after a bridge over Boulder Creek.

GPS COORDINATES N47° 35.007' W123° 14.016'

Hiking It

The trail begins as a well-maintained path that climbs moderately steeply through a second-growth forest of western hemlocks and western red cedars. Salal, vine maple, sword fern, and Oregon grape are abundant beneath the forest canopy. On your right, generally unseen Boulder Creek cascades along in a nearly continuous waterfall. At 0.3 mile you pass the signed but easy-to-miss grave site

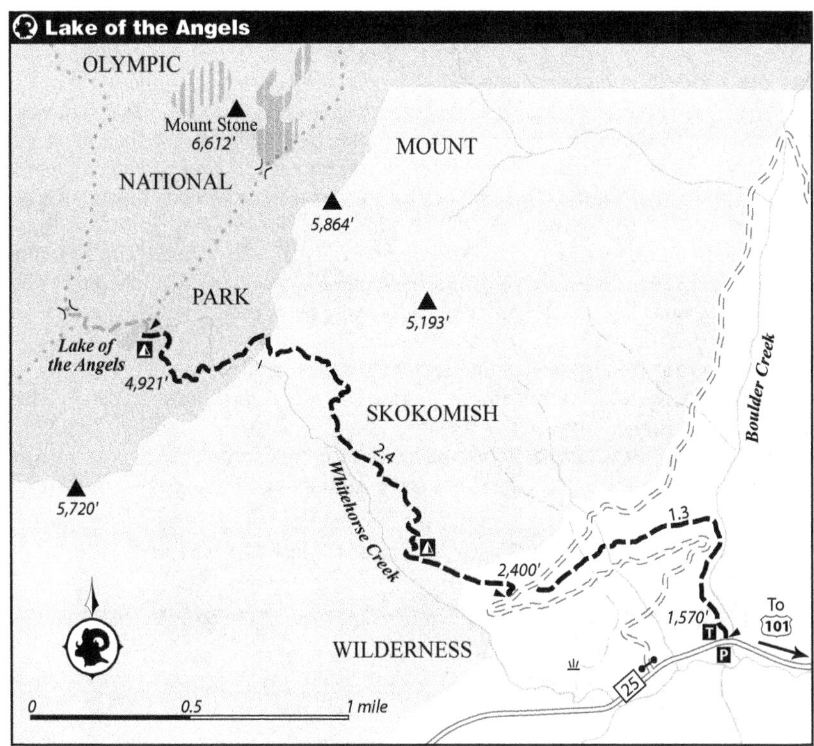

of Carl Putvin, who, the sign informs you, was a pioneer, trapper, and explorer who lived from 1892 to 1913. About 0.2 mile above this point, the trail climbs steeply around some huge moss-covered boulders before cutting left, away from the creek, and traveling at a gentler grade across a hillside. A few partial breaks in the forest here reveal tantalizing glimpses of rugged Mount Pershing to the south.

At 1 mile you cross a pair of rocky gullies where the trail is prone to washouts. In another 0.3 mile you meet a long-abandoned road (and the second trailhead mentioned above, where you can get a wilderness permit). Turn left (slightly downhill), and walk 25 yards to the resumption of the trail.

Now almost continuously steep, the trail makes a few short switchbacks and then traverses to a sign indicating your entry into the Mount Skokomish Wilderness. Shortly beyond this sign, at 1.7 miles, and just before you come to (but do not cross) tumbling Whitehorse Creek, is a mediocre campsite on the right. From here, more very steep climbing in short switchbacks leads to a relatively open avalanche chute at 2.3 miles that is choked with bracken fern, beargrass, and pearly everlasting.

Just 0.2 mile after the avalanche chute, you reach a gently sloping basin filled with an impenetrable tangle of slide alder. Directly ahead of you, at the northwest end of this basin, is a steep headwall where waterfalls cascade down from above. Lake of the Angels sits at the top of this imposing headwall. The rough trail climbs around the right side of the basin and then charges very steeply uphill, often over exposed rocks. In a couple of places you will need to grab onto rocks and roots to help pull yourself up.

Near the top of the headwall, the terrain opens up, becomes less steep, and features lots of huckleberries and good views. The trail's last 0.5 mile goes up and down, crossing a marshy meadow and several small creeks, and passing a shallow pond before depositing you on the northeast shore of Lake of the Angels. This scenic, teardrop-shaped lake is surrounded by rocky areas, meadows, and high-elevation conifers such as subalpine firs, Alaska yellow cedars, and mountain hemlocks. As always, never camp in the fragile meadows near the lake, but instead seek out places with harder surfaces away from the shore. The best views are from the south shore up to rugged Mount Stone.

Adventurous hikers can use the lake as a base camp for some fine explorations. Top goals include the views from atop the ridge to the west (accessible by an easy but unsigned boot path), the Stone Ponds (reached by a tough scramble through an obvious notch in the southeast shoulder of Mount Stone), and the top of a snow-filled gully high on the shoulder of Mount Skokomish to the southwest.

Mount Stone presides over Lake of the Angels in Olympic National Park.
photo by Douglas Lorain

3 Lena Lakes

RATINGS Scenery **9** Difficulty **4–8** Solitude **2**

ROUND-TRIP DISTANCE 6.2 miles to Lena Lake; 14.4 miles to Upper Lena Lake

ELEVATION GAIN 1,350' to Lena Lake; 3,900' to Upper Lena Lake

OPTIONAL MAP Green Trails *The Brothers (No. 168)*

USUALLY OPEN April–November for Lena Lake; July–October for Upper Lena Lake

BEST TIME Anytime it's open

AGENCY Hood Canal Ranger District (Olympic National Forest), 360-765-2200, fs.usda.gov/recarea/olympic/recreation/recarea/?recid=47691; Olympic National Park, Wilderness Information Center, 600 E. Park Ave., Port Angeles, 360-565-3130, nps.gov/olym

PERMIT National Park Service permit required for camping at Upper Lena Lake; it's a quota area, so reservations are required May–September; to request a reservation, email olym_wic_reservations@nps.gov as early as February 15. (*Note:* Olympic National Park is considering a new system for handling reservation requests, so check its website when planning your trip.) Permits are $8 per person per night; contact the park's wilderness information center for permits. Northwest Forest Pass required. No fires allowed above 3,500'.

Highlights

This trip gives you a choice: For an easier hike, follow the popular trail to attractive Lena Lake, a lower-elevation destination that is open most of the year. For more dramatic scenery, continue on a rougher trail into the high country to spectacular Upper Lena Lake, one of the most beautiful lakes in the Olympic Mountains. Hikers with children younger than teenagers should stop at Lena Lake.

Getting There

Drive 110 miles north of Portland on I-5 to Olympia and take Exit 104 for US 101. After 6 miles take Exit 101 to stay on US 101, and then drive 43.8 miles to a junction with paved Hamma Hamma Road near milepost 318. Turn left (west), drive 6.5 miles to a T-junction, turn right, and then go another 1.3 miles to the well-signed Lena Lake Trailhead.

GPS COORDINATES N47° 35.991' W123° 09.181'

Hiking It

The wide, heavily traveled, and gently graded trail soon leaves the river-bottom environment dominated by moss-draped big-leaf maples and gradually ascends a tangled forest of second-growth Douglas firs, western red cedars, and western hemlocks. The first 1.5 miles climb 14 switchbacks on a forested hillside before

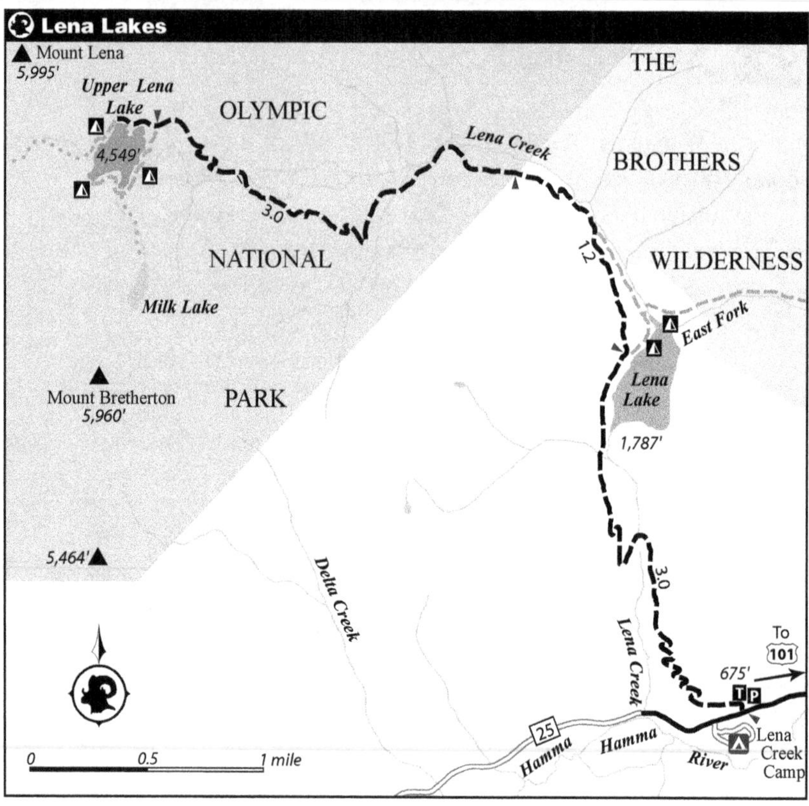

entering the lush canyon of loudly cascading Lena Creek. At 1.9 miles the trail crosses the creek on an unnecessarily large wooden bridge at a point where the stream flows underground and the creekbed is usually dry.

After the crossing, three more gentle switchbacks and a lengthy traverse lead to the south end of Lena Lake. Unfortunately, it is initially hard to get a good view of this large, deep, green-tinged lake because the trail stays on the heavily forested hillside well above the western shore. At 3 miles the trail splits. The trail to the right leads past a fine rocky viewpoint above Lena Lake before passing numerous excellent campsites on the lake's northwest and north shores. This is where hikers with children or those looking for a relatively easy hike should call it a night. Fires are allowed only in established campsites with metal fire rings.

To reach Upper Lena Lake, take the left fork (uphill) at the trail split, and follow a narrower trail that winds mostly uphill into the canyon of Lena Creek. After 0.4 mile go straight at the unsigned junction with a trail turning sharply right back toward Lena Lake. Your trail, which is rough in a few places but easy to follow, continues up the canyon and at 4.2 miles passes a sign marking your entry into Olympic National Park. Pets and weapons are prohibited beyond this point, as are fires above 3,500 feet elevation.

At 5 miles you cross a side creek on a convenient log, after which the trail gets steeper, with more roots, rocks, and mud. (You won't regret bringing a set of trekking poles.) Even with these obstacles, however, the route remains obvious and is not overly difficult. Numerous short, steep switchbacks now guide you into the high country, where forest openings provide enticing views east down the canyon of Lena Creek and up to a rugged ridge on the southwest shoulder of The Brothers. The trail makes a bridgeless crossing of Lena Creek at 6.3 miles just below a sliding waterfall, and then ascends several more short switchbacks to an open slope with views south of pyramid-shaped Mount Bretherton. Finally, at 7.2 miles, you reach a junction just above the northeast shore of Upper Lena Lake.

This gorgeous lake, which sits in the basin between Mount Lena to the north and Mount Bretherton to the south, is rimmed with forests of mountain hemlock and Alaska yellow cedar and open areas featuring an abundance of pink heather. Fires are not allowed at the lake, and hikers are required to camp in designated sites on the lake's northwest, southeast, east, and southwest shores. Composting toilets (with excellent views!) and bear wires for hanging food are provided for your convenience.

The lake is ideal for setting up camp and doing some exploring. A top goal is the rough boot path that goes west over a low pass before continuing to Scout Lake (no camping allowed) and the tiny but dramatically scenic Stone Ponds. You can also follow a scramble route to the top of Mount Lena or go south into the narrow basin containing Milk Lake.

Mount Bretherton provides a beautiful backdrop for Upper Lena Lake in Olympic National Park. *photo by Douglas Lorain*

Southern Mount Rainier and the Goat Rocks

The undisputed king of the Cascade Mountains, Mount Rainier rises 14,410 feet into the Pacific Northwest sky and is visible for hundreds of miles in every direction. The national park that surrounds the mountain is much beloved, not only by locals but also by admiring tourists from around the world. Only the southern part of the mountain is close enough for a reasonable weekend trip from Portland, but that includes some of the park's best scenery, including amazingly abundant wildflowers, enormous glaciers, stunning mountain views, plenty of wildlife, dozens of waterfalls—the list of wonders is almost endless.

Not far southeast of Mount Rainier is a less famous but just as mind-blowing mountain treasure: the Goat Rocks, the ruggedly scenic remains of an eroded volcano. The trails in both areas are justifiably popular, but with reservations in the national park and careful planning in the Goat Rocks Wilderness, it is possible to enjoy a welcome degree of solitude in your backcountry adventures. But even if you have to share it, the outstanding mountain scenery in both areas will delight you and keep you coming back time and again.

This alpine meadow sits just below Cispus Point (Trip 8, page 42) in the Goat Rocks Wilderness.

4 Goat Lake and Gobblers Knob

RATINGS	Scenery **8** Difficulty **6** Solitude **6**
ROUND-TRIP DISTANCE	6.8 miles to Goat Lake; 9 miles to Gobblers Knob
ELEVATION GAIN	1,650' to Goat Lake; 2,850' to Gobblers Knob
OPTIONAL MAP	Green Trails *Mount Rainier West (No. 269)*
USUALLY OPEN	Mid-July–October
BEST TIME	Mid-July–October
AGENCY	Cowlitz Valley Ranger District (Gifford Pinchot National Forest), 360- 497-1103, fs.usda.gov/recarea/giffordpinchot /recarea/?recid=31180; Mount Rainier National Park, nps.gov/mora
PERMIT	Wilderness permits required for all overnight camping within Mount Rainier National Park (but not at the recommended site at Goat Lake, which is outside the park); reserve permits online starting March 15. Reservation applications are $20 per party per trip (nonrefundable).

Highlights

The tiny Glacier View Wilderness, which borders the west side of Mount Rainier National Park, includes similar scenery to the park but avoids that more famous preserve's traffic jams and crowds. Long-distance hiking is limited by the small size of the wilderness, so most people who come here are day hikers. The area is large enough, however, for a wonderful one-night outing to quiet Goat Lake with access to a spectacular view of Mount Rainier from Gobblers Knob.

Getting There

From I-5, 67 miles north of Vancouver, Washington, take Exit 68 and travel 31 miles east on US 12 to a junction at the town of Morton. Turn left on WA 7 and drive 17 miles to a junction with WA 706. Turn right (east), proceed 11.1 miles to an unsigned junction near milepost 11, and turn left on gravel Forest Service Road 59. After climbing 4.3 miles, turn sharply right on Road 5920 and slowly drive 1.6 miles on this rough and rocky road to the road-end Mount Beljica/Lake Christine Trailhead.

GPS COORDINATES N46° 46.396' W121° 56.910'

Hiking It

The Lake Christine Trail starts in an ancient clear-cut now populated with 45-foot-tall Douglas and Pacific silver firs growing above a tangled mix of thimbleberry bushes, Sitka alders, fireweed, pearly everlasting, and various other shrubs, wildflowers, and grasses. The rocky path climbs very steeply 0.1 mile and then becomes more moderate when it enters uncut forest. In one switchback the intermittently steep path ascends through forest and then across a hillside choked with elderberries, bluebells, salmonberries, cow parsnip, devil's club, stinging nettle, and various other moisture-loving flowers and shrubs. At the top of the ascent, 0.8 mile from the trailhead, you arrive at the forested bowl holding tiny and rather shallow Lake Christine. Backed by a rugged, unnamed ridge to the east, this pretty little lake has nice views and features plenty of heather and other colorful wildflowers around its shore.

The trail circles to the right around the lake's south and east shores before reaching a pair of campsites just after a log bridge over the tiny inlet creek. From here the path pulls away from the lake and slowly climbs a meadowy ravine that is alive with midsummer wildflowers such as bistort, aster, wild carrot, Sitka valerian, arnica, groundsel, and pink heather. At 1.2 miles is a signed junction with a spur trail to the viewpoint atop Mount Beljica. This makes a good side trip, although better views will come later in the hike.

Go right at the junction, pass through a forested saddle, and then make a winding descent to a junction with Puyallup Trail at 1.8 miles. Turn right on this gently rolling trail as it rounds the north end of a ridge and then gradually

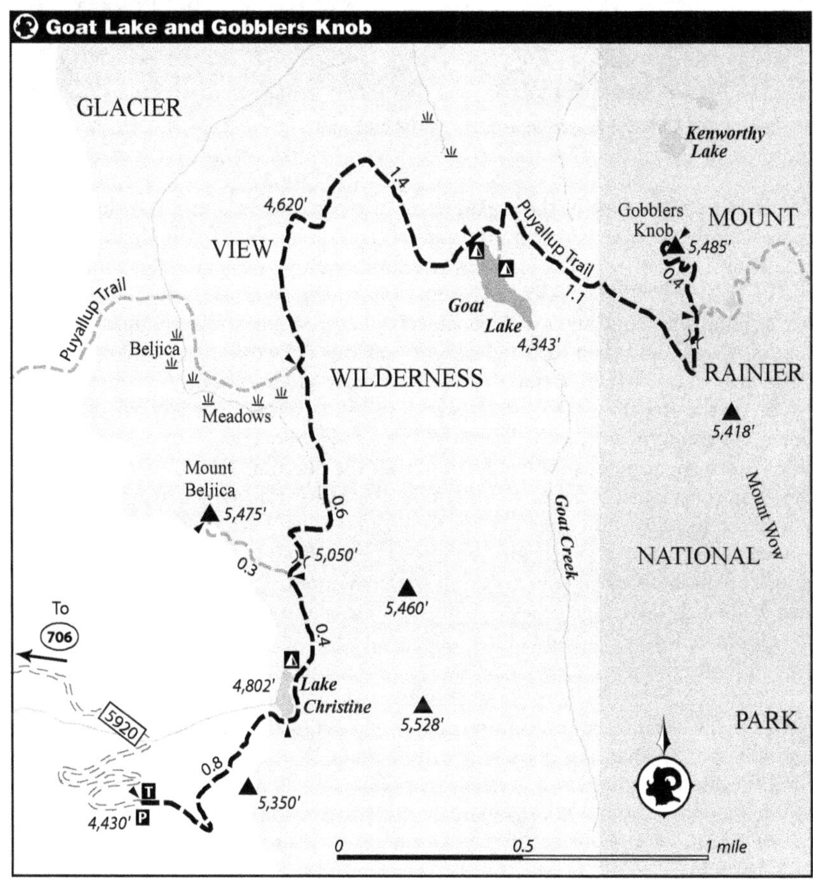

In spring Lake Christine is surrounded by colorful wildflowers. *photo by Douglas Lorain*

descends to a campsite at the northern tip of Goat Lake at 3 miles. Although not spectacularly scenic, this long and narrow lake is lovely, surrounded by stately forest with a narrow strip of grasses and flowers along the shore. The only views are of the long ridge of Mount Wow rising to the southeast. For a larger and better campsite, continue on the trail that goes east and a bit uphill from Goat Lake 0.1 mile, and then turn right on an obvious path that goes downhill about 150 yards to an attractive camp on the east shore of Goat Lake.

So far the scenery on this hike has been pleasant, but not particularly dramatic. For a big scenic payoff, set up camp at Goat Lake and spend the afternoon on a side trip to the top of Gobblers Knob. From the junction with the access trail to the camp on Goat Lake's east shore, take the main trail, which steadily ascends a forested hillside and enters Mount Rainier National Park after about 0.5 mile. Firearms, livestock, and pets are prohibited beyond this point. The trail then continues uphill, now mostly over open slopes, to a minor saddle at the top of a ridge. Just 100 yards down the other side of the ridge is a junction. Veer left (uphill) on the Gobblers Knob Trail and in 0.4 mile ascend 10 well-graded switchbacks to the staffed lookout building perched atop the rocky summit.

The views west of the route of this hike are superb, but you probably won't notice them because your attention will be drawn to the east and the breathtaking view of the towering mass of nearby Mount Rainier. Huge Tahoma Glacier tumbles down in an awesome display of white, while below that is a mantle of alpine meadows, rocky ridges, and forested valleys. This is one of the best views of the mountain anywhere. After plenty of time spent staring in awe, return the way you came.

5 Indian Henry's Hunting Ground and Pyramid Park

RATINGS Scenery **9** Difficulty **9** Solitude **5**

ROUND-TRIP DISTANCE 18 miles

ELEVATION GAIN 4,900'

OPTIONAL MAP Green Trails *Mount Rainier West (No. 269)*

USUALLY OPEN Late July–October

BEST TIME Late July–October

AGENCY Mount Rainier National Park, nps.gov/mora

PERMIT Required. All cars must also display an entry permit for the national park. Reservations are strongly advised: Mount Rainier National Park makes only 30% of its backcountry permits available on a first-come, first-serve basis. The rest are for hikers who made advance reservations. Because obtaining a permit for popular areas, especially on summer weekends, is extremely difficult, it is highly recommended that you reserve a permit in advance. Reservations are accepted starting on March 15, through the online request system only; you cannot make a reservation by phone. Cost is $20 per group and is nonrefundable. To obtain a reservation form, go to nps.gov/mora/planyourvisit/wilderness-permit.htm.

Highlights

Indian Henry's Hunting Ground is one of the most famous backcountry beauty spots in Mount Rainier National Park. This glorious meadow, with its bonanza of wildflowers, scenic ponds, and drop-dead-gorgeous views of Mount Rainier, certainly deserves the fame, but all that popularity has forced the park to protect this fragile area by closing the meadow to camping. Most hikers approach Indian Henry's along the Wonderland Trail from Longmire and spend the night at crowded Devils Dream Camp, a little over 1 mile south. But for adventuresome hikers who are willing to do some moderate cross-country hiking, there is a better and less crowded option. By hiking into Indian Henry's Hunting Ground on the little-used Kautz Creek Trail and continuing up to spectacular but off-trail Pyramid Park, you can avoid the crowds and spend the night at an amazingly beautiful alpine retreat with a dramatic up-close look at the rugged west face of Mount Rainier.

Getting There

From I-5, 67 miles north of Vancouver, Washington, take Exit 68 and travel 31 miles east on US 12 to a junction at the town of Morton. Turn left on WA 7 and drive 17 miles to a junction with WA 706. Turn right (east), enter Mount Rainier National Park after 14 miles, and continue another 3.4 miles to the Kautz Creek Trailhead. The parking lot is on the right. To obtain a permit (or to pick up your reserved permit), you will need to continue driving another 3 miles to Longmire and stop at the wilderness information center.

GPS COORDINATES N46° 44.227' W121° 51.614'

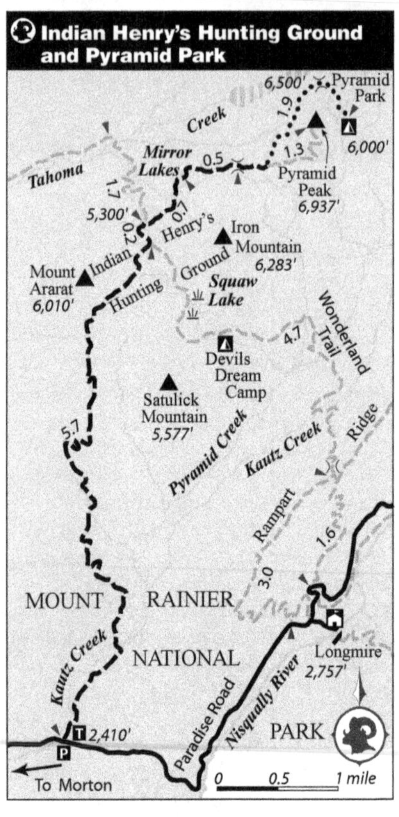

Hiking It

The trail starts next to a small sign on the north side of the highway across from the parking lot. Initially the path takes you over the remains of a massive debris and mud flow that devastated this valley in October 1947. The flow was triggered by heavy rains, which caused a partial collapse of the Kautz Glacier. Landslide events like this are fairly common on Mount Rainier, although they are usually smaller in size—a major one can cause extensive damage to park roads and trails, even forcing closures, so be sure to check conditions before hiking this route. On the remains of the 1947 slide, trees now crowd the area (mostly western hemlocks and western red cedars), but in more open and sunny areas, deciduous trees—especially red alders—predominate. The dense undergrowth is mostly composed of salal, along with various ferns and mosses.

Initially the trail is gentle, wide, and strewn with gravel to accommodate tourists interested in exploring the geology of the mudflow. At 1 mile, however, the trail crosses silty Kautz Creek on a seasonally installed log bridge and becomes a wilderness trail. The much narrower path now enters an old-growth forest unaffected by the 1947 mudflow and begins a long, persistent, and at times moderately steep climb. The way is viewless but shady and pleasant throughout. Numerous short switchbacks help keep the climb from becoming overly steep. You cross a trickling creek at about 3 miles (the first reliable source of clear water) then continue climbing in a series of short, steep switchbacks. Still not done with the uphill section, you ascend at a gentler grade on a wide ridge and slowly enter more open high-elevation terrain. Mount Rainier is frequently in view, while closer at hand are rocky buttes and increasing numbers of heather, huckleberries, and various wildflowers. A final short, steep uphill leads to a high point on the southeast shoulder of Mount Ararat (a name that significantly overstates the size of this small butte), and then you descend about 150 feet to a junction at 5.7 miles with the Wonderland Trail.

You are now smack in the middle of Indian Henry's Hunting Ground, a spectacular mountain meadow with acres of colorful wildflowers, several tiny ponds, a small ranger cabin, and some of the most photogenic views of Mount Rainier in the entire park. You turn left at the junction, almost immediately pass a spur trail to the ranger cabin, and 0.2 mile later come to a junction with the Mirror Lakes Trail. Turn right and gradually ascend 0.7 mile in rolling, wildflower-filled meadows to shallow Mirror Lake. Asahel Curtis made this view famous when he painted it for a postage stamp commemorating the national park in 1934. The scene is just as impressive today.

The trail rounds the right side of the tiny lake and then goes 100 yards to a sign saying END OF MAINTAINED TRAIL. Despite its now unofficial status, the trail remains very good and easy to follow as it climbs 0.4 mile and then descends a bit to a meadow-filled saddle with a great view of aptly named Pyramid Peak to the northeast. From here the trail continues to the top of Pyramid Peak, where you'll enjoy an absolutely out-of-this-world view of nearby Mount Rainier.

There is nowhere to camp on Pyramid Peak, so backpackers should go instead to Pyramid Park, a more-difficult-to-reach but equally spectacular destination. To reach it, follow the trail toward Pyramid Peak from the meadowy saddle about 0.3 mile, and then go cross-country to the left, angling moderately steeply uphill to a rocky, above-timberline ledge on the northeast side of Pyramid Peak. Follow this rugged ledge about 0.8 mile to a high, often windy saddle north of the peak, where you will enjoy up-close-and-personal views of Mount Rainier that are so incredible the word *great* just doesn't do them justice.

From this rocky saddle you scramble steeply downhill, going southeast across boulder fields, meadows, and scree slopes to the rolling meadowlands, springs, and tree islands of Pyramid Park. Tall but unnamed waterfalls drop into and off the edge of this alpine parkland, while the banks of the gently meandering creeks that cross the flats are choked with yellow monkey flower, western anemone, grass-of-Parnassus, and other wildflowers. There are also great views west of Pyramid Peak and northeast to Mount Rainier, which has a rather lopsided appearance from this angle. More distant views extend to the south and southeast, of the Tatoosh Range, Mount Adams, the Goat Rocks, and Mount St. Helens. You can camp almost anywhere in this parkland, although, as always, you should select a rocky or sandy area that is well away from the delicate alpine wildflowers and grasses. If you schedule more than one night here, you can visit all the waterfalls and enjoy the excellent scenery.

Hike to the top of Pyramid Peak for incredible views of Mount Rainier. *photo by Douglas Lorain*

6 Indian Bar and Cowlitz Park

RATINGS Scenery **9** Difficulty **8** Solitude **2**

ROUND-TRIP DISTANCE 15 miles to Indian Bar; 16 miles to Cowlitz Park

ELEVATION GAIN 4,000' to Indian Bar; 3,900' to Cowlitz Park

OPTIONAL MAP Green Trails *Mount Rainier East (No. 270)*

USUALLY OPEN Late July–mid-September

BEST TIME Late July–mid-September

AGENCY Mount Rainier National Park, nps.gov/mora

PERMIT Required. All cars must also display an entry permit for the national park. Reservations are strongly advised: Mount Rainier National Park makes only 30% of its backcountry permits available on a first-come, first-serve basis. The rest are for hikers who made advance reservations. Because obtaining a permit for popular areas, especially on summer weekends, is extremely difficult, it is highly recommended that you reserve a permit in advance. Reservations are accepted starting on March 15, through the online request system only; you cannot make a reservation over the phone. The cost is $20 per group and is nonrefundable. To obtain a reservation form and for further information, go to nps.gov/mora/planyourvisit/wilderness-permit.htm.

Highlights

One of the classic beauty spots in Mount Rainier National Park, Indian Bar is a fairly small but spectacular basin of abundant wildflowers, streaking waterfalls, and outstanding mountain scenery. There may be no more beautiful location in the Pacific Northwest backcountry. Unfortunately, there are only a handful of designated backpacker campsites at Indian Bar, and the place is justifiably popular, so it can be very hard to get a permit. Apply for a reserved permit well in advance, although even then it helps to be lucky.

For those willing to put in the extra time and effort required to visit a cross-country area, however, there is another option. Not far southwest of Indian Bar sits the off-trail camping zone of Cowlitz Park, a rolling land of alpine meadows, wildflowers, and numerous waterfalls. Although Cowlitz Park is harder to reach, it actually has a better view of the mountain than does Indian Bar. It is usually possible to obtain a permit for Cowlitz Park, but it is not a sure thing. The park currently allows only three parties a night to stay there, so it is often full as well, especially on weekends. Have an alternate plan in mind.

Getting There

From I-5, 67 miles north of Vancouver, Washington, take Exit 68 and travel 72 miles east on US 12 to a junction with WA 123, about 7.5 miles past the town of Packwood. Turn left, following signs to Mount Rainier National Park, and drive a little over 5 miles to a junction with Stevens Canyon Road. Turn left, immediately passing through an entrance station for the park, and drive 10 miles to the Box Canyon Trailhead, just before a bridge over Muddy Fork Cowlitz River.

GPS COORDINATES
N46° 45.937' W121° 38.088'

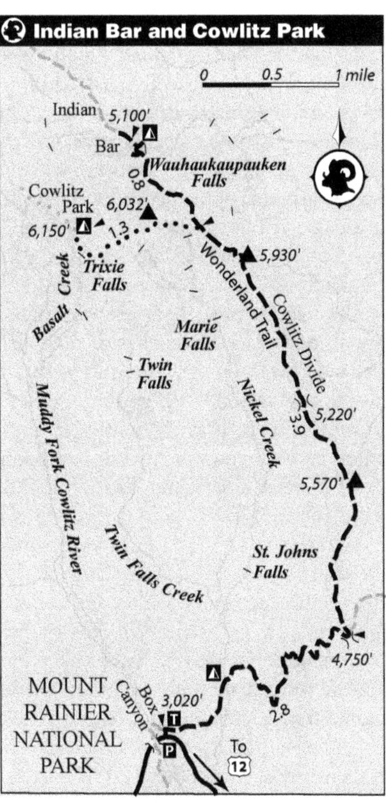

Hiking It

The trail departs from the north side of the road across from the parking lot and soon comes to a junction with the Wonderland Trail. It is worthwhile to turn left here and make a 0.2-mile side trip to check out Box Canyon, an extremely narrow cleft where the waters of the Muddy Fork Cowlitz River shoot through a steep-sided gorge.

After the short side trip, return to the junction and follow the Wonderland Trail as it gradually ascends a mostly forested hillside and then loses a little elevation before coming to a bridged crossing of Nickel Creek at 0.8 mile. There is a designated backpacker camping area on the left. The sites here are pleasant, but the camp area has poor drainage, so it tends to turn into a shallow lake after a hard rain.

After crossing Nickel Creek you make a long, switchbacking, generally viewless climb that gains some 1,500 feet in 2 miles to a junction with the Olallie Creek Trail at a wooded pass atop Cowlitz Divide. Keep left on the Wonderland Trail and climb in the forest 1 mile to a grassy knoll where you gain the first really nice views of the hike. From this point you can see Mount Rainier to the northwest as well as the rugged Cowlitz Chimneys to the north and down into the heavily forested Ohanapecosh Valley to the east. To the southwest is the jagged Tatoosh Range.

The trail's next section is wildly scenic as it descends to a saddle and then goes up and down (mostly up), never straying far from the top of Cowlitz Divide. The route is a mix of meadows and partial forest with frequent views that continue to improve as you get closer to the park's massive, glacier-clad centerpiece. Wildlife is common in this area. Look for black bears, elk, deer, and a variety of mountain birds. At 6.1 miles you come to the top of a knoll where the views of Mount Rainier are absolutely spectacular. With wildflowers in the foreground and trees framing the scene, this is a favorite spot to photograph the mountain. You can also look south to distant Mount Adams. From the knoll, the trail makes a moderately steep descent, following a ridgeline to the northwest 0.4 mile before leveling out in a rolling meadow.

If you are headed for Cowlitz Park, leave the trail at this meadow and go left (almost due west) through mostly open, rolling terrain. The hiking isn't overly difficult, but as with all cross-country travel, your progress will be slower and more challenging than it was on the trail. You soon cross two small creeks and then ascend rather steeply on a mostly rocky slope before passing on the south side of a small knoll. Continue west, now on more level terrain, and make your way gradually uphill, going west-southwest another 0.5 mile until you reach the drainage of Basalt Creek in the lower reaches of Cowlitz Park. On your left is a steep cliff over which creeks tumble in long drops. The most impressive of these cataracts is Trixie Falls on a small side stream feeding into Basalt Creek. Some of the best camps (there are no official or established sites in this off-trail zone) are along the lower reaches of the creek well above the cliffs. As always, choose a site well away from water and with a hard surface to avoid damaging the fragile alpine vegetation. You should expect to spend considerable time looking for a suitable site. It is worthwhile to explore the upper reaches of Cowlitz Park to enjoy its fine views of Mount Rainier and plentiful wildflowers.

If you have a permit to stay at Indian Bar, continue on the Wonderland Trail from the meadow where the Cowlitz Park route took off, and go downhill at a moderately steep grade until you come to the south end of Indian Bar. Just before the trail crosses the Ohanapecosh River, which here is only a creek, a trail goes left to a picturesque stone shelter. Camping here is generally restricted to groups of six or more people. The main trail crosses the "river" just above where the water plunges over thunderous Wauhaukaupauken Falls. Unfortunately, it is almost as hard to get a good look at the falls as it is to spell the name. Immediately after the crossing, a signed trail goes right on its way to the designated campsites of Indian Bar.

After setting up camp, take the time to do a bit of exploring. At a minimum, walk up the Wonderland Trail across the lovely and amazingly flat expanse of Indian Bar, with its waving grasses, gravel beds, and acres of wildflowers. The surrounding cliffs and ridges that enclose the basin host several impressive but unnamed waterfalls on small creeks that drain from the permanent snowfields and small glacier above. If you have the energy for a longer adventure, continue on the Wonderland Trail as it ascends a ridge above the green expanse of Ohanapecosh Park and then climbs over rocks and semipermanent snowfields to the views from Panhandle Gap, 3 miles from Indian Bar. Keep an eye out for wildlife, as Panhandle Gap is one of the better places in the park to see mountain goats.

WARNING Although the route to Panhandle Gap is very scenic, the way is often covered with snow and difficult to follow before about mid-August.

Mount Rainier from Peak 5,930 along Cowlitz Divide, Mount Rainier National Park
photo by Douglas Lorain

7 Dumbbell and Sand Lakes Loop

RATINGS Scenery **6** Difficulty **6** Solitude **6**
ROUND-TRIP DISTANCE 11.3 miles
ELEVATION GAIN 1,550'
OPTIONAL MAP Green Trails *White Pass (No. 303)*
USUALLY OPEN Mid-July–October
BEST TIME Late August–early September; early–mid-October
AGENCY Naches Ranger District (Wenatchee National Forest), 509-653-1401, fs.usda.gov/recarea/okawen/recarea/?recid=58395
PERMIT No permit required. Northwest Forest Pass required.

Highlights

The southern William O. Douglas Wilderness is a relatively gentle landscape of countless lakes, wonderful meadows, and attractive forests. Perhaps the area's most outstanding feature, however, becomes evident only from very late September through mid-October, when the millions of huckleberry bushes lining its lakes and meadows turn bright orange and red, putting on one of the better fall-color displays in our region. Fortuitously, this is also a time when crowds are few and the mosquitoes, which can be voracious in July and early August, are nearly gone. Late August to early September is also a nice time to visit, as the lakes are reasonably warm for swimming and you can feast on all those ripe huckleberries.

Getting There

From I-5, 67 miles north of Vancouver, Washington, take Exit 68 and travel 85 miles east on US 12 to White Pass. Continue east another 2.1 miles, then turn left into the signed Dog Lake Campground. The unpaved campground loop road passes the signed trailhead on the right after 0.1 mile.

GPS COORDINATES N46° 39.274' W121° 21.621'

Hiking It

The trail starts in a relatively open midelevation forest of mixed conifers with plenty of huckleberries, fireweed, grouse whortleberries, and numerous other low-growing flowers and shrubs scattered about on the forest floor. After just 0.1 mile of uphill hiking, you reach a fork at the start of the loop.

Bear right onto the Cramer Lake Trail and follow this wide, horse-pounded path as it traces a gentle course 1.2 miles to a camp immediately before a bridgeless crossing of North Fork Clear Creek. There is usually a log you can scoot across here (you might have to go upstream a bit to find one that's comfortable), but if that is missing, the creek crossing is generally an easy calf-deep ford. (Make sure you familiarize yourself with the proper way to safely ford a creek.)

After crossing the creek, the trail makes a gradual uphill traverse of a mostly forested hillside and then turns north and wanders gently uphill to Cramer Lake at

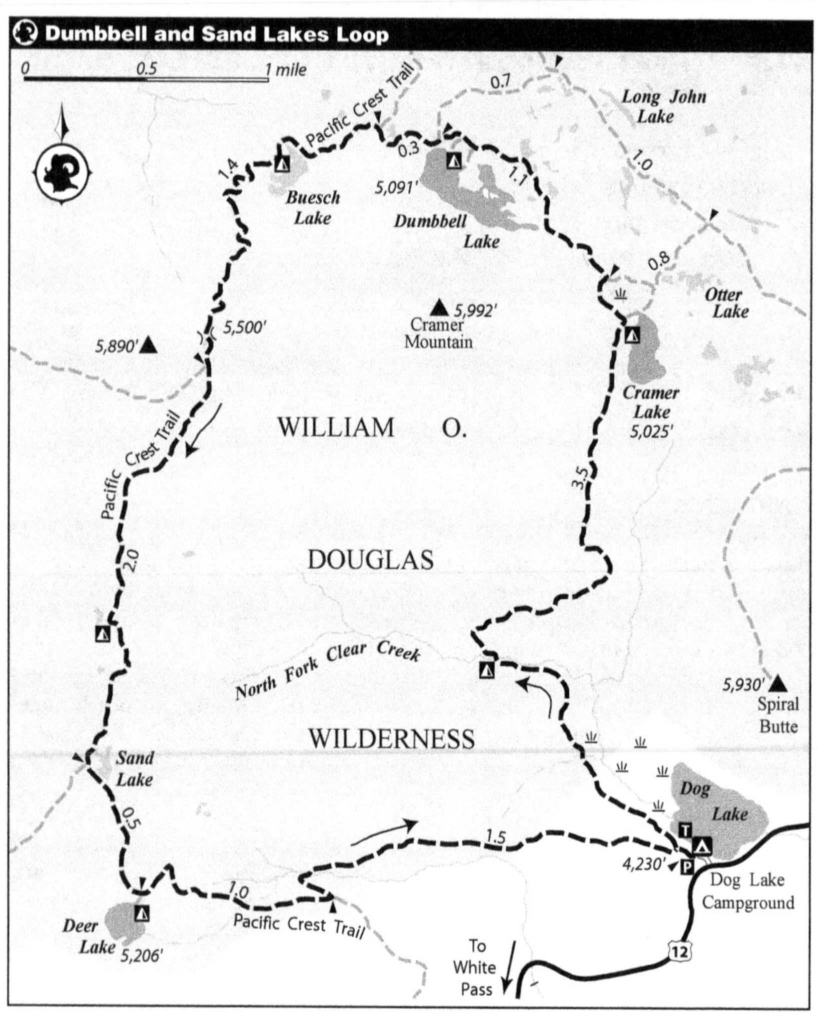

3.2 miles. The trail stays in the forest, so far back from this good-sized and attractive lake that it is easy to walk right past it without noticing. The lake is worth a visit, however, so watch carefully and follow any of several sketchy trails that branch right and lead to this forest-rimmed gem. It has a fine campsite at its northwest end.

Just beyond Cramer Lake is a junction at the southeast corner of a lush, grassy meadow. Watch for deer and elk here, especially early in the morning. This is only the first of several forest-rimmed meadows you will visit over the next few miles. All of these meadows feature plenty of wildflowers in mid- to late July and bright red and orange huckleberry bushes in early October. Keep straight at the junction and walk around the southwest side of the small meadow, coming to a second junction immediately after crossing a tiny creek. Turn left and climb a little more before catching a glimpse of large Dumbbell Lake. Unfortunately, this glimpse is all you will see of this scenic lake for some time, as the trail stays in the forest well back from the lake; instead, you pass several small but attractive ponds. After 0.4 mile you pass two unsigned but obvious use paths going left. These lead to well-located but somewhat exposed campsites near the northwest end of Dumbbell Lake.

The main trail finally approaches Dumbbell Lake at its northwest tip, where there is a (faintly) signed junction for Long John Trail. Go straight and follow a gentle path past more ponds and meadows 0.3 mile to a junction with the Pacific Crest Trail (PCT). Turn left (south) on this wide and well-graded trail, and walk 0.3 mile to beautiful, meadow-lined Buesch Lake. The trail skirts the north and west sides of the lake, passing a short side trail that leads to an exceptionally nice campsite above the west shore.

The PCT now climbs away from Buesch Lake, gradually ascending 0.8 mile to a broad pass with two shallow ponds before coming to a signed junction with the faint Cortright Creek Trail. Keep straight on the PCT and go gradually up and down 1.6 miles past tiny ponds and small meadows to a fine camp at a large and scenic pond just to the right (west) of the trail. From here you go downhill to a junction beside Sand Lake. The water in this lake recedes dramatically by late summer, reducing its attractiveness.

Keep left at the junction, still on the PCT, and after 0.6 mile come to a wide and heavily used side trail that goes right 80 yards to Deer Lake. There is a large and comfortable camping area above this nearly circular lake's northeast shore.

The PCT continues east from Deer Lake, gradually losing elevation as it follows the hillside above the tiny outlet creek of Deer Lake. About 1.1 miles from the lake, you come to a junction where you turn sharply left on Dark Meadow Trail. After 0.1 mile this path crosses a tiny creek in a meadow and then turns east and goes up and down 0.5 mile before descending to the junction just above Dog Lake Campground and the close of the loop. Turn right to return to the trailhead.

The PCT leads past Buesch Lake in the William O. Douglas Wilderness.
photo by Douglas Lorain

8 Cispus Point

RATINGS Scenery **7** Difficulty **4** Solitude **9**
ROUND-TRIP DISTANCE 5.6 miles (including side trip)
ELEVATION GAIN 1,400'
OPTIONAL MAP Green Trails *Blue Lake (No. 334)*
USUALLY OPEN July–October
BEST TIME July
AGENCY Cowlitz Valley Ranger District (Gifford Pinchot National Forest), fs.usda.gov/recarea/giffordpinchot/recarea/?recid=31180
PERMIT None

Highlights

This short but exciting hike takes you into a small but very attractive parcel of roadless terrain not far from Packwood, Washington. Because most hikers prefer the more famous trails around the scenic wonders of nearby Mount Rainier and the Goat Rocks, it's not surprising that few people visit Cispus Point. (On an early September weekend, there was not another car anywhere near the trailhead.) Those who do visit are rewarded not only with solitude but also with exceptional scenery, including spectacular 360-degree views that take in all of those much more crowded attractions.

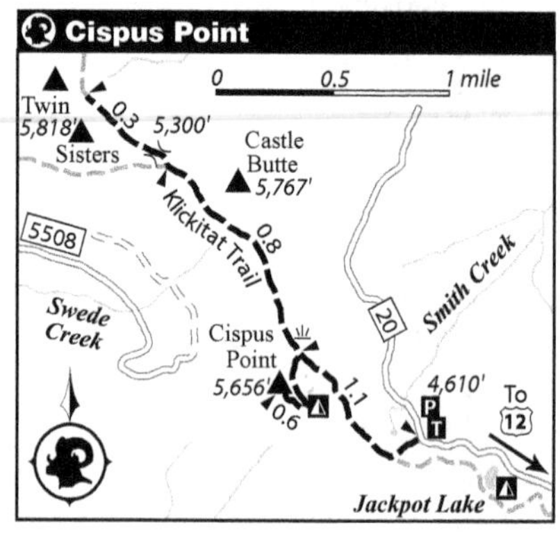

Getting There

From I-5, 67 miles north of Vancouver, Washington, take Exit 68 and travel 61 miles east on US 12 to an unsigned junction with Forest Service Road 20 near milepost 127.6. Turn right (south) on this narrow and sometimes rough gravel road. Continue on the main route 12.2 miles through several minor intersections. Park at a pullout on the left, about 0.5 mile past the (possibly unsigned, and certainly easy to miss) trailhead for Jackpot Lake (Klickitat Trail) and just before the road takes a sharp right.

GPS COORDINATES N46° 28.116' W121° 42.278'

Hiking It

The unsigned but obvious trail goes southwest along the edge of an old, now enthusiastically regrowing clear-cut for 0.2 mile to a junction with the Klickitat Trail. Turn right and wander through a forest of mountain hemlocks and Alaska yellow cedars, which provide lots of welcome shade but block most of the views. In July, wildflowers such as valerian, avalanche lily, columbine, wallflower, pink heather, bluebell, and lupine provide plenty of color, especially in places that get a bit more sun. Those breaks in the forest cover also provide views of bulky, snow-covered Mount Adams to the south.

At 0.4 mile you begin a steep and steady uphill traverse of an open, rocky slope directly beneath the imposing cliffs on the east face of Cispus Point. The ascent ends at a junction in a small meadow with a shallow seasonal pond. Look for marsh marigolds and western anemones growing in the wet soils here.

Campsites atop Cispus Point have spectacular views.

The trail that goes left at this junction is the route to Cispus Point. Since this is such an easy hike, however, it is worth spending a little extra time and energy on a short side trip. So drop your pack and take the trail to the right, hiking mostly on the level through an absolutely stunning open forest of subalpine firs and mountain hemlocks around the southwest side of massive Castle Butte. After 0.8 mile you come to a signed fork. The main Klickitat Trail goes left, but veer right, climb briefly to a saddle with a glimpse through thick trees of Mount Rainier, and then descend a little before turning north for a fun and scenic walk beneath the towering cliffs of Twin Sisters. (Keep your eyes peeled for mountain goats sunning themselves on the steep cliffs above.) This is the logical turnaround point for the side trip.

Back at the meadow junction, go south on the dead-end spur trail to Cispus Point, which climbs through forest then over open slopes before passing above a pair of small ponds with a couple of wildly scenic campsites. These camps are a bit exposed and the ponds are too shallow for either swimming or fishing, but they feature terrific views and plenty of solitude. The sunrises here can be spectacular.

The trail continues past the pond, ascending to a ridgetop where it switchbacks to the right and then climbs over loose, slightly slippery rock (be careful) to the cliff-edged top of Cispus Point. The views here are outstanding and include all of the big volcanic peaks of southern Washington—Rainier, Adams, St. Helens, and the eroded old volcano of the Goat Rocks. Again, look for goats resting on the various rocks and cliffs below. You can also look south to Oregon's Mount Hood and see countless smaller rocky ridges and summits closer at hand. Even though the hike is short, this is a fantastic place to sit and enjoy a snack while giving yourself a pat on the back and gazing across the better part of Washington state.

9 Packwood Lake and Coyote Ridge Loop

RATINGS	Scenery **8** Difficulty **3–9** Solitude **2–8**
ROUND-TRIP DISTANCE	9 miles to Packwood Lake; 25.4 miles for loop
ELEVATION GAIN	300' to Packwood Lake; 4,350' for loop
OPTIONAL MAPS	Green Trails *Packwood (No. 302)* and *White Pass (No. 303)*
USUALLY OPEN	May–November for Packwood Lake; late July–October for loop
BEST TIME	Late July–August
AGENCY	Cowlitz Valley Ranger District (Gifford Pinchot National Forest), 360-497-1100, fs.usda.gov/recarea/giffordpinchot/recreation/recarea/?recid=31180
PERMIT	Required; free at the trailhead. Northwest Forest Pass required.

Highlights

Packwood Lake is a huge subalpine gem with a scenic island and terrific views up to the snowy crags of Johnson Peak. It is also accessible along an easy trail from a trailhead reached by a good paved road. Not surprisingly, the place is very popular. What many visitors don't realize, however, is that the lake is only the starting point for a magnificent backcountry loop. The trail along Coyote Ridge is one of the finest high-elevation ridge walks in our region, with outstanding views, plenty of wildlife, and abundant wildflowers. The amazing thing is that the ridge is so little traveled that you may have the entire route to yourself.

Getting There

From I-5, 67 miles north of Vancouver, Washington, take Exit 68 and travel 64 miles east on US 12 to the town of Packwood. Near the north end of town, and immediately south of the Packwood Ranger Station/Work Center, turn right on Snyder Road, following signs to Packwood Lake Trail. This paved road, which becomes Forest Service Road 1260, climbs 3.8 miles to the large road-end parking lot and trailhead.

GPS COORDINATES N46° 36.520' W121°37.615'

Hiking It

The heavily used trail departs from the north end of the parking lot and gently climbs under the shade of tall Douglas firs and western hemlocks. All that shade limits the understory to a few salal, Oregon grape, elderberry, thimbleberry, and scattered forest wildflowers. The next 4.2 miles are easy hiking with very little elevation gain or loss, staying in generally viewless but pleasant forest. At the end of this section you descend a little to the west shore of Packwood Lake. This photo genic lake, with its large, forested island and views of Johnson Peak, is the destination of almost all hikers, so beyond this point you will enjoy much more solitude.

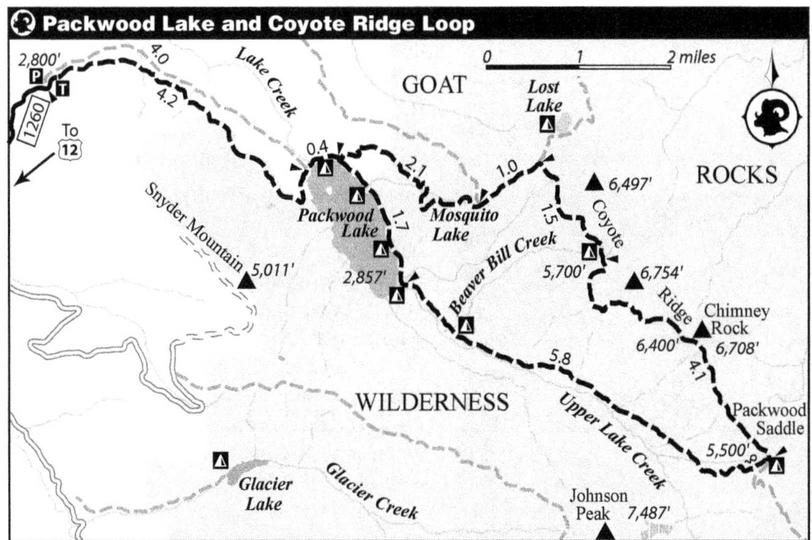

The trail passes a relatively new guard station just before a signed junction with the Pipeline Trail, an old road that parallels the hiker's trail and is often used by mountain bikers and motorcyclists to access the lake. Shortly after this junction your trail passes the historic 1910 log ranger station and then takes a bridge over the lake's dammed outlet creek. Shortly after this crossing are some fine campsites, featuring excellent views to the southeast of Johnson Peak rising over the waters of Packwood Lake.

At 4.6 miles the trail forks at the start of the recommended loop. Veer left (uphill) and immediately pull away from the lake as the trail steadily climbs at a moderately steep grade across a heavily forested hillside. The circuitous route ascends in switchbacks and winding traverses 2 miles before reaching a tiny, lily-pad-covered pond by the name of Mosquito Lake. Although this is not much of a lake, it does feature a decent campsite above its northwest shore.

The trail rounds the west and north sides of Mosquito Lake, and then continues 0.1 mile to an easy-to-miss junction. Stay straight on the main trail and contour 0.4 mile to a lovely wildflower meadow before climbing in forest 0.6 mile to a junction.

Veer right (uphill) on Coyote Ridge Trail and continue steadily uphill as the forest becomes more open, with mountain hemlocks, subalpine firs, Alaska yellow cedars, and other high-elevation trees replacing the lower-elevation types you saw earlier. At 9.2 miles you reach a fine campsite next to small Beaver Bill Creek, the last campsite and the last reliable water for several miles.

Beyond Beaver Bill Creek the trail ascends 300 feet to round the end of a ridge with great views of Mount Rainier to the northwest, and then settles into a pattern of ups and downs along the southwest side of Coyote Ridge. The scenery for the next 4 miles is stupendous, with views south to Mount St. Helens, down to Packwood Lake, and across the canyon to the snowy and jagged pinnacles of Johnson Peak and Old Snowy Mountain. Add to these distant vistas the fine, close-up views

Coyote Ridge affords impressive vistas of Johnson Peak's jagged pinnacles.
photo by Douglas Lorain

of impressive Chimney Rock, which sits atop Coyote Ridge, and you have a real winner. Wildlife is common as well. Look for pikas, elk, deer, and black bears, along with a wide variety of mountain birds. And don't forget the wildflowers! The mostly open slopes here are carpeted with flowers throughout the summer. Species include bellflower, spirea, beargrass, lupine, aster, pearly everlasting, false hellebore, buckwheat, partridgefoot, yarrow, bistort, and paintbrush. On the downside, the trail is narrow and eroded in places, so be careful where you step.

The trail reaches its highest point when it tops Coyote Ridge on the southeast side of Chimney Rock. From here you go steeply downhill on a narrow, gravel-strewn route, losing almost 900 feet to a junction at Packwood Saddle. There is a small campsite near this junction, with water available from a spring about 0.2 mile down the trail to the right.

The recommended loop trail goes right (downhill) from Packwood Saddle, but if you have the time and energy, it is worth taking a side trip that goes straight and climbs a little less than 1 mile to an extremely photogenic viewpoint on the shoulder of Egg Butte. The scene looking back down the length of rugged Coyote Ridge to the glacier-covered summit of Mount Rainier is outstanding. This is also a good place to look for the mountain goats for which Goat Rocks Wilderness is named.

Back at Packwood Saddle, turn west and descend steeply through dense forest past a spring and across several tiny creeks as you steadily lose elevation. The downhill continues 2.5 miles before finally bottoming out back in lower-elevation forest along Upper Lake Creek. From here the trail turns downstream, with only minor ups and downs for the next several miles as it follows the meandering creek. The walk used to involve a fair amount of scrambling around washouts from a major flood that swept through in 2006, but trail work since then has removed many of the fallen trees and made the washouts passable. Most of the route is now in good shape. The best place to camp is at 18.5 miles, immediately after you cross the lower end of Beaver Bill Creek.

About 0.6 mile of ups and downs past Beaver Bill Creek takes you to an inviting campsite at the southeast end of Packwood Lake. This camp features a good (if partially obstructed) view of Mount Rainier and offers the camper a chance to see ospreys flying over the lake. The camps at this end of the lake are much less crowded than those along the more easily accessible north shore. The trail goes around the east side of Packwood Lake, offering many fine views of this large, deep, and scenic lake and passing half a dozen possible campsites to a junction at the close of the loop at 20.8 miles. Go straight and return the way you came.

10 Heart Lake

RATINGS	Scenery **8** Difficulty **7** Solitude **6**
ROUND-TRIP DISTANCE	13.4 miles
ELEVATION GAIN	2,400'
OPTIONAL MAP	Green Trails *Blue Lake (No. 334)*
USUALLY OPEN	Late July–October
BEST TIME	Late July–October
AGENCY	Cowlitz Valley Ranger District (Gifford Pinchot National Forest), 360-497-1100, fs.usda.gov/recarea/giffordpinchot/recreation/recarea/?recid=31180
PERMIT	Required; free at the trailhead

Highlights

This relatively uncrowded trail samples all of the many charms of the Goat Rocks Wilderness. Starting in a lovely high-elevation forest, you ascend into flower-choked meadows along a ridge with amazing views of Packwood Lake and Mount Rainier, pass through a rocky basin below craggy Johnson Peak, and then descend to gorgeous Heart Lake in a scenic basin beneath meadowy slopes. Best of all, the lake features a wonderful campsite in a grove of trees with fine views and surprisingly few people.

Getting There

From I-5, 67 miles north of Vancouver, Washington, take Exit 68 and travel 63 miles east on US 12 to a poorly signed junction with Forest Service Road 48 near milepost 129.5. Turn right on this initially good gravel road, remaining on the main route and ignoring several minor intersections as the road steadily climbs. The road gets rough and steep in one spot just beyond a gravel pit, but if your vehicle has decent ground clearance, you should have no problem. The trailhead is on the right, 11.2 miles from US 12. There is a small parking area about 30 yards past the trailhead.

GPS COORDINATES
N46° 33.865' W121° 36.005'

Mount Rainier and Packwood Lake from the Lily Basin Trail *photo by Douglas Lorain*

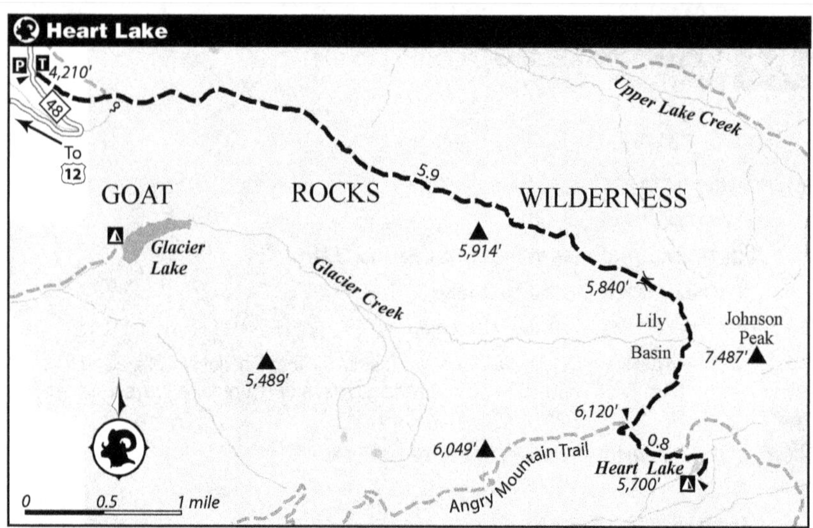

Hiking It

The Lily Basin Trail begins with a steady climb through a lovely forest of Douglas firs, western hemlocks, and Pacific silver firs, with an understory of beargrass and huckleberries. At 0.6 mile a horse trail splits off to the left. Go straight, still climbing, through a pleasant but generally viewless forest, and at about 1 mile begin following a wooded ridgeline.

As you traverse the north side of the ridge at about 3.5 miles, you hit the first of several breaks in the tree cover that reveal spectacularly photogenic views northeast of Mount Rainier with Packwood Lake and its distinctive island in the foreground below. At 4.3 miles you cross through a little saddle onto the south side of the ridge and enjoy good views of rugged Johnson Peak about 1 mile southeast.

After working its way east, the up-and-down trail cuts across the steep, rocky, and mostly open slopes on the west side of Johnson Peak above forested Lily Basin. Tiny creeks here provide the first water of the trip. There are fine views along this section, both of the forested canyon to the west and of imposing Johnson Peak to the east. The trail eventually climbs to the top of a ridge on the southwest side of Johnson Peak, where you enjoy terrific views to the southwest of Mount St. Helens, northwest to Mount Rainier, and south to a small part of Mount Adams. There is also a junction here with the Angry Mountain Trail.

You veer left (downhill) at the junction, make one quick switchback, and then descend a partly forested slope 0.6 mile to an unsigned fork with the spur trail to Heart Lake. Turn right and descend 0.2 mile to the lovely green-tinged pool, which is surrounded by meadows and backed by scenic ridges. (Wear long sleeves and prepare for some pretty serious mosquitoes near the lake through mid- to late August.) There are excellent camps near the outlet at the lake's west end.

11 Snowgrass Flat Loop

RATINGS	Scenery **10** Difficulty **7** Solitude **1**
ROUND-TRIP DISTANCE	14.3 miles (with many great side-trip options)
ELEVATION GAIN	3,000'
OPTIONAL MAP	USFS *Goat Rocks Wilderness*
USUALLY OPEN	Late July–October
BEST TIME	Late July–August
AGENCY	Cowlitz Valley Ranger District (Gifford Pinchot National Forest), 360-497-1100, fs.usda.gov/recarea/giffordpinchot/recreation/recarea/?recid=31180
PERMIT	Required; free at the trailhead. Northwest Forest Pass required.

Highlights

The sloping, flower-covered meadows of Snowgrass Flat are one of the most popular hiking destinations in Washington—with good reason because this is without question one of the premier hikes in the Pacific Northwest. The scenery is outstanding, with plenty of views of rugged mountains both near and far, a stunning glacial lake, thousands of acres of wildflowers, numerous scenic campsites, and gorgeous alpine ridges. If you like mountain scenery, then this country is beyond compare. It is highly recommended, however, that you time your visit for a weekday, or later in the fall, to make the crowd situation more tolerable.

Getting There

From I-5, 67 miles north of Vancouver, Washington, take Exit 68 and travel 62 miles east on US 12 to a signed junction with Forest Service Road 21 near milepost 128.4. Turn right (south), following signs to Chambers Lake, and stay on this good gravel road 13 miles to a junction. Turn left on Road 2150, drive 3 miles, and then veer right at a fork. Proceed 0.1 mile to a junction, go right on the trailhead loop road, and continue 0.4 mile to the scattered parking along the road for the popular Snowgrass Trailhead.

GPS COORDINATES

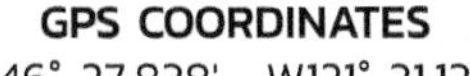

N46° 27.838' W121° 31.134'

Hiking It

You begin in a relatively open, midelevation forest of mixed conifers with an unusually high concentration of huckleberries and beargrass carpeting the forest floor. After just 0.1 mile there is a junction at the start of the

On a clear day, Mount Adams glimmers in the background of the Snowgrass Flat Loop hike.

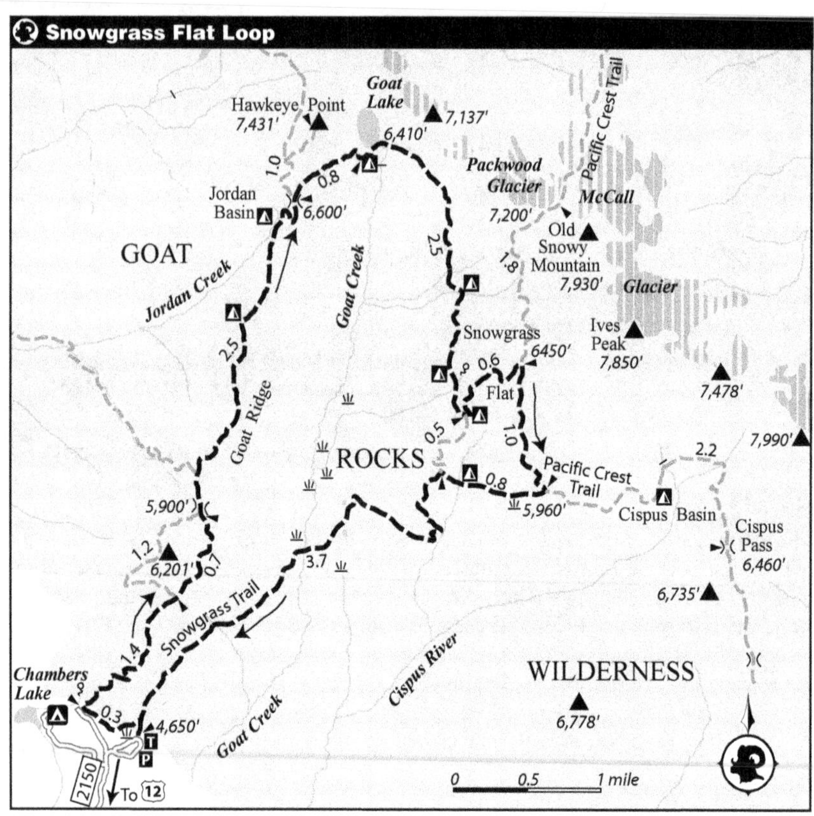

loop. For the recommended clockwise circuit, go sharply left on a horse trail, which soon passes a marshy lake before making a 0.3-mile traverse through forest and small wildflower meadows to a junction just 10 yards from a secondary trailhead (the well-signed Berry Patch Trailhead).

You turn right onto the Goat Ridge Trail and immediately begin a steady uphill, with the vegetation changing to the usual higher-elevation varieties as you ascend. At 1.7 miles go straight at a junction with an alternate side loop, and then climb a little more to a nice viewpoint looking east to the jagged summits of the Goat Rocks. From here you descend to a saddle and a reunion with the alternate loop trail.

Your trail goes straight, crosses to the west side of Goat Ridge, and then makes an up-and-down traverse with partial views looking north-northwest to Mount Rainier. Pass a junction with the faint Jordan Creek Trail, and then go up and down across a partially forested hillside that features several sloping wildflower meadows. From late July to mid-August the color show is terrific. Look for lupine, aster, columbine, pearly everlasting, yarrow, western anemone, bistort, pink heather, false hellebore, arnica, groundsel, cat's-ear, and a dozen other species.

At 3.6 miles you pass a grandly scenic campsite on a knoll on the left. This camp features outstanding views of the nearby ridges and canyons as well as distant Mount St. Helens. Unfortunately, the only nearby water is from seasonal trickles of snowmelt that are usually gone by late summer.

The trail now rounds a huge sloping basin beneath a scenic ridge and then climbs into Jordan Basin, which has reliable water, grandly scenic but exposed camps, and a (really) small pond. From here the trail climbs a pair of switchbacks to a 6,600-foot pass and a junction with Lily Basin Trail. A wonderful side trip from here goes left 0.4 mile, then right on the trail to the top of Hawkeye Point. Views from this summit extend to almost every major landmark for more than 50 miles.

You veer right and make a wildly scenic traverse of an open slope with several small trickling creeks. This slope, which is a sea of wildflowers in late summer, features breathtaking views of Mount Adams to the south and Snowgrass Flat and the Goat Rocks crest to the east. At the northeast end of the traverse, the trail descends to Goat Lake, a milky gem (the color comes from glacial silt) that is usually covered with ice until sometime in August. This scenic pool has good but exposed camps and an awesome setting beneath stark, rocky slopes and snowfields. Campfires are prohibited within 0.25 mile of the lake.

The trail crosses the lake's outlet creek well above a sloping waterfall you can hear but not see, and then contours across open slopes before entering the lower portion of Snowgrass Flat. This alpine paradise is a wonderland of scattered tree islands, bubbling creeks, great campsites, and profuse wildflowers. The trail goes up and down a little over 1 mile through this gorgeous meadowland before coming to an area with a confusion of trails, most of which soon dead-end at campsites. Veer left at the first major unsigned fork and, 150 yards later, reach a signed junction with Snowgrass Trail. Several trails converge here, but the unsigned ones are just dead ends that lead to campsites.

The fastest way back to the trailhead is to turn right on the Snowgrass Trail, but to visit the spectacular upper part of Snowgrass Flat, you should turn left and climb a series of lazy switchbacks to the flower-covered upper meadows and a junction with the Pacific Crest Trail (PCT). Great views are almost as common as the flowers here, with fine vistas south to Mount Adams and east to the nearby jagged summits of Ives Peak, Old Snowy Mountain, and a host of unnamed summits along the crest of the Goat Rocks. The whole area is a photographer's delight. Turning left (north) at the junction with the PCT will soon take you into above-timberline terrain and lead to miles of scenic hiking all the way to a ridgetop viewpoint just above Packwood Glacier. To loop back, however, you should turn right (south) on the PCT and descend through more lovely meadows 1 mile to a large cairn marking the junction with Bypass Trail. For a great side trip from here, continue straight (south) on the PCT 1 mile to scenic Cispus Basin, and then hike another mile up to the views from Cispus Pass.

The recommended loop goes sharply right at the junction onto the Bypass Trail, which goes downhill through forest to a hop-over crossing of a lovely creek. There are some good campsites at this crossing. Just 0.2 mile past this creek is a junction with Snowgrass Trail. Turn left and soon descend a series of well-graded switchbacks. From the bottom of these switchbacks, make a gentle, woodsy walk to a bridged crossing of Goat Creek, and then climb steadily before making a 1-mile contour across a forested hillside back to the junction 0.1 mile from the trailhead. Keep left to return to your car.

Mount St. Helens and Vicinity

Our world-famous resident volcano, Mount St. Helens, proved in the spring and summer of 1980 the dangers of having unresolved anger issues. In May of that year, it released 123 years of pent-up frustrations by literally blowing its top (more than 1,300 feet of which simply disappeared) and turning everything for a dozen miles or so to the north into a scorched wasteland. Although this event certainly altered its previous considerable beauty, it also increased its appeal. Ever since the (not so) little outburst, people have been flocking here to get a closer look at the damage. And that is understandable because this fascinating and strangely compelling landscape is like no other in North America.

Hikers have it even better than other tourists because the U.S. Forest Service, which oversees the national volcanic monument, has developed a network of exciting trails where hikers and backpackers can enjoy the scenery at a slower pace than car-bound tourists. If somehow you're unmoved by the volcanic landscape, the area just south and southeast of the mountain holds some superb trails that explore scenic canyons filled with clear streams, waterfalls, and old-growth forests.

The beloved Siouxon Creek hike (Trip 17, page 67) is accessible most of the year. *photo by Paul Gerald*

12 Dome Camp

RATINGS	Scenery **9** Difficulty **6** Solitude **3**
ROUND-TRIP DISTANCE	14.2 miles
ELEVATION GAIN	1,950'
OPTIONAL MAP	Green Trails *Mount St. Helens (No. 364)*
USUALLY OPEN	Mid-June–October
BEST TIME	Late June–mid-July
AGENCY	Mount St. Helens National Volcanic Monument, 360-449-7800, fs.usda.gov/recarea/giffordpinchot/recarea/?recid=34143
PERMIT	Northwest Forest Pass required. Backcountry camping permits are required for spending the night in the Mount Margaret Backcountry. Advance reservations are strongly encouraged, as the camps are very popular during the summer. There is no fee for the permit, but reservation fees are $6 per party. Overnight camping is allowed only at 8 designated sites; these must be reserved online at recreation.gov or by phone at 877-444-6777. Bicycles, stock, and fires are prohibited.

Highlights

The vast majority of the trails in the Pacific Northwest travel through miles of dense coniferous forests before ending at some ridge, lake, or other destination where you break out of the trees and can enjoy the view. In another 50 years or so that will probably be true of this hike as well. For now, though, this trail is a wonderfully open ramble with grand views, lots of wildflowers, and only a handful of scattered fir trees. This unusual scenery results from the dramatic handiwork of Mount St. Helens, which fills the skyline just a few miles southeast. On the cataclysmic morning of May 18, 1980, the volcano flattened the forests and generally destroyed this entire area. Walking through this devastated but recovering area is a hiking experience unlike anything else in North America.

WARNING Volcanic activity is ongoing at Mount St. Helens and is intermittently dangerous. In addition, this area's soft and unstable volcanic soils, with very little vegetation to hold them in place, make erosion and trail washouts a continuing problem. Trail closures for both reasons are common and may last for months. Check on current conditions before you travel here, so you don't waste a trip.

Water is scarce to nonexistent on this hike, and there are almost no trees to provide shade or protection from the wind. Be sure to carry extra water, sunglasses, a hat, and a windbreaker.

NOTE To protect this fragile and scientifically important area, all off-trail travel (even by a few feet) is prohibited.

Getting There

From I-5, 48 miles north of Vancouver, Washington, take Castle Rock Exit 49, following signs to Mount St. Helens National Volcanic Monument, and drive

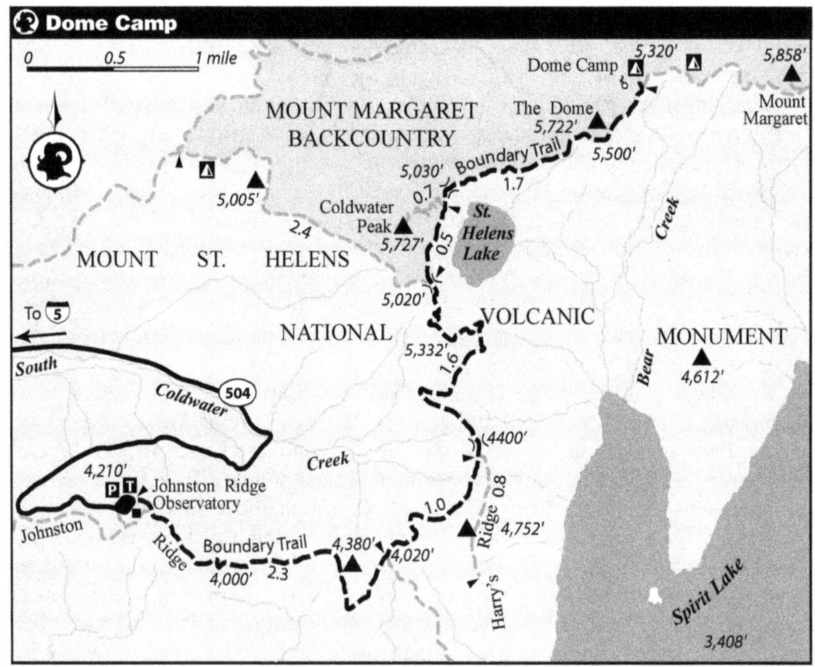

east on WA 504. Stay on this paved highway almost 44 miles, then veer right at a fork and proceed about 9 miles to the huge road-end parking lot for the Johnston Ridge Observatory and visitor center.

GPS COORDINATES N46° 16.533' W122° 12.964'

Hiking It

The initially paved, hiker-only trail departs from a large signboard at the northeast end of the parking lot. Vegetation is slowly reclaiming the surroundings. Look for willows, Sitka alders, a few scattered Pacific silver firs (now up to 20 feet tall), lupine, yarrow, pearly everlasting, wild strawberry, cliff penstemon, fireweed, and various other shrubs, grasses, and wildflowers. Look for them, that is, if you can take your eyes off the views of the mountain and the wildly eroded mudflows of the devastated area below.

After 100 yards the paved trail curves right on its way to the observatory, but you turn left on a gravelly path that goes gradually downhill. Careful inspection reveals that this "gravel" is actually a thick layer of pumice and coarse ash dropped by the volcano. Although this environment looks like a difficult place for animals to survive, keep an eye out for elk. Herds of 40 or more are fairly common, especially early in the morning. Binoculars will help you get a better look.

After 0.8 mile, the trail, which has been mostly downhill until now, changes to an up-and-down route along an open, undulating ridge. Views of the mountain are frequent, and you can also see northeast to Coldwater Peak and some of the higher summits in the Mount Margaret Backcountry. The trail makes a right turn (south) to go around a prominent high point, taking you to yet another fine view of the volcano at the end of the ridge. From here you can also see east for the first time to distant Mount Adams and down to log-choked Spirit Lake.

At 2.3 miles you go straight on the Boundary Trail at the junction with Truman Trail and wind mostly uphill through a particularly erosion-prone area where posts have been installed to help you locate the correct route. At 3.3 miles is a junction. Harry's Ridge Trail goes right 0.8 mile before dead-ending at yet another breathtaking viewpoint, this time featuring a particularly good perspective of Spirit Lake. Go left, still on the Boundary Trail, and steadily climb eight rather long switchbacks to the top of a ridge. From here you gain terrific, far-ranging views that include those looking south to Oregon's Mount Hood as well as north to Mount Rainier and the Goat Rocks. Deep, log-strewn St. Helens Lake sits in a basin between you and the rugged peaks of the Mount Margaret area.

The now narrow and rugged trail descends two short switchbacks before passing through a natural rock arch and going up and down along the side of a ridge to a junction in a saddle on the south side of prominent Coldwater Peak. The Coldwater Trail goes left, but you go straight on the Boundary Trail, which crosses the steep slope on the east side of Coldwater Peak well above St. Helens Lake.

At 5.4 miles is a junction with the 0.7-mile side trail that switchbacks up to the top of Coldwater Peak. Go straight, soon pass through another saddle, and then curve right (east), crossing a slope well above the north shore of St. Helens Lake. Atop the ridge on your left are some impressively jagged rock formations. The trail makes a final 500-foot climb to a high point on the south side of The Dome, a prominent rocky peak, before descending to the signed turnoff to Dome Camp at 7.1 miles. Situated high on a ridge just northeast of The Dome, this scenic camp boasts three designated tent sites and grand views. The only water is from a tiny spring near the lower designated campsite not far from the roofless outhouse. The spring is usually reliable but may stop flowing by late summer in particularly dry years. If the sites at Dome Camp are already taken, try to get a permit for Mount Margaret Camp, another 0.5 mile east along the Boundary Trail.

The peaks of the Mount Margaret area encircle St. Helens Lake. *photo by Douglas Lorain*

13 Goat Mountain and Green River Loop

RATINGS	Scenery **7** Difficulty **8** Solitude **8**
ROUND-TRIP DISTANCE	17.9 miles
ELEVATION GAIN	3,700'
OPTIONAL MAP	Green Trails *Mount St. Helens (No. 364)*
USUALLY OPEN	Late June–October
BEST TIME	Early July
AGENCY	Mount St. Helens National Volcanic Monument, 360-449-7800, fs.usda.gov/recarea/giffordpinchot/recarea/?recid=34143
PERMIT	None

Highlights

In the northern part of the Mount St. Helens National Volcanic Monument, only a few miles but seemingly a world away from the crowds that gather near the volcano, this wonderful loop hike explores the edge of the volcano's recovering devastated area. The loop has it all: high ridges with outstanding views; a mountain lake that is ideal for swimming; a lush river valley with huge old-growth forests; and, most surprisingly, very few people. In fact, the trails are more commonly used by equestrians than by hikers. Despite the horses, though, the trails are in good shape.

Getting There

From I-5, 20 miles north of Vancouver, Washington, take Exit 21 and travel 23.5 miles east on WA 503 to a junction. Go straight on WA 503 Spur and proceed 24.2 miles to a junction immediately past the Pine Creek Information Station. Go straight, now on Forest Service Road 25, and drive 25.6 miles to a major intersection. Turn left on FS 99, following signs to Windy Ridge; go 9.2 miles; and then turn right on single-lane paved FS 26 (this road is often closed due to washouts; call ahead for the latest conditions). Proceed 4.6 miles to a junction about 100 yards after the turnoff into the Ryan Lake Interpretive Site. Turn left on gravel FS 2612 and drive 0.4 mile to a large gravel trailhead parking lot on the right.

GPS COORDINATES N46° 21.389' W122° 04.182'

Hiking It

The trail begins from the west end of the parking lot and winds uphill at a steep grade through an old clear-cut now populated by 20-foot-tall Douglas firs, western hemlocks, Pacific silver firs, western white pines, and Engelmann spruces. The sun can be oppressive here on hot summer days, but it also provides life-giving light to many wildflowers, including Queen Anne's lace, penstemon, paintbrush, lousewort, and wild rose. Wildlife is also common. Look for elk, deer, black bears, coyotes, ruffed and blue grouse, and various small birds.

At 1 mile the trail enters a pristine forest and you enjoy shade while you continue climbing. At 1.8 miles you reach the end of a ridgeline, make a sharp left, and then continue uphill in a lichen-draped forest. About 0.5 mile and four short switchbacks later, you leave the forest and finally enter the enchanting world atop Goat Mountain Ridge. This ridge is on the edge of the devastated area, so the forests on the north side of the ridge survived, while those to the south were killed by clouds of fast-moving, super-heated gas. Two factors have allowed this area to recover more quickly than places nearer the volcano: first, plants had a shorter distance to go to recolonize the area, and second, the ground this far from the mountain was not completely sterilized by the searing heat, so some seeds managed to survive and sprout shortly after the eruption. As a result, wildflowers now abound in the meadows atop the ridge, including such colorful varieties as yarrow, lupine, wild strawberry, buckwheat, larkspur, and lomatium. Small trees have also colonized the ridgetop. But even with all the interesting geology and botany, it is the views that are this area's biggest attraction. Most impressive is the vista south over the deep chasm of the Green River Valley to the rugged, snowy crags of the Mount Margaret Backcountry. Rising behind these crags are the dramatic gray-streaked walls of the steaming crater of Mount St. Helens. If you can pry your admiring eyes away from this scene, look north to massive Mount Rainier, south to pointed Mount Hood, and east to bulky Mount Adams, each ominously awaiting its own inevitable opportunity to create volcanic mayhem.

For the next 1.5 miles the trail goes up and down near the top of the ridge, providing nonstop spectacular views. Near the western end of the traverse, you cut across the south side of a ruggedly scenic high point on the ridge and then drop to a saddle. From here you enjoy your last good view south of the devastated area and the Mount Margaret Backcountry. The pass also supports some of the best flower fields along the entire loop.

From the saddle, the trail steadily descends a brushy slope on the north side of the ridge then enters forest, and at about 4.5 miles passes a pair of unsigned but obvious junctions with side trails to campsites on Deadmans Lake. This lovely, forest-rimmed lake has a unique sandy shoreline, a result of the huge quantities of ash and pumice that dropped here during the eruption. The resulting "beach" provides a fun way to wade out into the deeper water for a swim.

Just beyond Deadmans Lake the main trail comes to a junction with the Tumwater Mountain Trail. Go straight and follow a roller-coaster route along a woodsy ridge. The vegetation is primarily open forests of subalpine and other true firs mixed with western white and lodgepole pines. Views are limited to a few glimpses of Mount Rainier to the north, but the flowers are abundant, especially in late June and early July.

About 2.4 miles from Deadmans Lake is a four-way junction. Take the downhill trail left, and descend two steep switch-

Goat Mountain Ridge from Goat Mountain Saddle, Mount St. Helens National Volcanic Monument *photo by Douglas Lorain*

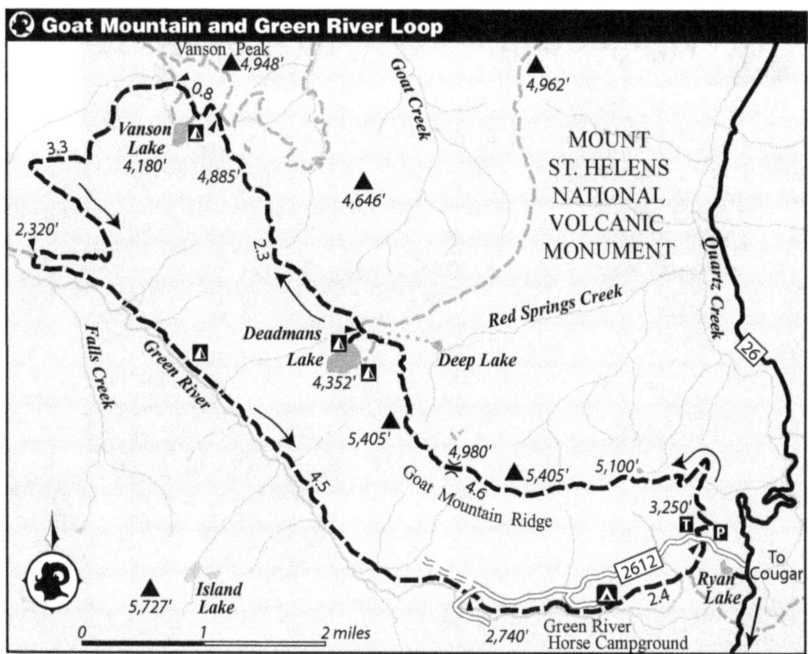

backs to a poorly marked junction. The trail to the left drops steeply to a campsite on the northeast shore of Vanson Lake. The main trail goes straight, descends to a junction with another spur to Vanson Lake, and soon reaches yet another trail junction. You go left, cross a small creek below a pretty little meadow, and then descend steadily through forest 3.2 miles to a junction with the Green River Trail.

Turn left (east) on the Green River Trail and follow this joyful, low-elevation route as it slowly ascends through an impressive old-growth forest of towering Douglas firs, never far from the clear water of misnamed Green River. After 1.4 miles you pass a pair of fine riverside campsites. Elk tracks and droppings are abundant in this area, so keep an eye out for these animals as you hike. Shortly after the campsites you take a dilapidated wooden bridge over a side creek and then go up and down 0.6 mile before leaving the forest and entering the recovering devastated area. Tall snags left behind by the blast frame sweeping views both up to Goat Mountain Ridge on your left and, on your right, of the many waterfalls on creeks dropping into the canyon from the peaks and lakes of the Mount Margaret Backcountry. Young fir trees are returning to this zone, but they still have a long way to go to match the big, old trees you passed farther downstream. The wildflowers, however, have made a more rapid recovery, with plenty of bunchberry, lupine, columbine, daisy, spirea, and other species blanketing the area.

At 15.5 miles you cross a gravel road and then gradually make your way upstream through the devastated area to the Green River Horse Campground. The trail skirts the camp area and then climbs more noticeably, passing a junction with a trail going to the right before returning to the trailhead.

14 Mount Margaret Backcountry Lakes

RATINGS Scenery **8** Difficulty **6** Solitude **4**

ROUND-TRIP DISTANCE 12.2 miles to Panhandle Lake; 15.8 miles to pass above Shovel Lake

ELEVATION GAIN 2,400' to Panhandle Lake; 3,100' to pass above Shovel Lake

OPTIONAL MAP Green Trails *Mount St. Helens (No. 364)*

USUALLY OPEN July–October

BEST TIME Mid- to late July

AGENCY Mount St. Helens National Volcanic Monument, 360-449-7800, fs.usda.gov/recarea/giffordpinchot/recarea/?recid=34143

PERMIT Northwest Forest Pass required. Backcountry camping permits are required for spending the night in the Mount Margaret Backcountry. Advance reservations are strongly encouraged, as the camps are very popular during the summer. There is no fee for the permit, but reservation fees are $6 per party. Overnight camping is allowed only at 8 designated sites; these must be reserved online at recreation.gov or by phone at 877-444-6777. Bicycles, stock, and fires are prohibited.

Highlights

The Mount Margaret Backcountry is a very scenic area in the rugged peaks north of Spirit Lake, filled with attractive mountain lakes, rocky peaks, flower fields, and great viewpoints. The region has been a popular hiking destination for decades, although its character changed dramatically (to use a woefully inadequate word) on May 18, 1980, when Mount Margaret's larger and more hot-headed neighbor literally blew its stack, blasted out the world's largest clear-cut, and obliterated the entire neighborhood. Slowly, vegetation and trails are returning to this region, providing hiking opportunities that are scenic and fascinating from both a botanical and a geological point of view. To protect the fragile environment, all off-trail travel is prohibited and hikers may camp only at designated sites.

Getting There

From I-5, 20 miles north of Vancouver, Washington, take Exit 21 and travel 23.5 miles east on WA 503 to a junction. Go straight on WA 503 Spur and proceed 24.2 miles to a junction immediately past the Pine Creek Information Station. Go straight, now on Forest Service Road 25, and drive 25.6 miles to a major intersection. Turn left on FS 99, following signs to Windy Ridge; go 9.2 miles; and then turn right on FS 26. Drive 0.9 mile, then turn left into the large parking lot at the Norway Pass Trailhead.

GPS COORDINATES N46° 18.268' W122° 04.932'

Hiking It

The trail begins from the north side of the parking lot, soon crosses a little creek, and then goes gradually uphill through a landscape that continues to recover from the 1980 blast. In addition to the obvious lack of big trees, remaining evidence of the eruption comes in the form of downed logs and sand on the trail. Careful analysis reveals that the substance isn't really sand but a mix of fine-grained ash and pumice, several feet of which fell here during the eruption. Various shrubs, including snowberries, huckleberries, and willows, now grow atop this material, along with wildflowers. Some of the more common blossoms include yarrow, fireweed, pearly everlasting, paintbrush, groundsel, and cliff penstemon. The few trees are mostly Pacific silver firs with some western hemlocks and Douglas firs. Although some of the trees are now well over 20 feet tall, they remain few and far between, putting shade at a premium. Water is also rare, so bring plenty.

At 1.1 miles is a junction. Go right, climb to the top of a small spur ridge, and then make a mostly level traverse to Norway Pass and a junction with the Independence Pass Trail. Here Mount St. Helens rather suddenly makes its appearance onstage and, like any great performer, really steals the show. The gaping crater, which often emits an ominous cloud of steam, is on full display, as is the huge (and still growing) lava dome that now fills most of the crater.

Between you and the volcano sits Spirit Lake, about 20% of which is still covered with a mat of floating logs. The logs are the result of trees that were instantly killed and toppled by a fast-moving cloud of superheated gas. The dead logs were then swept back into the lake by an enormous, avalanche-produced wave of water out of the lake. The scene is like nothing else in North America and produces memories that are likely to last a lifetime.

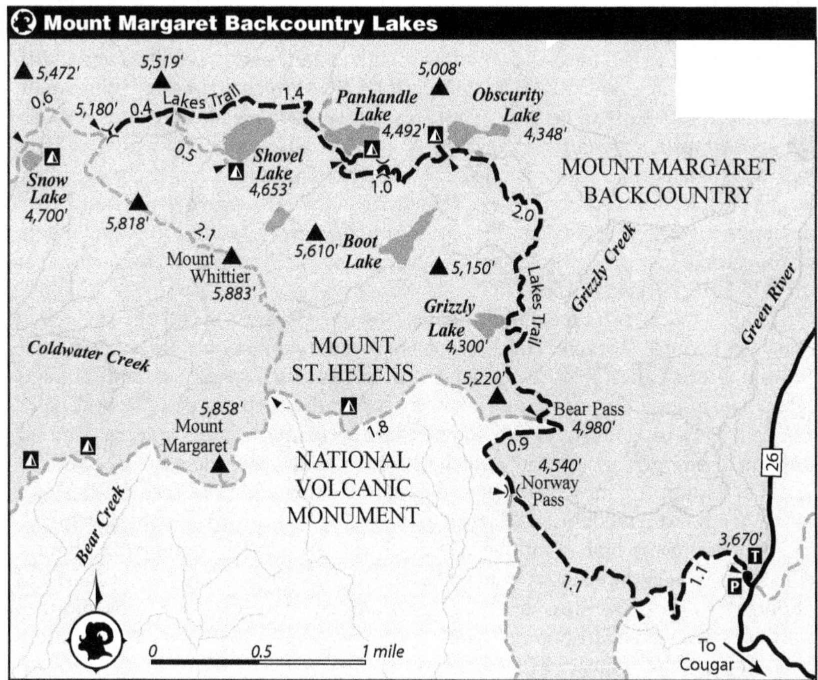

Steep cliffs rise above Grizzly Lake.
photo by Douglas Lorain

After several minutes (or hours) of gaping in awe, go right at the junction, and wind your way uphill to another junction at 3.1 miles. Turn right on Lakes Trail #211 and ascend 0.1 mile to a viewpoint at Bear Pass. From here the previously described view of Mount St. Helens is joined by views of two older volcanoes, Mount Adams to the east and Mount Rainier to the north.

To reach the lakes, descend at a steep grade on a narrow and often dangerously eroded trail that winds 0.8 mile across a steep hillside, over little ridges, and past massive deadfall to Grizzly Lake. This deep and lovely lake is set in a steep-walled cirque basin and is surrounded (as are all lakes in this devastated region) by regrowing shrubs, downed logs, and a few young trees. In spring and summer the undergrowth looks thick and healthy. Alpine wildflowers have regained a foothold, especially pink heather and white partridgefoot. Like a smaller version of Spirit Lake, Grizzly Lake has many logs floating on it. To the west rise steep slopes and cliffs that are still largely devoid of trees. It is a dramatic spot, and one that is well worth taking some time to admire, although camping is not allowed.

Cross the lake's outlet creek, and then make a mile-long sidehill traverse with lots of minor ups and downs to Obscurity Lake, which is backed by a small, unnamed rocky butte to the northwest. A short spur trail leads to a cluster of designated campsites along the inlet creek at the lake's west end. As with all camps in the devastated area, there is no shade and almost no protection from the wind.

The trail climbs steadily from Obscurity Lake to a narrow pass and then descends toward deep Panhandle Lake. About halfway around the south shore of this scenic lake, a downhill spur trail leads to the designated campsites near the lake's inlet creek.

Either Obscurity or Panhandle Lake is a fine place to spend the night, but don't stop your hike there. After setting up camp, take the time for a terrific side trip along the Lakes Trail to the west. The trail, which steeply ascends a ridge, offers some incredibly dramatic views down into the deep cirque of Shovel Lake. The tall, snow-streaked cliffs of Mount Whittier rise above the cirque, making for dramatic photographs. As you gain elevation, you also gain increasingly excellent views of Mount Adams to the east and Mount Rainier and the Green River Valley to the north. You might also be fortunate enough to see the herd of elk that spends its summers in the high meadows of this region. At a ridgetop junction about 1 mile from Panhandle Lake, a spur trail goes left and drops steeply to the west end of Shovel Lake, where there are a couple of designated campsites. The main trail continues straight from this junction, contouring 0.5 mile to a wide pass and a junction with the Whittier Ridge Trail.

NOTE The map shows an enticing loop possibility that goes southeast on the Whittier Ridge Trail to a junction with the Boundary Trail. A hiker could then turn east and walk back to Bear Pass to close out the loop. Unfortunately, the Whittier Ridge Trail has become so faint that it barely exists, and it's so dangerously steep that it should only be contemplated by daring and athletic hikers with no fear of heights. It is especially dangerous if snow remains on the trail or if there have been recent rockslides and landslides (which happen almost every year). It is safer and usually better to simply return the way you came.

15 Lewis River Trail

RATINGS Scenery **5** Difficulty **2** Solitude **6**

ROUND-TRIP DISTANCE 5.2 miles (or more, depending on your ambitions)

ELEVATION GAIN 200'

OPTIONAL MAP Green Trails *Lone Butte (No. 365)*

USUALLY OPEN April–November

BEST TIME Mid-April–mid-October

AGENCY Mount St. Helens National Volcanic Monument (Gifford Pinchot National Forest), 360-449-7800, fs.usda.gov/recarea/giffordpinchot/recarea/?recid=34143

PERMIT None

Highlights

Draining off the snowfields of Mount Adams, the clear-flowing Lewis River cascades along through some of the most impressive forests and wooded canyons of our region. A trail once followed this magnificent stream all the way from the farmlands in the lower valley to the alpine terrain of the high country, but logging roads have long since destroyed virtually all of it. A much-shortened yet still worthwhile segment remains, however, and it is a joy to hike, with great camps, a fine swimming hole, good fishing, and some of the most impressive big trees in our region.

Getting There

From I-5, 20 miles north of Vancouver, Washington, take Exit 21 and travel 23.5 miles east on WA 503 to a junction. Keep straight on WA 503 Spur and proceed 24.2 miles to a junction immediately past the Pine Creek Information Station. Turn right on paved Forest Service Road 90, drive 5.2 miles, and then turn sharply left on gravel Curly Creek Road (FS 9039). Proceed 0.7 mile to the signed Curly Creek Falls Trailhead immediately after a bridge over Lewis River.

NOTE The access road to the trailhead is closed December–March for winter wildlife protection.

GPS COORDINATES N46° 03.615' W121° 58.236'

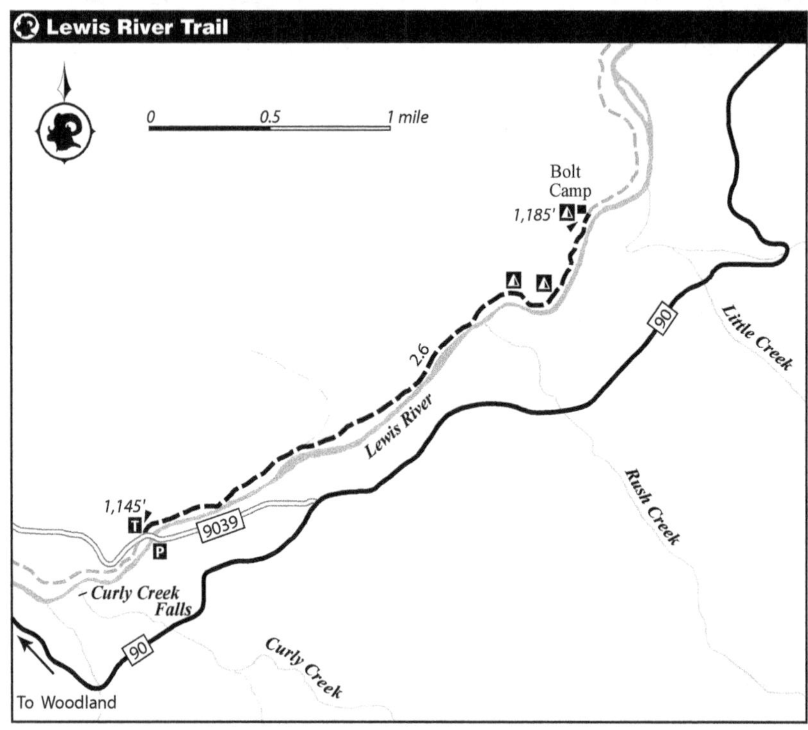

Hiking It

Head upstream on a trail that parallels the north bank of the beautifully clear and rushing Lewis River. As pretty as the water is, rivaling the stream for your attention are the trees. Huge, old Douglas firs and western red cedars mix with western hemlocks and moss-draped big-leaf maples, vine maples, and red alders in a grand display that resembles a living cathedral. Beneath this green canopy is a dense understory of salal, Oregon grape, sword fern, maidenhair fern, and various mosses and forest wildflowers.

After just a few yards, there is a fork in the trail. The 25-yard downhill path to the right provides quick access to the river, but the main trail keeps left on the hillside above the water. Like most river trails, this wide route includes several small ups and downs, but it is generally a long, gradual uphill either on the hillside a little above the river or on heavily forested, river-level flats. There are also several places where you can visit the water, do a little fishing, let the kids splash around, or just sit back and be soothed by the sounds of a flowing stream.

At 2.3 miles you pass a nice campsite just past where Rush Creek enters on the other side of the river. About 100 yards later is an even better campsite, this one right beside a superb swimming hole complete with a rope swing so you can do your best Tarzan imitation before plunging into the deep water. It is hard to imagine a more pleasant and enjoyable spot for a family backpacking trip.

Just 0.3 mile past this campsite is the Bolt Camp shelter, which has several fine tent sites clustered around a wooden shelter. The shelter, with bunks for four campers, makes an extremely inviting overnight spot if it happens to be raining, as it often does.

Stronger hikers who want a bit more exercise can continue upstream on the Lewis River Trail another 6.7 miles, passing through fine forests and enjoying continuously attractive riverside scenes the entire distance. A particularly noteworthy highlight comes at just over 7 miles from the trailhead when you climb to a fine clifftop viewpoint above the river. By making a short car shuttle, you can turn this into a fun point-to-point, 9.3-mile hike that exits at an upper trailhead (the Lewis River/Quartz Creek Trailhead; see next hike) on FS 90.

Check out 43-foot-tall Lower Lewis River Falls.

16 Quartz Creek

RATINGS	Scenery **5** Difficulty **3** Solitude **8**
ROUND-TRIP DISTANCE	9.2 miles
ELEVATION GAIN	750'
OPTIONAL MAP	Green Trails *Lone Butte (No. 365)*
USUALLY OPEN	April–November
BEST TIME	June–mid-October
AGENCY	Mount St. Helens National Volcanic Monument (Gifford Pinchot National Forest), 360-449-7800, fs.usda.gov/recarea/giffordpinchot/recarea/?recid=34143
PERMIT	None

Highlights

Quartz Creek is that most precious of rarities in our region, a significant lower-elevation watershed that has largely escaped the ravages of the chainsaw. Although there are a few logging scars in the creek's lower reaches, the generally undisturbed condition of the watershed ensures that the stream runs beautifully clear and cold beneath a green canopy of old-growth trees. That alone would make a visit here

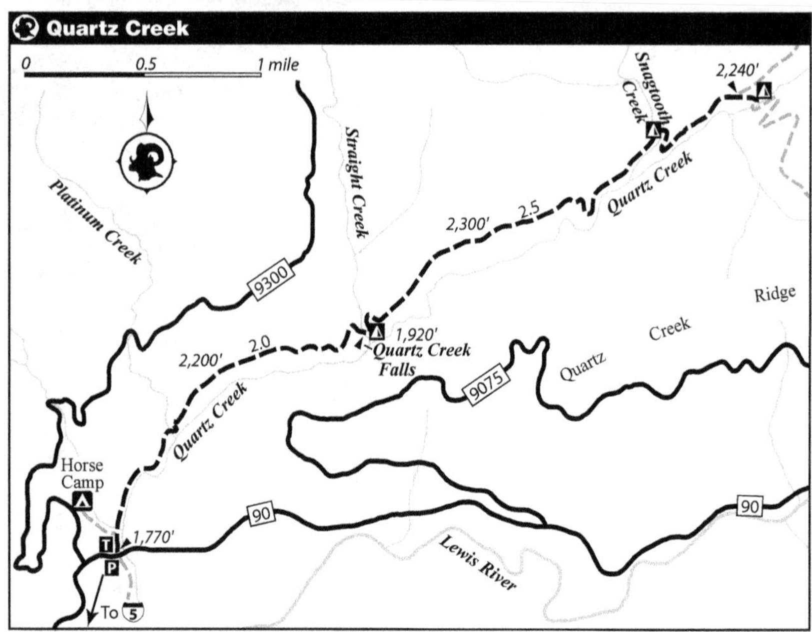

worthwhile, but the creek also has waterfalls, wildlife, and plenty of solitude, so despite the lack of distant views, hiking here is a joy.

Getting There

From I-5 north of Vancouver, Washington, take Exit 21 and travel 23.5 miles east on WA 503 to a junction. Go straight on WA 503 Spur and proceed 24.2 miles to a junction immediately past the Pine Creek Information Station. Turn right on paved Forest Service Road 90 and drive 17 miles to a trailhead pullout just before a bridge over Quartz Creek. For the latest road conditions, call the Mount Adams Ranger District, 509-395-3402.

GPS COORDINATES N46° 10.961', W121° 50.931'

Hiking It

The trail goes upstream on the west side of clear-flowing Quartz Creek through a lush, old-growth forest of massive Douglas firs, western hemlocks, and western red cedars. After just 60 yards go straight at an unsigned junction with a spur trail that goes left to a horse camp. The trail then closely follows the creek 0.4 mile before crossing Platinum Creek and making two uphill switchbacks that mark the beginning of a series of steep ups and downs. Although this part of the hike takes you well away from the creek, it compensates you with good, if partially obstructed, views of the creek canyon and surrounding ridges.

At 2 miles the trail descends to a crossing of Straight Creek. In late summer this is a simple rock-hop crossing, but early in the season it can be a wet and treacherous ford. There is a spacious and comfortable campsite on the north side of this crossing. Just downstream from this campsite, at the confluence of Straight and Quartz Creeks, is 20-foot-tall Quartz Creek Falls, which drops into an inviting (but frigid!) swimming hole.

Past Straight Creek the trail makes a short, fairly steep climb and then skirts the edge of a recovering clear-cut before gradually descending once again to Quartz Creek. You continue upstream to a rock-hop crossing of Snagtooth Creek at 4.1 miles and, 150 yards later, pass a mediocre campsite. To reach the best overnight spot in the canyon, continue another 0.4 mile to a fork, bear right (downhill), and walk 0.1 mile to an inviting campsite just before a chilly ford of Quartz Creek. Enjoy being serenaded by the soothing "river music" of a forest stream.

17 Siouxon Creek

RATINGS Scenery **7** Difficulty **2** Solitude **4**
ROUND-TRIP DISTANCE 7.6 miles
ELEVATION GAIN 700'
OPTIONAL MAP Green Trails *Lookout Mountain (No. 396)*
USUALLY OPEN March–November
BEST TIME May–October
AGENCY Mount St. Helens National Volcanic Monument (Gifford Pinchot National Forest), 360-449-7800, fs.usda.gov/recarea/giffordpinchot/recarea/?recid=34143
PERMIT None

Highlights

Three of the trademark features of the Pacific Northwest—big trees, clear creeks, and lovely waterfalls—are all on spectacular display along Siouxon Creek. Flowing through an almost unlogged low-elevation valley, Siouxon Creek runs clear and cold, just the way a natural stream should flow in this part of the world. When combined with the majestic old-growth forest and several stunning waterfalls, this trip makes for a great introduction to the Northwest outdoors. The trail is popular with mountain bikers, so hikers should expect to meet some cyclists along the way.

Getting There

From the intersection of WA 502 and WA 503 in downtown Battle Ground, Washington, drive 16.8 miles north on WA 503 to a junction in Chelatchie, just after the Mount St. Helens National Volcanic Monument Headquarters. Turn right on NE Healy Road and drive 9.2 miles to a poorly signed junction, where you bear left onto single-lane, paved Forest Service Road 57. Drive another 1.3 miles, and then turn sharply left on FS 5701. Follow this rough, paved road 3.7 miles to its end at a trailhead parking lot.

GPS COORDINATES N45° 56.795' W122° 10.657'

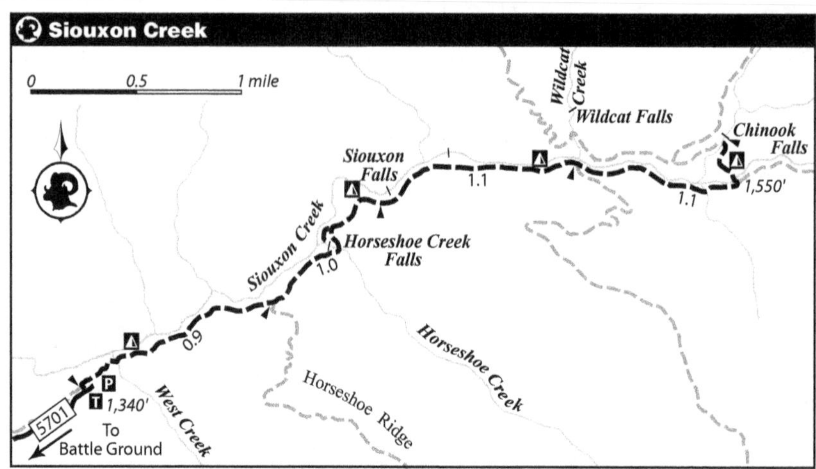

Hiking It

The trail departs from the north side of the lot and drops 50 feet to a junction with the Siouxon Creek Trail. Turn right and descend through a lovely forest composed predominantly of western hemlocks. On the forest floor are downed nurse logs sprouting a new growth of mosses, sword ferns, oxalis, and young saplings. After 0.1 mile of downhill, you reach and cross West Creek on a flat-topped log bridge. The walls of this creek's lush canyon are draped with mosses and ferns. Immediately after the bridge, you pass the first of this trip's many excellent campsites along clear Siouxon Creek. Although it occasionally approaches the water, the trail generally travels in small ups and downs, staying about 50 feet above Siouxon Creek. At 0.9 mile is the signed junction with the Horseshoe Ridge Trail.

The Siouxon Creek Trail goes straight and does a series of small ups and downs, alternating between creek-level flats covered with a tangle of vegetation and hillsides sprouting tall cedars, firs, and hemlocks. Several tiny tributary creeks cross the trail, providing ample water for plants such as devil's club and salmonberry. Cross Horseshoe Creek on a plank bridge just above lacy Horseshoe Creek Falls and, about 100 yards later, come to a junction with a 0.1-mile spur trail to a viewpoint at the base of this impressive falls.

About 0.2 mile after Horseshoe Creek Falls is a camp with a little wooden bench where you can sit and enjoy a classic view of nearby Siouxon Falls, a twisting cataract with a deep swimming hole at its base.

WARNING The scramble down to this swimming hole is steep and difficult, especially if conditions are wet.

A short distance farther upstream, you come to a smaller waterfall and then hike past a series of unsigned side trails that lead to terrific campsites and lunch spots that are perfect places for the kids to play or for adults to quietly contemplate nature.

At 3 miles you reach the unsigned junction with the upper end of the Horseshoe Ridge Trail, which bears uphill to the right. You stay straight on the lower path and walk 0.7 mile to a junction next to a bridge. The official Siouxon Creek

Trail continues straight, reaching Forest Service Road 58 in about 4.5 miles, but our more attractive route turns left, crosses the bridge above a deep pool of water, and wanders through forest less than 0.1 mile to a pair of excellent campsites. From here the trail follows Chinook Creek upstream about 0.2 mile to the base of Chinook Falls, a scenic 50-foot drop over a sheer cliff. This is a great place to enjoy the scenery while having a snack and watching the kids play in the water.

If you are up for a bit more exploring, cross Chinook Creek and make a short traverse across a hillside to a junction with the Chinook Trail. Turn left and travel gently downhill 0.5 mile to a bridgeless but easy crossing of Wildcat Creek, a little above where this stream joins Siouxon Creek. Turn right at an unofficial junction, and climb 0.2 mile to a viewpoint at the base of impressive, 100-foot-tall Wildcat Falls. Having enjoyed your fill of trees, creeks, and waterfalls, return the way you came.

Waterfalls are a highlight of the Siouxon Creek Trail. *photo by Paul Gerald*

Mount Adams and Indian Heaven

Bulky Mount Adams, which at 12,276 feet ranks second in our region only to Mount Rainier in both height and girth, towers over the Cascade Range well to the east of most other major Cascade volcanoes. This easterly location requires you to drive a bit farther to reach the mountain, but it also has some distinct advantages. First, the longer drive means that this peak, while just as scenic as its rivals, gets fewer visitors on its wildflower-covered slopes. Second, being farther east means that it is common, especially in the summer, for the clouds that frequently hang onto the western slopes of the Cascade Mountains to dissipate by the time they reach Mount Adams, leaving this glacier-clad behemoth in brilliant sunshine. Not far southeast of Mount Adams is a somewhat less dramatic but equally beautiful area called Indian Heaven. This gentle landscape hides hundreds of small lakes, open forests, and stunningly beautiful meadows. The wilderness here is especially attractive in early October, when the vine maples and huckleberry bushes turn red and orange, putting on one of the finest fall-color displays in the Pacific Northwest.

True to its name, Junction Lake (Trip 23, page 88) serves as the meeting spot for several trails. *photo by Douglas Lorain*

18 Dark Meadow via Jumbo Peak

RATINGS	Scenery **8** Difficulty **8** Solitude **8**
ROUND-TRIP DISTANCE	14 miles; 15.8 miles with side trip to Sunrise Peak
ELEVATION GAIN	3,100'; 4,000' with side trip to Sunrise Peak
OPTIONAL MAPS	Green Trails *Blue Lake (No. 334)* and *McCoy Peak (No. 333)*
USUALLY OPEN	Late June–October
BEST TIME	Early–mid-July
AGENCY	Cowlitz Valley Ranger District (Gifford Pinchot National Forest), 360- 497-1103, fs.usda.gov/recarea/giffordpinchot /recarea/?recid=31180
PERMIT	None

Highlights

If you like ridge walks through acres of wildflowers, past scenic rock formations, and to great viewpoints, then this is the trail for you. The Juniper Ridge Trail traces the entire length of its 13-mile-long, north-south-oriented namesake ridge, and hiking the entire distance is one of the finest ridge walks in our region. Since the full trail is more than most people want to tackle in a weekend, you might prefer this shorter version that hits most of the best sections, including the most interesting rock outcroppings and some of the best viewpoints. Although various species of wildflowers are abundant throughout, the real star of the show is beargrass, which in early to mid-July of favorable years puts on an amazing show of millions of tall stalks with clusters of tiny white blossoms.

Views from Jumbo Peak make the climb worth the extra effort. *photo by Douglas Lorain*

The entire length of this trail is open to motorcycles, so be aware that you may meet oncoming traffic. One consequence is that trails may be badly eroded in places. One tip for avoiding most motorized traffic is to hike early in the season before trail maintenance has been completed; downed logs will keep many motorcyclists off the trails.

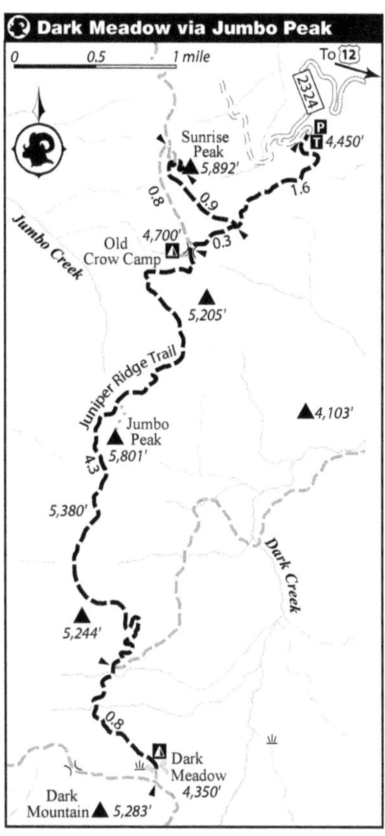

Getting There

From I-5, 67 miles north of Vancouver, Washington, take Exit 68 and drive east on US 12 for 48 miles to a junction at Randle. Turn right (south) on WA 131, following signs to Mount St. Helens, and go 1 mile to a junction. Turn left onto Forest Service Road 23 and stay on this good paved road 18.1 miles, past several intersections, to a major junction. Bear right, still on FS 23, which is now a winding one-lane road, proceed 4.6 miles, and then veer right onto gravel FS 2324, following signs to Sunrise Peak Trail. Drive this steep, narrow, and sometimes rough road 5.4 miles, fork left (uphill) at a junction, and continue a final 0.3 mile to the road-end turnaround and trailhead.

NOTE As of this writing, FS 2324 was washed out about 0.1 mile in from FS 23, making the trailhead inaccessible, but rangers expected it to be repaired and reopened soon.

GPS COORDINATES N46° 20.124' W121° 44.604'

Hiking It

From the trailhead you can see your first goal, pointed Sunrise Peak, rising on the ridge to the west. To reach it, the trail winds up a side ridge partly in forest, but mostly across open, southeast-facing slopes with good views and plenty of wildflowers. At 1.6 miles is a junction. An excellent and highly recommended side trip goes right and makes a moderately steep climb 0.6 mile up the mostly open southwest side of Sunrise Peak to a junction. From there you turn right and switchback uphill another 0.3 mile to the top of Sunrise Peak. A metal handrail helps to steady you on the final, rocky 50 feet. Views from here include all the nearby ridges and valleys, as well as the three major volcanic peaks of southern Washington: Mounts Rainier, Adams, and St. Helens. In the distance to the south you can also see horn-shaped Mount Hood in Oregon.

Back on the main trail, you descend across grassy slopes 0.3 mile to an open saddle and a junction with the Juniper Ridge Trail. Turn left and, 100 yards later, meet an unmarked boot path that leads right 0.1 mile to Old Crow Camp. This is a scenic location in a lovely green basin, but the only water comes from snowmelt or a tiny, unreliable creek. The trail now climbs a series of open slopes north of prominent Jumbo Peak. Fires swept over this ridge in the early 1900s, and the forests still haven't recovered. As a result there are frequent excellent views and plenty of sunshine for colorful July-blooming wildflowers. Look for lupine, larkspur, paintbrush, wallflower, lomatium, cat's-ear, yarrow, tiger lily, and phlox, among others. You can also expect to see hummingbirds, seemingly hundreds of which are attracted to the colorful, nectar-bearing flowers. The best views are looking north to Sunrise Peak, Mount Rainier, and the Goat Rocks.

After making an irregular but very scenic climb, you reach the northern base of Jumbo Peak. The easiest way to reach the top of this cliff-edged high point is to scramble up the trailless north ridge. The views are well worth the extra sweat. The main trail loops around the towering cliffs on the west side of Jumbo Peak and then comes to an open ridge south of the peak.

From the high, open slopes around Jumbo Peak, the trail goes down along the ridge and then steeply descends to the east. Initially you travel through a dense forest where snow often blocks the trail in early summer, but then you leave the forest and switchback down open slopes. Go left (downhill) at an unmarked junction with a long-abandoned trail and continue to a junction with little-used Dark Meadows Trail #263. Go straight and travel through brush and open forest, crossing several seasonal creeks on the way to misnamed Dark Meadow. This two-tiered, emerald-green gem sits beneath the cliffs and brushy slopes of Dark Mountain and is a good place to enjoy the wildflowers and watch for elk. (It's actually named not for any lack of sunshine or cheer, but for a prospector named John Dark who built a cabin here in 1895.) The animals often spend their evenings enjoying the pleasant diversions of bugling at one another and wallowing in the mud. There are some nice camps beside the meadow and plenty of water, at least until about late July. You should expect mosquitoes in this marshy environment in early summer. Just beyond the camps, the trail goes through an open forest between the two levels of Dark Meadow before arriving at a T-junction with the 53-mile Boundary Trail. This motorcycle-plagued pathway leads to many fine destinations, but these are beyond the scope of a short backpacking trip.

19 Foggy Flat and Avalanche Valley

RATINGS	Scenery **10** Difficulty **10** Solitude **5**
ROUND-TRIP DISTANCE	13.5 miles to Foggy Flat; 24.4 miles to Avalanche Valley
ELEVATION GAIN	1,300' to Foggy Flat; 4,800' to Avalanche Valley
OPTIONAL MAP	Green Trails *Mount Adams (No. 367S)*
USUALLY OPEN	Late July–early October

Mount Adams towers over Avalanche Valley. *photo by Douglas Lorain*

BEST TIME August–early September

AGENCY Mount Adams Ranger District (Gifford Pinchot National Forest), 509-395-3400, fs.usda.gov/recarea/giffordpinchot/recarea/?recid=31184; Yakama Nation, 509-865-5121, yakamanation-nsn.gov

PERMIT Required. U.S. Forest Service permits are free at the trailhead. Hikers must also obtain a permit for entry onto the Yakama Indian Reservation around Avalanche Valley. Crossing the boundary of the reservation without a permit is considered trespassing. Entry permits cost $5 per vehicle (good for five days) and can be purchased at the kiosk along the road near Mirror Lake. Online permit sales may be available soon at ynwildlife.org.

Highlights

Avalanche Valley is one of that handful of indescribably spectacular places that every Northwest backpacker should visit at least once in their hiking lives. The joyful springs, lovely ponds, acres of wildflowers, and, most of all, amazing views of the massive east face of Mount Adams make this one of our region's most outstanding backcountry locations. Getting there involves a long and fairly difficult hike, but almost every hiker who has made the effort swears it is worth it.

NOTE The portion of this hike from Devils Garden to Goat Butte, in the Yakama Indian Reservation, was devastated in the 2015 Cougar Creek Fire, and at the time of this writing, was still closed. Rangers hope it will reopen in summer 2020; even if it's open, definitely call ahead to check conditions and current regulations.

Getting There

Drive 60 miles east of Portland on I-84 to Hood River, take Exit 64, and cross the toll bridge into Washington ($2 as of 2019). Turn left (west) on WA 14, drive 1.6 miles to a junction, then turn right (north) on WA 141 ALT. Proceed 2.2 miles, turn left on WA 141, and go 19.5 miles to a junction just before you enter the small town of Trout Lake. Turn right (north), following signs to Mount Adams Recreation Area, and drive 1.3 miles to a fork. Bear left onto Forest Service Road 23 and remain on this paved then good gravel road through several intersections 24 miles to a prominent junction. Turn right on FS 2329 and follow this paved route to Takhlakh Lake. Drive past the campground at this popular lake and follow the narrow gravel road as it winds through forest and past trailheads 9.5 miles to a junction with paved FS 5603. Turn right and drive 1.5 miles to the well-marked PCT/Potato Hill Trailhead.

GPS COORDINATES N46° 19.515' W121° 30.357'

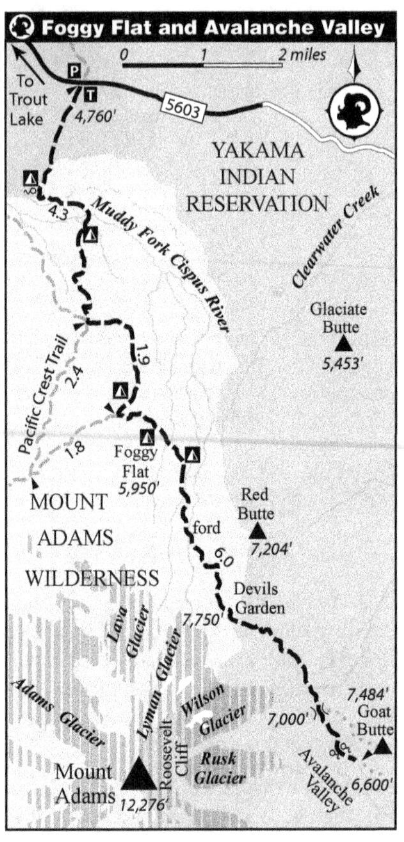

Hiking It

Walk south on the wide Pacific Crest Trail (PCT) as it gradually climbs through a lodgepole-pine forest 1.9 miles to a large lava flow. The trail then rounds the end of this jumbled mass of dark rock and comes to cheerful little Lava Spring, where there is a fine campsite. After following the edge of the lava flow another 0.5 mile, the trail angles away from the rock and goes briefly through forest to a bridged crossing of Muddy Fork Cispus River, a torrent of silt-laden glacial water. Just 0.1 mile later you cross a clear but unnamed creek that has a good campsite on its south bank.

At 4.3 miles is a four-way junction with Muddy Meadows Trail. Turn left and ascend through generally viewless forest 1.9 miles before passing a nice campsite and coming to a junction with Highline Trail. Turn left and make a series of steep little ups and downs (more ups than downs) before coming to a lush, flat meadow called Foggy Flat. A clear stream flows through this green oasis, and there are excellent camps in the nearby forest. To the south, Mount Adams crowns the entire scene. As always, do not camp on the fragile meadow vegetation. Since the creek at Foggy Flat is the last good source of clear water for several miles, it is important that hikers fill their water bottles here.

The Yakama Nation allows overnight camping in a limited number of existing sites only in Avalanche Valley, so Foggy Flat is the last good, wide-open camping area on this trip. The best plan is to set up your tent, get a good night's sleep, and then begin early the next morning on the long but very rewarding day hike into Avalanche Valley.

Beyond Foggy Flat the trail soon leaves the forest and enters a rugged area of boulders and glacial outwash. At the edge of this wasteland is a mediocre but acceptable camp near a small, reasonably clear creek. As the trail continues uphill, the views, especially to the north of distant Mount Rainier and the Goat Rocks, become ever more impressive. Another consequence of the increase in elevation is a change in vegetation. The dense forest of earlier in the trip is replaced by a few weather-stunted mountain hemlocks and whitebark pines. Even grass is rare in this rocky and inhospitable environment. The path climbs steeply beside the upper reaches of Muddy Fork Cispus River, a boisterous glacial stream, and then drops briefly to cross the creek. Snowbridges provide reasonably safe passage across the torrent for most of the summer, but you should probe carefully with an ice ax or a walking stick to avoid thin spots. If the snowbridge has collapsed, the crossing may be very difficult or even dangerous. Have a rope on hand to assist weaker members of your group across. After crossing the creek, look for huge rock cairns on the far side, and follow these as the trail resumes climbing through this above-timberline moonscape.

You climb moderately steeply through more boulder fields and lava until you reach a small, flat area covered with volcanic cinders. Here you will enjoy fine views of Red Butte, a prominent cinder cone about 1 mile northeast, and the distant icy summit of Mount Rainier. The trail finally tops out at about 7,750 feet on an exposed ridge called Devils Garden. Winds are almost constant here, so you may have to take cover behind one of the large rock cairns to rest and enjoy the view. Do not attempt this exposed section in bad weather.

The route now turns east and enters the Yakama Indian Reservation. Beyond this point the trail exists only by virtue of hikers' boots, as the Yakamas do not maintain this remote route. In places the trail is sketchy and rough, but experienced hikers should have no difficulty. To ensure that the Yakama tribe is not forced to impose restrictions on public use, it is important that you never build fires and always treat the land with special care.

The scenic tour goes east to a small drop-off and then descends steeply over a semipermanent snowfield into a little basin. From here you turn south and cross rolling alpine terrain that is both varied and attractive, with many large boulders, pretty meadows, small creeks, and rocky ridges. Unfortunately, water sources in this sandy, volcanic soil sometimes dry up by late summer, so come prepared for a dry walk. Since the trail is easy to lose in this open terrain, you will need to watch carefully for small cairns that hikers have put up to aid in navigation.

The trail gradually descends to cross a couple of usually flowing creeks draining out of Wilson Glacier, and then climbs a little to a low saddle northwest of prominent Goat Butte. From this saddle the trail descends past some springs to two small but scenic ponds before dropping to the glorious expanse of Avalanche Valley. A large, gushing spring gives birth to a good-size creek of extremely cold water at the head of the meadows, while colorful wildflowers carpet the area. The craggy edge of Goat Butte forms a beautiful backdrop along the meadow's eastern edge. It will be hard to notice any of these features, however, as your attention will naturally be turned to the jaw-dropping view of Mount Adams to the west. Cliffs and 4,000-foot-high ramparts support streaking waterfalls that pour out of Rusk and Klickitat Glaciers, shimmering in the sun. Higher still rises Roosevelt Cliff, then more glaciers, and finally the rounded summit of the great volcano. The scene is truly outstanding and well worth several hours of gazing to appreciate.

If you have time for some exploring, go back up to the trail saddle northwest of Avalanche Valley, and then climb southeast along a ridge to the summit of Goat Butte. The view from here of Mount Adams to the west and the semidesert of central Washington to the east is about as good as views get.

20 High Camp and Killen Creek

RATINGS	Scenery **9** Difficulty **6** Solitude **4**
ROUND-TRIP DISTANCE	8.2 miles to High Camp; 8.4 miles to Killen Creek; 10.4 miles combined
ELEVATION GAIN	2,350' to High Camp; 1,800' to Killen Creek; 2,650' combined
OPTIONAL MAP	Green Trails *Mount Adams (No. 367S)*
USUALLY OPEN	Mid-July–October
BEST TIME	Late July–August
AGENCY	Mount Adams Ranger District (Gifford Pinchot National Forest), 509-395-3400, fs.usda.gov/recarea/giffordpinchot/recarea/?recid=31184
PERMIT	Required; free at trailhead

Highlights

Aptly named High Camp sits at timberline on the northwest shoulder of Mount Adams, and, like most high-elevation locations, offers views that are absolutely stupendous. Most impressive are those looking up to the hulking mass of the nearby mountain, but you can also enjoy distant views to other volcanic peaks, including Mounts Hood, Rainier, and St. Helens, and look across thousands of square miles of forested ridges and valleys. The sunsets from this camp are frequently breathtaking. But like most timberline locations, High Camp is very exposed to the weather. Winds are nearly constant (good for keeping bugs at bay, but bad for almost everything else), and if a storm is on the way, it can be mighty uncomfortable. For an alternate destination a bit lower on the mountain, try Killen Creek, which has lesser views but provides more comfortable camping. Here you will find an often crowded but nice camp amid a protective grove of trees, a delightful waterfall, and a pretty little pond with a superb reflection of Mount Adams. The two locations are close enough to be combined in a single hike but are also worth enjoying separately on different trips.

Getting There

Drive 60 miles east of Portland on I-84 to Hood River, take Exit 64, and cross the toll bridge into Washington ($2 as of 2019). Turn left (west) on WA 14, drive

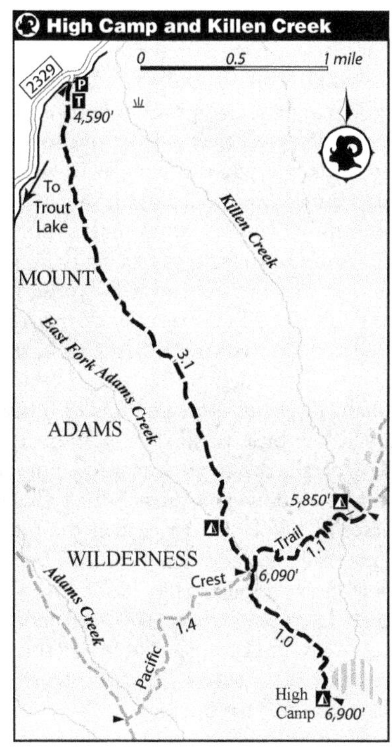

1.6 miles to a junction, then turn right (north) on WA 141 ALT. Proceed 2.2 miles, turn left on WA 141, and go 19.5 miles to a junction just before you enter the small town of Trout Lake. Turn right (north), following signs to Mount Adams Recreation Area, and drive 1.3 miles to a fork. Bear left onto Forest Service Road 23 and remain on this paved then good gravel road through several intersections 24 miles to a prominent junction. Turn right on FS 2329 and follow this paved route to a junction with the entrance road to popular Takhlakh Lake Campground. Go straight, follow the narrow gravel road 4.4 miles, and then turn right into the Killen Creek Trailhead.

GPS COORDINATES

N46° 17.304' W121° 33.164'

Hiking It

The trail winds its way south, initially on an old jeep road, but then following a pleasant trail through a forest of lodgepole pines and other conifers with a dense understory dominated by beargrass and tall huckleberry bushes. The steadily uphill route is mostly in viewless forest but with plenty of small wildflowers and an unusual variety of mushrooms along the way to keep your interest. Unfortunately, the trail is often very dusty, due to heavy horse use and a thick layer of light-gray ash dropped here by Mount St. Helens.

At about 2.5 miles the terrain becomes much more interesting when you enter some large meadows with lots of wildflowers. As with most mountain meadows, what is blooming depends on the season, with marsh marigold, shooting star, western anemone, and avalanche lily dominating in early summer; paintbrush, lupine, phlox, and pink heather taking over in midsummer; and gentian rounding out the show in late summer and early fall. The uphill slope in these meadows is more gradual than it was in the forest and is frequently interspersed with level stretches.

Shortly after passing a shallow, seasonal pond, the trail crosses tiny East Fork Adams Creek, which flows for most of the summer and has a nice campsite in a nearby grove of trees. A bit more uphill hiking through meadows takes you to a four-way junction with the Pacific Crest Trail (PCT) at 3.1 miles.

If you are heading for High Camp, go straight at the junction and resume your uphill progress on a trail that takes you into increasingly rocky terrain. You are rapidly approaching timberline now, so what trees you find are mostly stunted whitebark pines. The trail skirts around a rocky cliff, and then passes a series of small meadows and semipermanent snowfields before making a final uphill push in short, rocky switchbacks to the small, mostly level plain holding High Camp. There are a few twisted pines here but generally little else to provide shelter from the wind. Water is available either from seasonal snowmelt creeks or from lingering snow patches. Campfires are prohibited at this and any other site above the PCT.

In good weather the explorations from High Camp are magnificent. There are no trails, but you can wander to your heart's content up rocky moraines, through alpine meadows, over old lava flows, and past small waterfalls. If you are really ambitious, you can even make your way up to the base of Adams Glacier. The views are outstanding, especially up to the rugged ramparts of Mount Adams. Be sure to navigate carefully, however, because if the clouds move in, it can be very difficult to find your way back through this bleak, trailless terrain.

If you are visiting Killen Creek, return to the PCT junction and turn north on that well-traveled pathway as it winds its way up and down past meadows, over small ridges, and through bits of forest almost 1 mile to a gorgeous meadow with a shallow little pond that is often fringed with thousands of tiny white flowers. Best of all, the pond features a fine view of Mount Adams. After rounding this small meadow you cross Killen Creek just above a beautiful sloping waterfall, descend a hillside just east of the falls, and come to a junction with an obvious spur trail that goes left to a nice but overused campsite in a grove of trees. This deservedly popular spot has a lovely setting just below the falls and access to a fairly large pond about 100 yards northwest with a superb view of Mount Adams. Less crowded campsites are available if you hunt around in the forests and rocky areas to the west or by searching upstream along Killen Creek. As always, camp at least 100 feet from water.

Mount Adams from Killen Creek Meadows *photo by Douglas Lorain*

21 Horseshoe Meadow and Crystal Lake

RATINGS Scenery **7** Difficulty **6–8** Solitude **7**

ROUND-TRIP DISTANCE 14 miles to Horseshoe Meadow; 20 miles to Crystal Lake

ELEVATION GAIN 1,400' to Horseshoe Meadow; 1,900' to Crystal Lake

OPTIONAL MAP Green Trails *Mount Adams (No. 367S)*

USUALLY OPEN Mid-July–October

BEST TIME Late July–early October

AGENCY Mount Adams Ranger District (Gifford Pinchot National Forest), 509-395-3400, fs.usda.gov/recarea/giffordpinchot/recarea/?recid=31184

PERMIT Required; free at the trailhead. Northwest Forest Pass required.

Highlights

Although the Pacific Northwest has thousands of miles of trails leading to impressive and worthwhile locations, often the best and most beautiful spots are hidden just off the maintained paths. One such gem is Crystal Lake, on the southwest side of Mount Adams. Although little more than a pond, the lake is perfectly situated to provide drop-dead gorgeous views of its neighboring glacier-clad peak. But because this lake is not on an established trail, relatively few hikers make the detour to find and enjoy this spot. An alternate destination for hikers with a little less time and energy is Horseshoe Meadow, which also features a tremendous view of the mountain and has better displays of wildflowers. Some of these areas were severely burned in the 2012 Cascade Creek Fire, which consumed much of the forest around Horseshoe Meadow but—silver lining—allowed more open and dramatic views of the various peaks.

Getting There

Drive 60 miles east of Portland on I-84 to Hood River, take Exit 64, and cross the toll bridge into Washington ($2 as of 2019). Turn left (west) on WA 14, drive 1.6 miles to a junction, then turn right (north) on WA 141 ALT. Proceed 2.2 miles, turn left on WA 141, and go 19.5 miles to a junction just before you enter the small town of Trout Lake. Turn right (north), following signs to Mount Adams Recreation Area, and drive 1.3 miles to a fork. Veer right and proceed 0.7 mile to another fork, where you go left onto Forest Service Road 80. Stay on this initially paved, then gravel road about 9 miles to Morrison Creek Campground, where you turn right and continue 2.5 miles on rough dirt FS 500 to the South Climb Trailhead near Cold Springs Campground. This trailhead parking area fills quickly with climbers looking to go up Mount Adams, so try to arrive early.

GPS COORDINATES N46° 08.140' W121° 29.868'

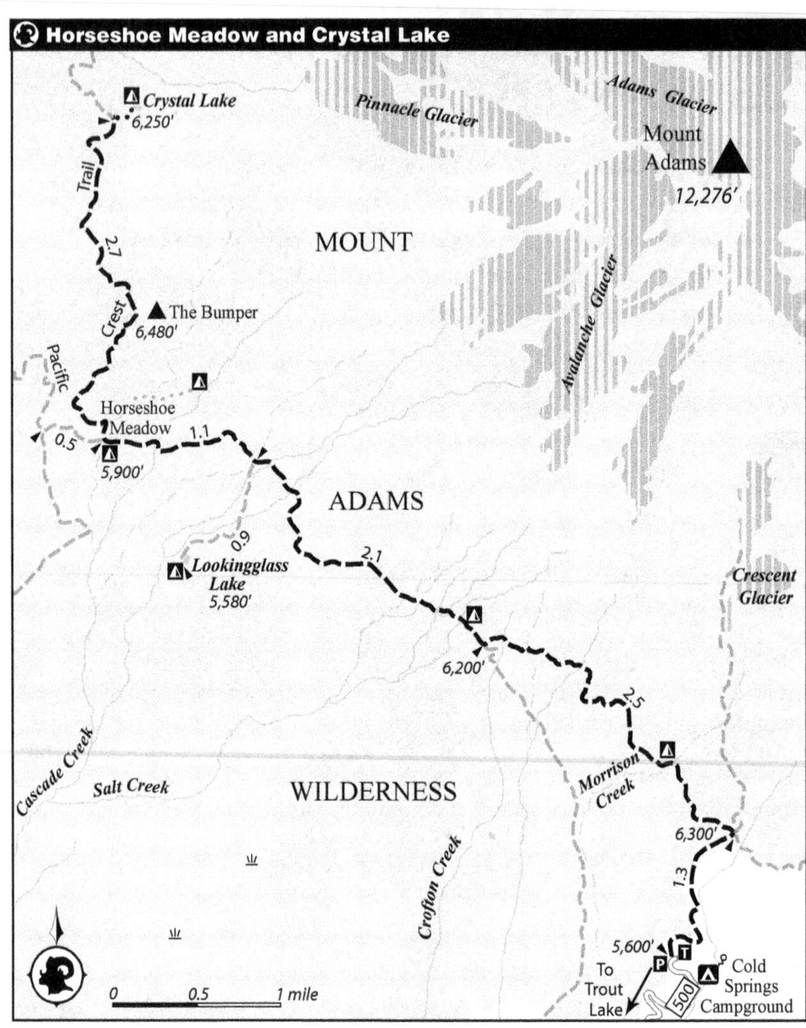

Hiking It

Stark evidence of the 2012 Cascade Creek Fire greets you right at the trailhead, allowing early peeks of Mount Adams gleaming ahead. Walk north on a wide trail (actually a long-abandoned jeep road) as you gradually gain elevation in an open forest of mountain hemlocks and subalpine firs. With each step the surroundings become increasingly alpine in nature, with more wildflowers and fewer trees. At 1.3 miles is a four-way junction with the Round-the-Mountain Trail. The well-used path that goes straight (uphill) is the most popular climbing route up Mount Adams. The ascent is long and tiring, but not technically difficult. If you want to make the attempt, keep in mind that from May through September all climbers are required to have a Cascade Volcanoes Pass when venturing above 7,000 feet on the mountain. As of 2020, daily passes cost $10 per person for a weekday or $15 for a weekend day and are available at the Mount Adams Ranger Station in Trout Lake or the Cowlitz Ranger Station in Randle. Exact change or a check is required.

For this trip you turn left (west) at the junction and begin a long, gently rolling traverse that leads over a small ridge to a nice view of Mount Adams. The visibly scorched terrain is generally open, with a few mountain hemlocks adding patches of shade and variety. At 2.1 miles you cross intermittent Morrison Creek (camps nearby), and then continue the easy up-and-down hike. On clear days this area provides some fine views looking south to Oregon's Mount Hood. After crossing some old lava flows and a few usually dry creekbeds, you come to a junction with the Shorthorn Trail at 3.8 miles. Keep straight and soon reach Salt Creek, where there are some scenic camps.

The trail continues west, maintaining its remarkably level grade. Although the trail is mostly gentle, the surrounding landscape is not, much of it consisting of jumbled rock and sand deposited here in a massive landslide in 1921. Another huge debris slide came down this side of Mount Adams in 1997, although that one did not get as far down as the trail. In late 2006, several significant washouts occurred along this section when many of the creeks flooded and washed away the unstable soils. On top of that are the effects of the 2012 fire, which tend to make slides and washouts even worse. Be sure to check on current conditions before attempting this hike.

As the trail continues into the burn zone, the alpine terrain becomes gentler. Soon the trail crosses two branches of aptly named Cascade Creek just before reaching a junction. The trail to the left leads down to tiny Lookingglass Lake, which is ringed by scorched trees but has some pleasant camps. Your trail goes

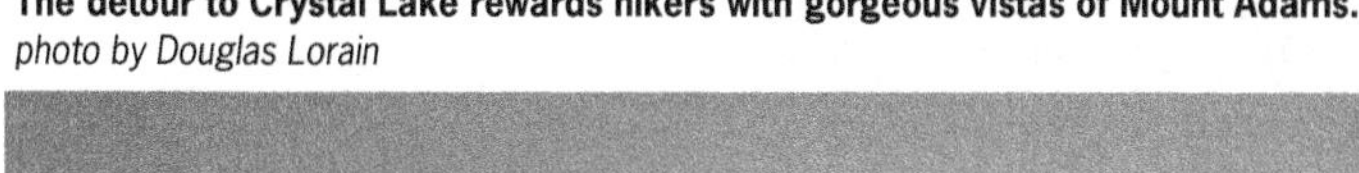

The detour to Crystal Lake rewards hikers with gorgeous vistas of Mount Adams.
photo by Douglas Lorain

straight and continues west 1.1 miles to the welcome expanse of Horseshoe Meadow. This large and remarkably flat meadow, despite having lost many of its surrounding tall trees to the blaze, is covered with tiny wildflowers in July and August and features an excellent view of Mount Adams. The tiny creek crossing Horseshoe Meadow sometimes dries up by midsummer, but if water is available, there are excellent camps near the creek crossing. Unfortunately, equestrian parties often use these camps, so expect plenty of horse apples and that distinctive equine aroma. For privacy and more-reliable water, consider walking cross-country up to the northeast corner of the meadow and then scrambling uphill past a waterfall on the right branch of the intermittent creek to a lovely pumice-covered meadow, where there are nice mountain views, good camps, and water from a permanent tributary of Cascade Creek.

At the west end of Horseshoe Meadow is a junction with the Pacific Crest Trail (PCT). Turn right (north), gain a little elevation along a minor ridge, and then make an up-and-down traverse of numerous small ridges and gullies on a circuitous course to the north. Views of Mount Adams are blocked by ridges, but there are nice vistas to the west of distant Mount St. Helens. You round a ridge, and then, about 2.7 miles from where you started on the PCT, you begin to lose elevation along the side of a second ridge. Immediately after beginning this descent, turn right (east) off the trail and walk cross-country up a grassy gully 0.2 mile. From there you turn left and climb a rocky area with scattered trees to small Crystal Lake. The lake has no fish and is too cold for comfortable swimming, but the view of Mount Adams across the glassy waters is superb. Be sure to camp at least 100 feet away from water in this pristine area.

22 Sunrise Camp

RATINGS Scenery **9** Difficulty **8** Solitude **5**

ROUND-TRIP DISTANCE 8 miles

ELEVATION GAIN 2,650'

OPTIONAL MAP Green Trails *Mount Adams (No. 367S)* (but the trail alignment is inaccurate)

USUALLY OPEN Late July–September

BEST TIME August and September

AGENCY Yakama Nation, 509-865-5121, yakamanation.org/tract-d.php

PERMIT Yakama tribal permits are required both to enter and to camp in this area, known as Tract D of the Mount Adams Recreation Area. Crossing the boundary of the reservation without a permit is considered trespassing. Entry permits cost $5 per vehicle (good for five days) and can be purchased at the kiosk along the road near Mirror Lake. Camping permits cost $10 per group, good for 24 hours, and can be purchased at the self-service drop box at Mirror Lake or at the trailhead. Camping is allowed in existing sites only; there are 15 sites at Sunrise Camp.

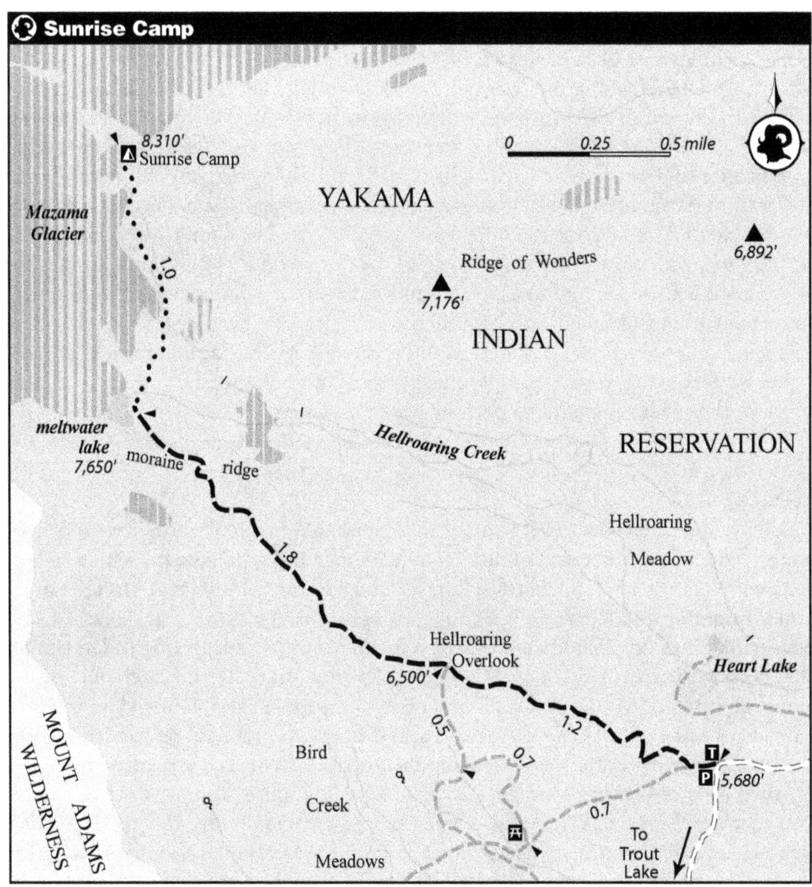

Highlights

Sunrise Camp, as the name suggests, is an excellent place to watch a sunrise, but there is much more to recommend this trip than just the fine early-morning show. Located high above timberline on the east slopes of Mount Adams in the Yakama Indian Reservation, the camp is also a great place to observe mountain goats, take in extensive views, get up close and personal with a glacier, and fill your lungs with clear mountain air. The hike, however, is not for everyone, as the upper part of the route involves boulder-hopping and off-trail scrambling. At least one member of the party should be familiar with cross-country travel. The camp is also very exposed, so bring a sturdy tent, and do not attempt this hike in bad weather.

NOTE Sadly, the hike includes areas that were devastated in the massive 2015 Cougar Creek Fire, and at the time of this writing, the entire area was still closed, but rangers hope it will reopen in summer 2020. Even if it's open, definitely call ahead to check conditions and current regulations before setting out.

Getting There

Drive 60 miles east of Portland on I-84 to Hood River, take Exit 64, and cross the toll bridge into Washington ($2 as of 2019). Turn left (west) on WA 14, drive 1.6 miles to a junction, then turn right (north) on WA 141 ALT. Proceed 2.2 miles, turn left on WA 141, and go 19.5 miles to a junction just before you enter the small town of Trout Lake. Turn right (north), following signs to Mount Adams Recreation Area, and drive 1.3 miles to a fork. Veer right on what becomes Forest Service Road 82 and drive 2.6 miles on this paved road to a multiway junction at a Sno-Park, where the road turns to gravel. Continue on FS 82, following signs to Bird Creek Meadows, and proceed 6.4 miles on this good gravel road to another fork. Go straight on what quickly becomes a rough dirt road and slowly bounce along 4.2 miles to a tribal pay station and road junction beside scenic little Mirror Lake. After buying your entry permit, go straight at the junction and drive 1.1 miles to the spacious trailhead parking area on the left.

GPS COORDINATES N46° 09.218' W121° 25.504'

Hiking It

The wide and often dusty trail (actually a long-abandoned road) goes west through a lovely high-elevation forest of mountain hemlocks and subalpine firs with a rather sparse understory of huckleberries, lupines, and various wildflowers. After 0.1 mile you go right at a junction onto a foot trail signed as MOUNTAIN CLIMBERS TRAIL. This path winds uphill at an uneven but sometimes steep grade through a landscape that becomes increasingly open as you gain elevation. Initially you catch only occasional glimpses of Mount Adams, but these become more expansive and impressive as you continue uphill. The vegetation also changes to more alpine varieties, with wind-twisted whitebark pines replacing the previous trees, and low-growing flowers such as late-August-blooming gentians becoming more dominant. At 1.2 miles you reach Hellroaring Overlook, where there is an outstanding view of the wide, steep-sided canyon of Hellroaring Creek and up to glacier-clad Mount Adams. To the north you can see a tall waterfall dropping over the headwall of Hellroaring Canyon. Your route will take you a little above the top of this falls.

Above Hellroaring Overlook an unmaintained trail continues uphill, generally staying near the edge of the drop-off into Hellroaring Canyon. There are several unsigned use paths in this area, but if you stay close to the rim and stick with what appears to be the main route, it is hard to go wrong. If you lose the trail, look for occasional cairns or orange blazes on rocks to help get you back on track. As you continue gaining elevation, the trees become smaller and then disappear entirely, leaving only rocks, grasses, small wildflowers, and plenty of amazing views. To the south you can see Mount Hood and the high points of the Columbia River Gorge. To the east extend the forested Simcoe Mountains and the dry plains of eastern Washington. Most impressive of all, straight ahead to the north rises Mount Adams, covered with rocks, snow, and massive flows of ice.

Because this trail is not maintained or signed and it travels through harsh and rocky terrain, you should expect to do some wandering around to find the correct route. This doesn't affect the scenery, but you need to realize that the mileages given here are only approximations. At about 2.7 miles you come to the top of a

From a moraine below Mazama Glacier, Mount Adams lies in the distance.
photo by Douglas Lorain

large moraine, left behind by the retreating Mazama Glacier. Turn left and go up the spine of this rocky moraine for about 100 yards, and then bear right on an obvious trail that makes a rough and rocky up-and-down traverse for 0.3 mile to a possible emergency campsite near a stark and unnamed meltwater lake at the base of Mazama Glacier. A few rocks have been piled around the tent site to provide at least some shelter from the frequent winds. The lake is a spectacular spot, filled with floating icebergs for the two months each year it is not frozen over entirely. You can see a small part of the top of Mount Adams over a ridge to the north.

Above the meltwater lake, the way is only a general route. There is no tread visible amid the rocks, although a few cairns have been built to assist hikers with navigation. Fortunately, staying on course is surprisingly easy, as you simply make your way up toward the left side of an obvious flat-topped ridge that extends east from the shoulder of Mount Adams. The easiest route to this destination crosses the meltwater lake's silty outlet creek and then climbs over rocks and snowfields going almost due north. You will cross a couple of very silty meltwater creeks along the way, but these crossings are easy rock-hops.

You reach the low point in the ridge at 4 miles, where you are greeted with a tumbling creek flowing from the icy base of nearby Mazama Glacier. Sunrise Camp is located on a large sandy flat with several tent sites. Once again, campers have stacked up low rock walls to provide some protection from the almost constant winds. Even so, the area is very exposed, so you will need a sturdy tent with plenty of guy wires. If you can tear your eyes away from the amazing scenery, be sure to check the nearby rocky areas for mountain goats. Often the animals will wander right through camp, so guard your food carefully. Never approach the goats, which are unpredictable and have very sharp horns.

It is possible to scramble from Sunrise Camp to Avalanche Valley (see Trip 19, page 74), which you can see well below you to the north-northeast. However, the way is unmarked, steep, rough, and potentially dangerous. Depending on conditions, you may have to cross glaciers, and you will certainly have to negotiate steep rocky areas that are extremely difficult and even dangerous for all but the most experienced hikers. It is better to return the way you came.

23 Lemei and Blue Lakes Loop

RATINGS Scenery **7** Difficulty **4** Solitude **5**

ROUND-TRIP DISTANCE 12.3 miles (with many shorter options)

ELEVATION GAIN 1,800'

OPTIONAL MAPS Green Trails *Lone Butte (No. 365)* and *Wind River (No. 397)*

USUALLY OPEN Late June–October

BEST TIMES Late August; early–mid-October

AGENCY Mount Adams Ranger District (Gifford Pinchot National Forest), 509-395-3400, fs.usda.gov/recarea/giffordpinchot/recarea/?recid=31184

PERMIT Required; free at the trailhead. Northwest Forest Pass required.

Highlights

The Indian Heaven Wilderness is a gentle mountain landscape that covers a high volcanic plateau in the Washington Cascades southwest of Mount Adams. Instead of featuring a towering, glacier-clad mountain like many other wilderness areas in our region, this wilderness protects hundreds of lakes and beautiful subalpine meadows amid an open mid-elevation forest. Hiking here is relatively easy because elevation gains are generally small and there seems to be a new lake with fine campsites around every bend. Although in July the wildflowers are terrific, that is when the bugs in this area (sometimes called Mosquito Heaven) can number in the trillions—and that's just counting the clouds hovering around your head. As a result, it is best to give this area a wide berth in July and early August—a couple hundred miles should do it. Fall-color time in early October is a much better time to visit, as the huckleberry bushes will be bright orange and red, the meadows golden brown, and the vine maples a stunning scarlet. Best of all, you probably won't see a single bug. Late August is also a good time for this trip, especially if you are a fan of eating tasty huckleberries.

NOTE Although part of this loop is on abandoned trails that are no longer maintained nor shown on the newer maps, they are still easy to follow and fun to hike.

Getting There

From Portland, take I-84 east 40 miles to Cascade Locks, take Exit 44, and almost immediately veer right to loop around and cross the Columbia River on the Bridge of the Gods (a $2 toll applies, as of 2019). Turn right on WA 14, go 6.1 miles, and then turn left (north) on the signed road to Carson. After 0.9 mile go straight at an intersection in the middle of Carson, and then proceed 4.9 miles to a junction. Turn right on Old State Road, proceed 0.1 mile, and then turn left on paved Forest Service Road 65. (Note that there's currently some flood damage on this road; for lower-clearance vehicles, the Forest Service recommends using FS 6507 instead; from Carson, stay on Wind River Highway/Meadow Creek Road 28 miles, then

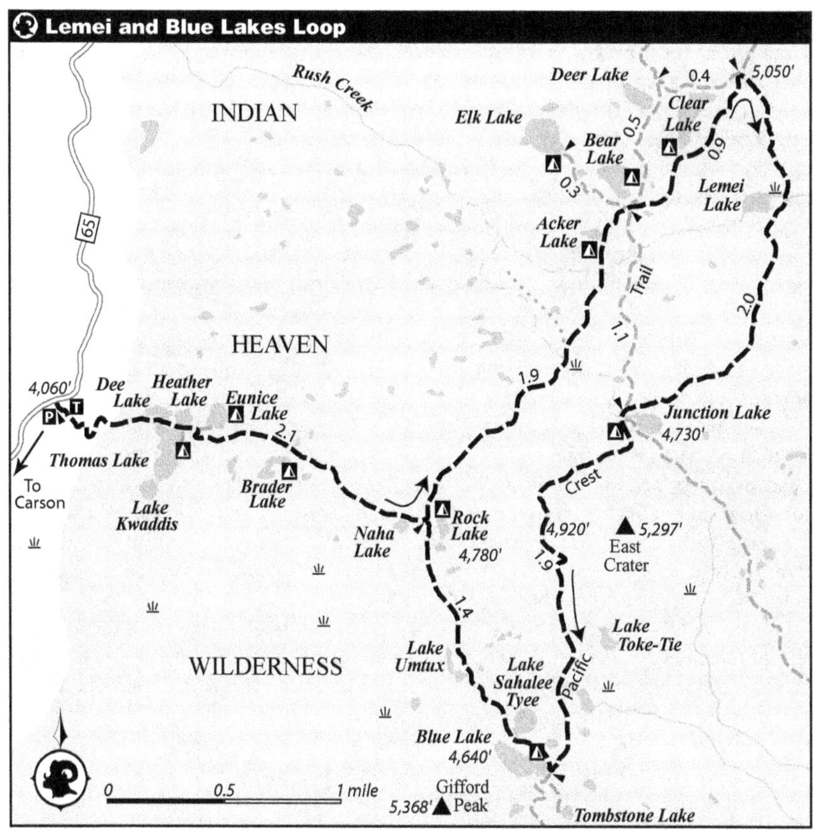

turn right onto FS 6507. Drive 4 miles to FS 65, turn left, and find the trailhead on your right.) High-clearance vehicles can follow FS 65 for 11.1 miles to a four-way junction, where you go straight, still on paved FS 65. After 2 more miles you come to a fork where the pavement ends. Keep right on FS 65 and proceed a final 6.8 miles on good gravel to the signed Thomas Lake Trailhead on the right.

GPS COORDINATES N46° 00.348' W121° 50.352'

Hiking It

The trail starts in an old clear-cut but soon leaves this unattractive area, enters the Indian Heaven Wilderness, and travels through a lovely mid-elevation forest of mountain hemlocks and Pacific silver firs. Tall blueberry and huckleberry bushes crowd the trail and make tempting reasons to stop and enjoy the harvest from late August to mid-September. The route is uphill but never steep, and is easy enough for hikers of any age or ability. After 0.5 mile you reach the first lakes when the trail cuts through the narrow strip of forested land separating large Thomas Lake on the right (south) from smaller Dee and Heather Lakes on the left (north). All three lakes have fish and are good for swimming. With such easy trail access, it is not surprising that these lakes are very popular. Still, they make excellent destinations for hikers with young children. The Forest Service prohibits camping in the fragile strip of land between the lakes and requires that backpackers use only sites designated by cedar posts with engraved camp symbols. Some of the best legal sites are along the east shore of Thomas Lake.

Near the southeast end of Heather Lake, a spur trail goes straight 120 yards to a campsite beside pretty Eunice Lake. The main trail goes right at this junction, makes a short but steep climb up a forested ridge, and then levels out as you enter the high plateau of Indian Heaven. This plateau is covered with forests and delightful meadows that are lined with low-growing huckleberries and heather. Unseen to the south is off-trail Brader Lake, which you can wander down to and camp beside with a reasonable chance of privacy. The main trail continues straight, passing through more small meadows and strips of forest as it gradually climbs to an unsigned but obvious junction at 2.1 miles, just 75 yards west of shallow Rock Lake.

The official trail goes sharply right (south) here and is the way you will return if you take the recommended loop. For now, turn left on a section of the old Cascade Crest Trail and follow this winding and often badly eroded route as it goes downhill in fits and starts, mostly through forest, for 0.7 mile before entering the large meadows in the center of Indian Heaven. These grassy expanses are stunningly attractive with plenty of wildflowers and several small ponds. In early to mid-October the color show is outstanding.

In the middle of one of these meadows, the trail crosses a deep but sluggish section of misnamed Rush Creek, where kids can amuse themselves for hours hunting for frogs or looking at small fish. Just beyond this crossing you may notice a faint old trail that angles off to the left. Go straight on the main route, which is often marked with posts across the meadows, and wander north to a fine campsite beside lovely Acker Lake. This lake is rarely crowded and makes a fine place to spend the night.

Beyond Acker Lake the old trail makes a short but steep climb up a forested hillside to a multiway junction. Through the trees to the north you can see deep Bear Lake. The main trail at this junction is the Pacific Crest Trail (PCT), which goes north–south. Another official trail goes left on its way to Elk Lake. Your route, however, goes straight across the PCT to the east, following another old trail that winds uphill beside a little gully. After about 0.2 mile look for a use path that continues upstream along the gully for about 50 yards to a fine campsite at the south end of large Clear Lake. This is a particularly beautiful lake, as its north end is backed by a scenic talus slope.

Clear Lake *photo by Douglas Lorain*

The main trail wanders up and down through the forests east of Clear Lake, eventually coming to a junction at 4.9 miles. Turn sharply right here onto the maintained Lemei Trail. This winding route takes you south through more meadow-and-forest country for 0.5 mile to the large meadow holding marshy Lemei Lake. This is an excellent place to eat lunch and enjoy the view to the east of distant Lemei Rock. The trail then makes a short uphill before heading southwest, mostly in forest, another 1.5 miles to Junction Lake. This narrow lake features fine campsites and, true to its name, several trail junctions.

Turn south on the PCT, ignoring a junction with the East Lemei Trail that goes along the south side of Junction Lake, and climb a bit before making a long loop around the forested flanks of an old cinder cone called East Crater. At the south end of this traverse, you lose elevation and then reach a junction at the eastern end of Blue Lake at 8.8 miles. Turn right at this junction, leaving the PCT, and soon pass some superb campsites above the northeast shore of the lake. This is a fairly popular but very scenic place to spend the night because the deep, clear lake is backed by the impressive cliffs of Gifford Peak to the southwest. Backpackers are required to camp at sites designated by cedar posts with camp symbols.

To close out the loop, follow the trail as it goes uphill, rounds the shore of Lake Sahalee Tyee (more designated camps here), and then reenters meadow country as it winds past Lake Umtux and a series of nearby ponds back to the junction near Rock Lake. Turn left and return past Thomas Lake the way you came.

24 Lake Wapiki

RATINGS Scenery **7** Difficulty **6** Solitude **6**

ROUND-TRIP DISTANCE 9.6 miles

ELEVATION GAIN 2,500'

OPTIONAL MAPS Green Trails *Lone Butte (No. 365)* and *Mount Adams—West (No. 366)*

USUALLY OPEN Late June-October

BEST TIME Late August; early October

AGENCY Mount Adams Ranger District (Gifford Pinchot National Forest), 509-395-3400, fs.usda.gov/recarea/giffordpinchot/recarea/?recid=31184

PERMIT Required; free at the trailhead. Northwest Forest Pass required.

Highlights

Filling the center of a colorful old volcanic crater, Lake Wapiki is one of the crown jewels in the string of watery gems that populate Washington's Indian Heaven Wilderness. There are two ways into the lake; the eastern approach is shorter and involves less elevation gain but travels through viewless forest the entire way. The more attractive and recommended option comes in from the north and west on a scenic route that visits lovely Cultus Lake, passes several beautiful meadows,

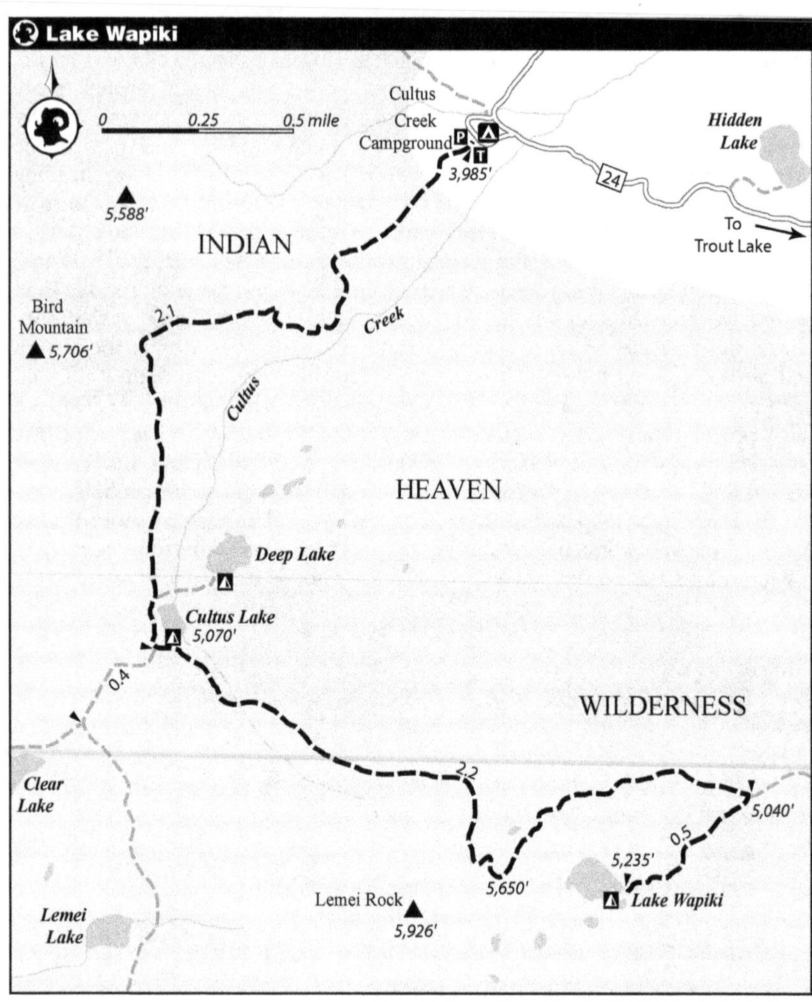

takes you to a fine viewpoint, and nearly touches the jagged crags of dramatic Lemei Rock. Overall, it is a tasty package, and you can make it even tastier if you time your visit for late August, when the huckleberries are ripe. As with other trips in Indian Heaven, avoid July and early August, when you will be plagued by clouds of buzzing, blood-sucking mosquitoes.

Getting There

Drive 60 miles east of Portland on I-84 to Hood River, take Exit 64, and cross the toll bridge into Washington ($2 as of 2019). Turn left (west) on WA 14, drive 1.6 miles to a junction, and then turn right (north) on WA 141 ALT. Proceed 2.2 miles, turn left on WA 141, and go 19.6 miles to the small town of Trout Lake. Stay on WA 141 through town (veering left at the fork), and continue 8 miles to a junction. Paved Forest Service Road 60 goes straight, but turn right on good gravel FS 24 and continue 9.1 miles to Cultus Creek Campground. Turn left and follow the dirt campground loop road 0.2 mile to the signed trailhead.

GPS COORDINATES N46° 02.863' W121° 45.299'

Hiking It

Walk southwest from the campground through a dense but attractive forest of mixed conifers featuring grand firs, Douglas firs, Engelmann spruces, and western hemlocks. The forest floor is covered with a thick blanket of beargrass, vanilla leaf, and false hellebore, but the most common understory species here, as it is throughout Indian Heaven, is huckleberries. After crossing a trickling creek, the trail begins going steeply uphill. At 1.4 miles you briefly break out of the trees for a fine view of Mounts Adams and Rainier and then return to forest and continue uphill, although now at a more gradual grade.

The terrain opens up at 1.5 miles, where the forest is interspersed with delightful subalpine meadows filled with grasses, wildflowers, and low-growing huckleberry bushes. In early October these bushes turn bright orange and red, making for a great display of color. In addition to being beautiful, these meadows provide fine views of nearby rugged peaks, such as Bird Mountain and Lemei Rock.

At 2 miles you reach Cultus Lake and a signed junction with the short side trail to aptly named Deep Lake, which features a view of distant Mount Adams. Huckleberry bushes line the shores of both Deep and Cultus Lakes, as they do all meadows and bodies of water in this wilderness.

Above the southwest end of Cultus Lake are a very good campsite and a trail junction. To reach Lake Wapiki, turn left on the Lemei Trail, which for the next mile or so climbs through stunningly beautiful meadows that come alive in late July with the blossoms of pink heather, white partridgefoot, blue lupine, and numerous other colorful wildflowers. At 3.4 miles the trail tops a ridge that radiates off the northeast shoulder of jagged Lemei Rock. From here you turn left to cross a small open area with outstanding views down into the deep bowl holding Lake Wapiki and northeast to snow-covered Mount Adams.

The trail now makes a rather steep descent, losing 600 feet in 0.9 mile, to a signed junction with a 0.5-mile uphill spur trail leading to the east end of Lake Wapiki. There are several fine campsites at this scenic lake that allow you to put up your tent and spend a lazy afternoon fishing or just gazing in admiration at the lake and its surrounding ridges. Because this is one of our area's best swimming lakes, you will probably want to plunge in and give that a try as well.

Lemei Rock, Indian Heaven Wilderness
photo by Douglas Lorain

Oregon Coast and Coast Range

The dramatic north coast of Oregon is a land of rugged headlands, offshore rocks, abundant wildlife, sandy beaches, and generally excellent scenery. But despite its allure, it's not actually an easy place to find a good backpacking route. Most coastal trails are too short or have no camping options for backpackers, partly because the rules that govern camping on Oregon beaches limit the options for staying overnight. In the Coast Range, backpacking options are also fairly limited, with only a few hiking destinations that have reasonable camping available. But the rare trails to campsites along salmon streams or at the handful of small lakes hidden amid the dense forests and rugged ridges of these mountains are worth seeking out. The lower elevations of the coast and Coast Range are a good choice in the off-season, when the Cascade Mountains are still covered in a thick blanket of white.

You may have to wait until the fog lifts, but views from Tillamook Head (Trip 25, page 96) can be incredible.

25 Tillamook Head

RATINGS	Scenery **6** Difficulty **4–5** Solitude **4**
ROUND-TRIP DISTANCE	3 miles (from the south); 8.8 miles (from the north)
ELEVATION GAIN	820' (from the south); 1,200' (from the north)
OPTIONAL MAP	USGS *Tillamook Head*
USUALLY OPEN	All year (but very muddy in winter)
BEST TIME	March–June
AGENCY	Ecola State Park, 503-436-2844, oregonstateparks.org
PERMIT	None required to camp, but you must purchase a day-use pass ($5) to enter Ecola State Park. Overnight parking is prohibited inside the park and at both trailheads, so you'll need to either arrange for someone to drop you off or leave your car in a public parking area outside the main trailhead lot. (The latter option is more appealing in Seaside than in Cannon Beach, as the access road to the south trailhead makes for an awfully long trek on a paved road with no pedestrian walkway).

Highlights

Tillamook Head is a towering headland that rises more than 1,000 feet above the pounding surf of the Pacific Ocean between Cannon Beach and Seaside. This imposing landmark is protected in Ecola State Park, truly one of Oregon's crown-jewel parks. Along a route taken by Captain William Clark, Sacagawea, and other members of the Lewis and Clark Expedition, the park is crossed by an enjoyable and historic section of the Oregon Coast Trail that passes through lush coastal rainforests and visits several fine viewpoints. Unlike most other trails along the Oregon Coast, this one also includes a designated backpackers' campsite, allowing hikers to extend their stay and enjoy the scenery a little longer.

WARNING Signs at the trailhead correctly warn of steep trailside cliffs along this route. Over the years, these cliffs have claimed the lives of more than a few unwary hikers and numerous dogs whose owners failed to have the animals leashed. Please be careful, and always keep dogs leashed.

Getting There

Take US 26 about 70 miles northwest from Portland to its junction with US 101.

To reach the north trailhead, go north on US 101 for 3.1 miles, and then turn left at a light at the south end of Seaside onto Avenue U. Proceed 0.2 mile, and then turn left (south) on Edgewood Street, which becomes Sunset Boulevard, and continue 1.4 miles to the road-end trailhead across from an apartment complex. No overnight parking is allowed in the trailhead lot, so either arrange for someone to drop you off or park in a public space in town and walk to the trailhead.

For the south trailhead, go south from the US 26/US 101 junction and drive 2.9 miles to the turnoff for Cannon Beach. Turn right and wind downhill 0.5 mile to a stop-signed junction with the signed road into Ecola State Park. Turn right onto East Fifth Street and go 1.7 miles to the pay station and, immediately thereafter, the turnoff for the Ecola Point Picnic Area, on the left. It was once possible to start the hike at Ecola Point, but a section of the trail washed out in 2017. Repairs are under way, but for now it's closed to thru-hiking. Instead, go right at the junction and drive 1.6 miles to the road-end picnic area and trailhead at Indian Beach. Although the hike from the south section is short, it's important to arrive early, especially on summer weekends; Indian Point is popular with surfers and kayakers, but parking is limited, so there are often long lines of cars waiting to get in.

GPS COORDINATES N45° 59.036' W123° 57.769' (north trailhead)
N45° 55.868' W123° 58.696' (south trailhead)

Hiking It

Northern Trail: From the north trailhead, the signed Oregon Coast Trail sets off through a typically dense coastal rainforest dominated by massive old Douglas firs, western hemlocks, and Sitka spruces. The mossy trunks of some of these giants rise hundreds of feet into the sky. Beneath this shady canopy, the forest floor is covered with salmonberry, sword fern, salal, and hundreds of unusually large deer ferns. The trail goes steadily uphill as it ascends more than a dozen irregularly spaced switchbacks, which help to keep the grade from becoming too steep. Cool ocean breezes make the hike more comfortable and keep you from becoming overheated.

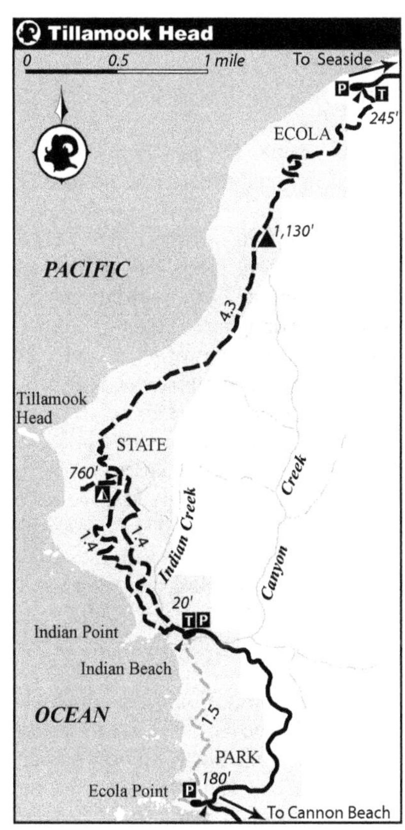

The trail levels off when it rounds the woodsy top of Tillamook Head near 1.7 miles. Several wooden boardwalks here span areas that are prone to becoming muddy. Shortly after you start to go downhill, you come to the hike's first good viewpoint, a high overlook where you can look west over the endless expanse of the Pacific Ocean and south along the precipitous cliffs to a string of offshore rocks. Atop one of the larger rocks, about 1.2 miles out to sea, sits the old Tillamook Rock Lighthouse (nicknamed Terrible Tilly, thanks to its notoriously stormy waters). The lighthouse was decommissioned in 1957, about 20 years after an epic storm smashed its Fresnel lens and lantern room. When it's not shrouded in fog, Tilly makes an impressive photo subject.

The Pacific Ocean sparkles below Tillamook Head. *photo by Paul Gerald*

The trail now goes up and down (mostly down) through dense woods punctuated by a series of dramatic cliff-edge viewpoints several hundred feet above the crashing waves of the misnamed Pacific Ocean. If you can pry your eyes away from the views, this is a good area to look for bald eagles, which are frequently seen soaring above the headland or perched on trees near the trail.

At 3.8 miles you pass an overlook signed CLARK'S POINT OF VIEW, which Captain William Clark of the Lewis and Clark Expedition considered one of the best he had ever seen. From here you descend a series of short switchbacks and come to a four-way junction with an old gravel service road. Turn right and walk 50 yards to the designated Hikers' Camp, complete with three sturdy log shelters with wooden sleeping platforms, a covered picnic table, a fire grate, and an outhouse. The shelters are comfortable and provide protection from the rain, but they are available only on a first-come, first-serve basis. Another option is to set up your tent in one of the flat areas a little to the west of the shelters. Beware of mice around the camp and guard your food accordingly. Finding water near the camp is difficult. There is a tiny seasonal creek a bit to the east, but it cannot be relied upon, especially in summer. The best plan is to pack in any water you will need.

The trail continues west another 0.15 mile, leading downhill past the remains of an abandoned military fortification to yet another stunning viewpoint of Tillamook Rock Lighthouse. (If you're here early in the morning, the view is likely to be obscured by fog; don't despair, as the fog usually lifts by midmorning. It's worth the wait!)

Southern Trail: If you are approaching along the shorter trail from the south, take the Clatsop Loop Trail that begins next to the restroom building at Indian Beach, and walk north along an abandoned gravel road. Twisted Sitka spruce trees beside the trail frame photogenic views of Indian Beach to the west. After just 80 yards you come to a junction and the start of a loop.

Go straight, staying on the old gravel road, cross tiny Indian Creek, and soon enter a dark "forest primeval" of tall Sitka spruces and western hemlocks. Salmonberry bushes, sword ferns, oxalis, and other shrubs and wildflowers carpet the forest floor. The old road/trail goes steadily uphill at a moderate grade and passes numerous numbered markers that an interpretive brochure (available at the trailhead) translates into interesting information about this area's natural and human history.

At 1.4 miles the trail abruptly stops climbing, makes a sharp left turn, and proceeds west 150 yards to a signed four-way junction. The Oregon Coast Trail (the northern approach described above) goes right, the return route of the Clatsop Loop goes left, and straight ahead is Hikers' Camp.

For variety on the return, take the western leg of the Clatsop Loop Trail, which goes south from the four-way junction just east of Hikers' Camp. This circuitous footpath goes up and down through dense forest 0.2 mile and then begins a steady descent. A series of six switchbacks descends through increasingly open forests and past a small brushy meadow to a pair of excellent viewpoints of rugged Tillamook Head to the north and Tillamook Rock Lighthouse to the west. After a bit more downhill hiking you reach another fine viewpoint, this one complete with a comfortable bench. From here you can look south to Indian Beach, distant Ecola Point, and numerous offshore rocks, including one prominent arch. The trail finishes its journey by going 0.1 mile down to a bridge over Indian Creek and the close of the loop at the junction with the old road. Turn right to return to the trailhead.

26 Soapstone Lake

RATINGS Scenery **5** Difficulty **1** Solitude **9**

ROUND-TRIP DISTANCE 2.4 miles (including loop around lake)

ELEVATION GAIN 250'

OPTIONAL MAP USGS *Soapstone Lake* (trail not shown)

USUALLY OPEN All year (except during winter storms)

BEST TIME April–November

AGENCY Clatsop State Forest, Astoria District, Oregon Department of Forestry; 503-325-5451; tinyurl.com/clatsoprecreationguide

PERMIT None

Highlights

The trail to Soapstone Lake is a pleasant and easy backpacking outing that makes an excellent choice for families with children. The trail to the lake is short but diverse, including areas of dense forest, some relatively open second-growth woodlands, a small meadow, and a lovely creek, all leading to a lake at trail's end. Wildlife is common and the lake is surprisingly scenic, so there is plenty to appreciate, regardless of your age or hiking abilities. Be aware that because the Clatsop

State Forest manages this land as a working forest, hikers should expect periodic trail closures due to timber harvest activity. Call ahead for the latest conditions.

Getting There

From Portland, go west on US 26 to the junction with OR 53 near milepost 9.5. Turn left (south), drive 4.8 miles, and then turn left on a gravel road signed SOAPSTONE LAKE TRAILHEAD. Proceed 0.4 mile on the narrow road to the signed trailhead and parking area.

GPS COORDINATES N45° 50.846' W123° 45.734'

Hiking It

The wide, smooth, and gently graded trail travels through a second-growth forest dominated by western hemlocks towering above a thick mat of oxalis, various ferns, and thimbleberry bushes. Several huge stumps with old logging springboard holes attest that the forest here was once composed of much larger specimens. The trail crosses two often-dry creeks on wooden bridges, and then at 0.3 mile gradually loses a little elevation before crossing a small grassy meadow where a homestead was once located. In late summer this meadow delights the visitor with ripe blackberries and blooming goldenrods. During the winter and early spring, you may see elk here, especially in the early morning.

At the far end of the meadow is a log bridge across clear Soapstone Creek. After the crossing, you climb a rather steep set of wooden stairs and then wander uphill through a lovely forest of impressive old Douglas firs before coming to a T-junction near the north end of Soapstone Lake. To reach the lake's only real campsite, turn right at the junction and walk 50 yards uphill to a spacious and comfortable site on the left.

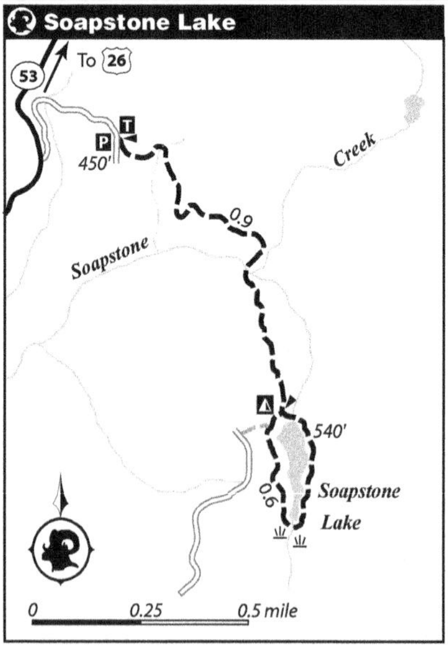

The lake is fun to explore, and a trail going all the way around its shore makes this easy. A clockwise tour takes you over a bridge spanning the outlet creek and past several inviting picnic spots to a fine little rocky beach near a beaver lodge along the east shore. This is a good spot to fish for cutthroat trout or for kids to observe the lake's abundant population of rough-skinned newts. From here the loop trail continues to a boardwalk over a skunk-cabbage bog at the lake's south end, and then goes up and down along the west shore to a junction with a trail to a nearby logging road. Turn right and walk a few yards downhill to the campsite and the trail back to your car.

The Soapstone Lake Trail is easy to reach and great for backpacking with kids.

Columbia River Gorge

Cutting a nearly sea-level canyon through one of North America's greatest mountain ranges, the mighty Columbia River has created a scenic treasure right at Portland's doorstep. The Columbia River Gorge (or simply the Gorge, as locals refer to it) is a land of countless waterfalls, towering cliffs, howling winds, and dramatic scenery. Sadly, the massive Eagle Creek Fire of 2017 scorched nearly 50,000 miles of forest, resulting in the closure of about 60 miles of trails in the Gorge, including the beloved Eagle Creek Trail and the Dublin Lake–Tanner Butte hike described in the previous edition of this guide. Many dedicated souls are working hard to repair the trails, but downed trees and other fire damage mean the work is slow and dangerous; at the time of this writing, the Eagle Creek Trail and several others are expected to be closed for many years. Luckily, some of the best backpacking trails skirt the edges of the fire-damaged areas, and several of these have reopened. One important caveat: If you hike a trail near a burn zone, respect all posted closure signs, and don't venture off-trail, for your own safety. The U.S. Forest Service also strongly recommends not hiking trails in the burn area if the forecast calls for strong winds or rain. For an updated map of the closed areas, go to gorgefriends.org/trails.

Though the Eagle Creek Fire will have a lasting impact on parts of the Gorge, other parts of it seem nearly unaffected. It's a vast territory, and its east–west orientation provides for strikingly varied vegetation zones. In just 50 miles you can move from lush rainforests in the west to a treeless desert of sagebrush and dry grasses in the east. Hiking in this vertical landscape is often challenging but highly rewarding. Possible overnight destinations include not only the familiar stream canyons and waterfalls along the trails closest to Portland but also remote lakes in the forested mountains both north and south of the river, as well as high ridges with excellent views of the rugged canyonlands below. It's easy to see why the Gorge has been a popular local outdoor destination for more than 100 years.

The Herman Creek Trail (Trip 29, page 109) passes several lovely streams along its route.

27 Silver Star Mountain

RATINGS	Scenery **8** Difficulty **7** Solitude **6**
ROUND-TRIP DISTANCE	12.5 miles
ELEVATION GAIN	2,600'
OPTIONAL MAPS	Green Trails *Bridal Veil (No. 428)* and *Lookout Mountain (No. 396)*
USUALLY OPEN	Mid-May–mid-November
BEST TIME	Mid-June–mid-July; October
AGENCY	Mount St. Helens National Volcanic Monument, 360-449-7800, fs.usda.gov/giffordpinchot
PERMIT	None

Highlights

As seen from Portland, Silver Star Mountain is that long, brownish ridge to the northeast that frustratingly blocks the view of Mount Adams. But once you're standing on this ridge, nothing obstructs the views, and you can see not only Mount Adams but pretty much everything else for 50 miles in any direction. And it's not just the views that make a visit here worthwhile. In 1902 the massive Yacolt Burn swept over this peak, killing nearly all the trees. The forests never grew back, so despite its relatively low elevation, the peak has an open, almost alpine appearance, with plenty of sunshine to nourish thousands of acres of wildflowers in June and July. Those same alpinelike meadows turn a burnished red-gold in the fall, which also means cooler temperatures and no bugs. Most hikers who visit this area make it a day hike. But a campsite near a little-known spring just southwest of the summit allows backpackers to spend the night, watch a terrific sunset, and even see the lights of Portland twinkling far below.

Several routes lead to the summit, and every one of them is outstanding, but most require a high-clearance four-wheel-drive vehicle to access. The main Silver Star Trailhead has become impossible to reach without four-wheel drive, so we're recommending the longer and even more scenic trail that starts from the Bluff Mountain Trailhead to the east (still not a great road, but manageable if you drive carefully).

Getting There

From the intersection of WA 502 and WA 503 in downtown Battle Ground, Washington, drive 5.7 miles north on WA 503. Turn right on NE Rock Creek Road, which soon becomes Lucia Falls Road, and proceed 8.6 miles. Turn right on Sunset Falls Road and drive 7.4 miles to a junction at the entrance to Sunset Campground. Turn right and cross the East Fork Lewis River on gravel Forest Service Road 41. Stay on often potholed and bumpy FS 41 approximately 9 miles to a large parking area just as the road makes a hairpin turn.

GPS COORDINATES N45° 46.856' W122° 09.966'

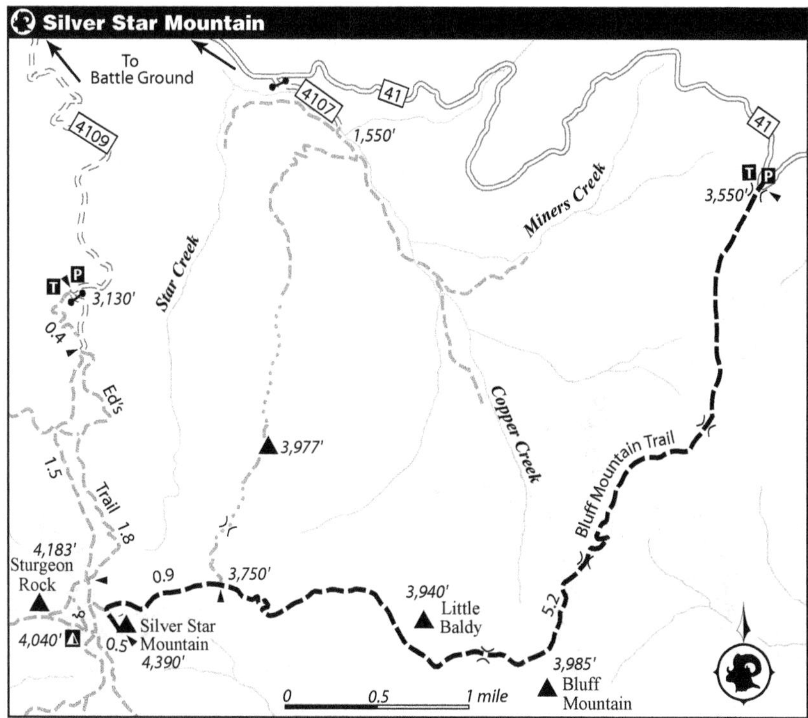

Hiking It

The Bluff Mountain Trail starts as an old jeep road, long since closed to motor vehicles, that undulates along a scenic, mostly open ridgetop. The route provides extensive views and is carpeted with a delightful mix of small Pacific silver fir trees, huckleberry and serviceberry bushes, beargrass, and a wide array of wildflowers. There are dozens of varieties, but the most common are lupine, wild carrot, paintbrush, iris, yarrow, valerian, tiger lily, and golden pea.

After 2 up-and-down miles, you descend to a small saddle where the road ends and the trail veers right. From here the path loses more elevation in one long switchback to another, more prominent saddle and then cuts across the north side of Bluff Mountain, where in early summer you may encounter lingering snow patches and small runoff creeks. After completing the traverse, the trail climbs to and crosses another saddle, this one in dense timber, and then traverses the open, view-packed talus slopes on the south and west sides of pyramid-shaped Little Baldy. Here you'll have great views of the impressive crags of Silver Star Mountain to the west. Still traveling toward that goal, the well-graded trail uses two short switchbacks to work its way gradually up an open ridge with lots of beargrass.

Five miles along the trail you'll reach a signed junction with the rarely used Starway Trail heading off to your right; continue straight (west) at the junction, then climb through the forest on the north side of Silver Star Mountain, where

Arch along Ed's Trail near Silver Star Mountain *photo by Douglas Lorain*

snowdrifts usually remain into late June. The trail ends at a multiway intersection, where you encounter a closed jeep road and Ed's Trail. (If you have lots of excess energy or feel like taking a day hike the next morning, you can make a skinny loop of Ed's Trail, heading north toward the Silver Star Trailhead and then returning to the summit on the nearly parallel Silver Star Trail.)

Turn left (south) on the jeep route and climb 200 yards to a road junction. To reach the summit, bear left and ascend a rock-strewn old road about 0.2 mile to the high saddle between the twin summits of Silver Star Mountain. The north summit is slightly higher and has better views. On very clear days you can see not only the nearby volcanic peaks already mentioned but also south to Mount Jefferson and the Three Sisters in Oregon, and northwest to Washington's Olympic Mountains.

To reach the small campsite, return to the junction 0.2 mile below the summit, and go south (downhill) along a jeep track 0.2 mile to a junction. Turn right, walk 50 yards, then turn right again onto an unsigned but obvious trail. This path goes 80 yards to a small but reliable piped spring with a fine campsite nearby.

28 Soda Peaks Lake

RATINGS	Scenery **6** Difficulty **5** Solitude **7**
ROUND-TRIP DISTANCE	4.6 miles
ELEVATION GAIN	1,300'
OPTIONAL MAP	Green Trails *Lookout Mountain (No. 396)*
USUALLY OPEN	June–November
BEST TIME	Mid-June–early October
AGENCY	Mount Adams Ranger District (Gifford Pinchot National Forest), 509-395-3402, fs.usda.gov/recarea/giffordpinchot/recarea/?recid=31184
PERMIT	Free at the trailhead

Highlights

With its clear, greenish waters backed by an encircling ridge of forests and talus slopes, Soda Peaks Lake makes an attractive destination. The hike is short but sometimes steep, making it a good choice for backpacking with enthusiastic kids or for a spontaneous getaway that doesn't require hitting the trailhead at the crack of dawn. Trout jump almost continuously, enticing the angler, while the waters are warm enough for swimming by early–mid-July. All in all, this tranquil spot makes a great place for a quiet night in the wilderness.

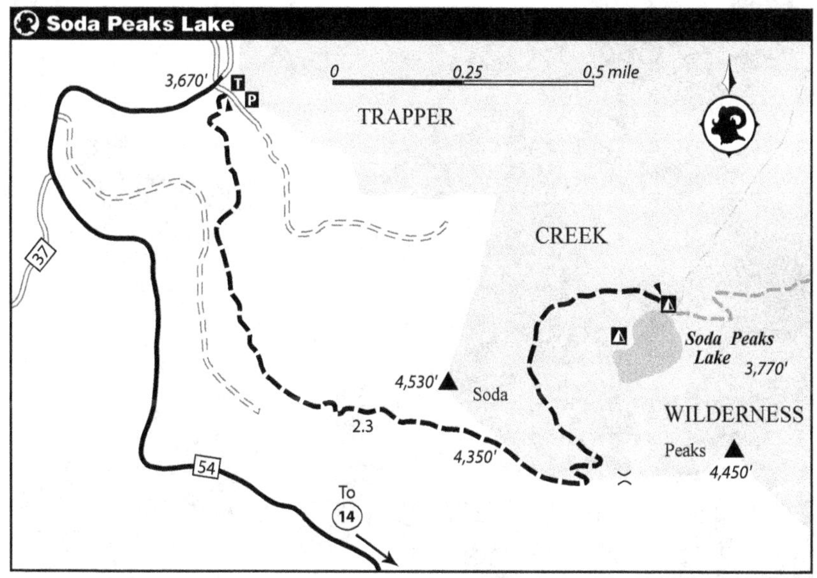

Getting There

From Portland, drive east 40 miles on I-84 to Cascade Locks, take Exit 44, and almost immediately veer right to loop around and cross the Columbia River on the Bridge of the Gods (there's a $2 toll, as of 2019). Turn right on WA 14, go 6.1 miles, and then turn left (north) on the signed road to Carson. Proceed on Wind River Parkway 8.6 miles. Turn left on Hemlock Road, following signs to Wind River Visitors Center, and go 0.3 mile to a four-way junction. Turn right on Szydlo Road, which after 3.5 miles narrows to one-lane pavement and becomes Forest Service Road 54. Go 9.5 more miles, staying on FS 54 at all intersections, to a four-way junction at the end of the pavement. Turn right and park almost immediately near an open gate. There's room for five or six cars. There's no obvious sign at the trailhead (thanks to vandalism), but the start of the trail opposite the parking area is easy to spot, and there is a large wooden signboard a few yards up the trail from the road.

GPS COORDINATES N45° 53.445' W122° 03.950'

Hiking It

The trail begins in a patch of young evergreens (regrowing after an old clear-cut) but soon enters an equally attractive mature forest of stately hemlocks and firs. Huckleberry bushes, avalanche lilies, and beargrass are among the most common of the abundant plants crowding the forest floor. In the first 0.3 mile, the up-and-down trail skirts a couple of old clear-cuts, which are rapidly filling in but still

Soda Peaks Lake caps a short but sometimes steep trail.

sparse enough to provide some glimpses of the epic surroundings; in particular, stay alert for a terrific view of Mount Adams to the northeast.

After this, you reenter the dense, mature woods and begin a steady, steep climb. The route closely follows an east-west-oriented ridgeline nearly to the top of the western summit of the two Soda Peaks, and then cuts across the forested south side of that peak to arrive at an open ridgetop viewpoint. From here you can look north to such snowy landmarks as Mount Rainier and the Goat Rocks, as well as down to the shimmering waters of Soda Peaks Lake, just visible through a screen of tree branches.

To reach the lake, the trail descends nearly to the saddle between the two Soda Peaks, then makes a sharp left to begin its descent of the north side of the ridge. You switchback twice down the heavily forested hillside as the trail winds gradually down to a signed day-use area and then to a campsite just beyond the outlet on the north shore of Soda Peaks Lake. Views to the ridge rising above the south shore make a nice backdrop for an evening meal. The lake is fun for youngsters to explore, as the water is reasonably warm and has lots of trout, crayfish, and newts to keep kids interested.

29 Herman Creek Trail

RATINGS	Scenery **6** Difficulty **5–8** Solitude **7**
ROUND-TRIP DISTANCE	14.6 miles to Cedar Swamp Camp; 19 miles to Mud Lake
ELEVATION GAIN	2,850' to Cedar Swamp; 3,700' to Mud Lake
OPTIONAL MAP	Green Trails *Bonneville Dam (No. 429)*
USUALLY OPEN	Mid-March–November for Cedar Swamp; mid-May–early November for Mud Lake
BEST TIME	April–June
AGENCY	Columbia River Gorge National Scenic Area, 541-308-1700, fs.usda.gov/crgnsa
PERMIT	None. Northwest Forest Pass required.

Highlights

Herman Creek is one of the major streams of the Columbia River Gorge, and the trail up its long canyon leads to a number of interesting and worthwhile destinations. In the wake of the 2017 Eagle Creek Fire, it also provides a chance to see the effects of wildfire up close; the trail is open and generally in good shape, but it passes through several areas of visually striking blackened tree trunks and scorched ground. Although the trail generally stays in the forests on the hillside well above cascading Herman Creek, it passes beneath several tall, wispy waterfalls on side streams. Backpackers have several options for spending the night, but the best locations are Cedar Swamp Camp and Mud Lake. Both are very attractive and far from any crowds.

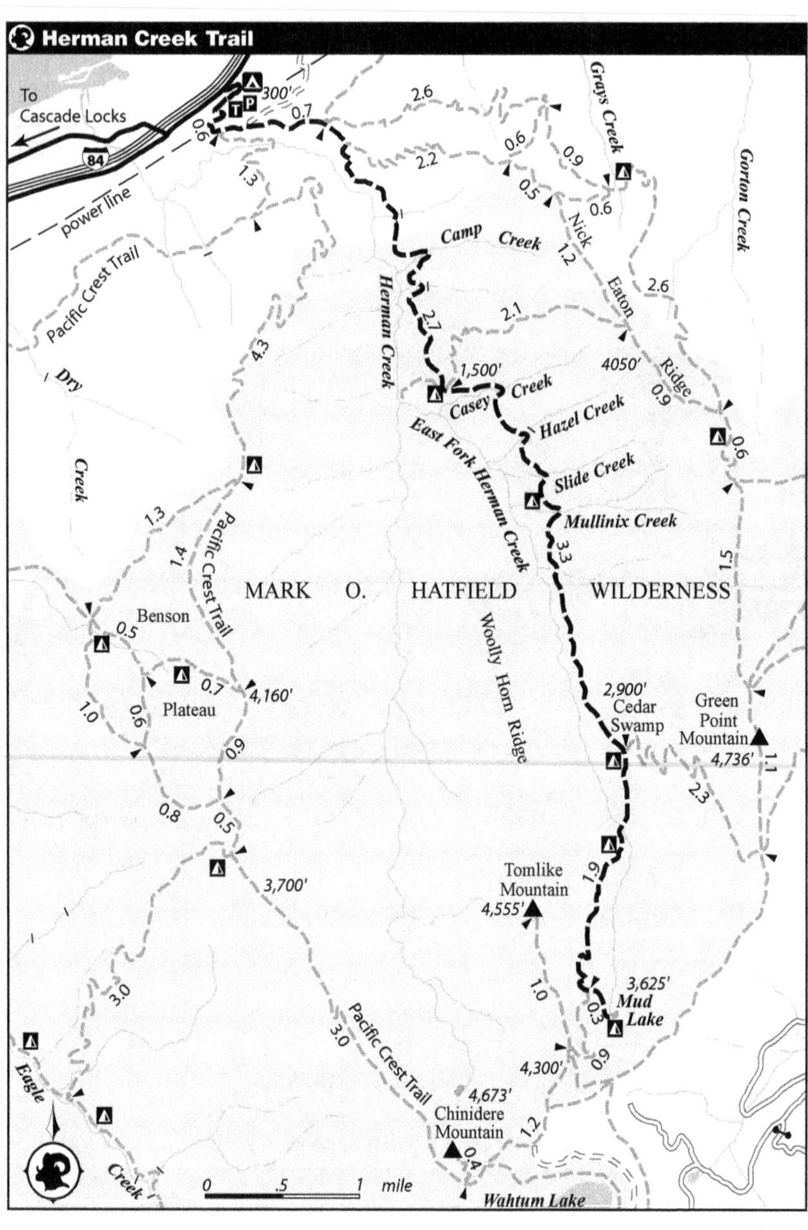
Herman Creek Trail
To
Cascade Locks
84
power line
Pacific Crest Trail
300'
0.7
0.6
1.3
2.6
2.2
0.6
0.9
0.5
0.6
Grays Creek
Gorton Creek
Camp Creek
Nick
1.2
Eaton
2.6
Herman Creek
2.7
2.1
4.3
Dry
Creek
1,500'
Casey Creek
4050'
Ridge
0.9
Hazel Creek
East Fork Herman Creek
Slide Creek
0.6
Mullinix Creek
3.3
1.3
1.4
Pacific Crest Trail
1.5
MARK O. HATFIELD WILDERNESS
Benson
0.5
Woolly Horn Ridge
0.7
4,160'
Plateau
1.0
0.6
2,900'
Cedar
Swamp
Green
Point
Mountain
4,736'
0.9
1.1
2.3
0.8
0.5
3,700'
Tomlike
Mountain
4,555'
1.9
3.0
1.0
3,625'
Mud
Lake
0.3
Pacific Crest Trail
3.0
4,300'
0.9
Eagle
4,673'
Chinidere
Mountain
1.2
0.4
Creek
0 .5 1 mile
Wahtum Lake

Getting There

From Portland, drive east 43 miles on I-84, and take the exit for the weigh station, 1.2 miles past Exit 44 (Cascade Locks). Continue through the weigh station, and turn right on Frontage Road at the four-way junction. Stay on Frontage Road 1.7 miles, then turn right at the entrance road for the (now closed) Herman Creek Campground. Go 0.3 mile up this one-lane paved road, following signs to the trailhead parking lot.

GPS COORDINATES N45° 40.955' W121° 50.559'

Hiking It

The trail departs from the west end of the parking lot and winds steadily uphill in several turns and switchbacks through a stately forest of Douglas firs, western hemlocks, and big-leaf and vine maples. At 0.4 mile you pass under a set of power lines and then continue uphill to a fork at 0.6 mile. Already, evidence of the Eagle Creek Fire is obvious in the scorched tree trunks surrounding the trail; you'll be walking through the burn for several more miles. Bear left, still on Herman Creek Trail, and proceed gradually up a mostly forested hillside to a switchback in an abandoned dirt road. Bear right and follow this old road as it steadily climbs 0.4 mile, then levels off before continuing 0.2 mile to a signed junction.

You go straight and travel slightly downhill along a heavily wooded hillside. Swift-flowing Herman Creek can be heard but not seen in the canyon on your right. At 2.2 miles you pass beside a tall, lacy waterfall on an unnamed little creek, and shortly thereafter enter the Mark O. Hatfield Wilderness. The trail then ducks into the canyon of Camp Creek, crossing this small stream without the benefit of a bridge. From here you hike gradually uphill through a relatively open forest to a fine campsite at the junction with Casey Creek Trail at 4 miles. To obtain water here, you must follow a steep and unsigned 0.3-mile side trail that goes down to a once mossy but now scorched-clear little glen at the confluence of Herman and East Fork Herman Creeks.

Keep straight at the junction, staying on the Herman Creek Trail, and go gradually uphill. The forest here is composed mostly of western hemlocks, Douglas firs, and western red cedars, but there are also lots of vine maples in the understory, which add a touch of color in late October. About 0.8 mile from the Casey Creek junction, you pass below a trickling waterfall on Hazel Creek, and then cross Slide and Mullinix Creeks, the latter perhaps getting your feet wet before midsummer. There is a fair campsite on the right about 100 yards before you cross Mullinix Creek.

The trail continues with its long, slow, steady ascent, always in forest and crossing several trickling creeks along the way to a junction just before spacious Cedar Swamp Camp at 7.3 miles. Situated in a grove of big, old trees, this camp is a good destination for a moderate overnight trip.

If you are continuing beyond Cedar Swamp, go straight at the junction and walk on the mostly level trail for 0.4 mile through a wet area crowded with devil's club to a crossing of what is left of East Fork Herman Creek. The crossing is an easy ford (or sometimes a rock-hop), but if you prefer to keep your feet dry, you can usually find a log a little upstream from the trail crossing. About 100 yards

You'll see evidence of fire on parts of the Herman Creek Trail.

after the crossing, you'll find a nice camp. The best sites are at the end of a short, unmarked spur trail that goes left toward the creek.

The trail soon resumes its steady uphill into higher-elevation forest with lots of beargrass on the forest floor. After passing through a small meadow, climb a little more to a junction at 9.2 miles with the 0.3-mile spur trail to tiny Mud Lake. Although it is marked with a very small brown sign on a tree on your left, this junction is easy to miss, so watch carefully. The lake amply rewards your vigilance, with fine views of a talus slope to the southeast, a scenic grassy shoreline, and a nice campsite above the southwest shore. Look for ducks and beavers on the lake, especially in the evening and early morning.

Although Mud Lake is the recommended turnaround point, hikers looking for a more challenging trip can make a very scenic 23.3-mile loop that returns to the trailhead via the Pacific Crest Trail over Benson Plateau. Excellent side trips off this route include Wahtum Lake and Tomlike and Chinidere Mountains.

30 North, Bear, and Warren Lakes

RATINGS Scenery **6** Difficulty **1–6** Solitude **6**

ROUND-TRIP DISTANCE 1.6 miles to North Lake; 2.6 miles to Bear Lake; 6.8 miles to Warren Lake

ELEVATION GAIN 190' to North Lake; 480' to Bear Lake; 2,100' to Warren Lake

OPTIONAL MAPS Green Trails *Bonneville Dam (No. 429)* and *Hood River (No. 430)*

USUALLY OPEN Mid-May–mid-November

BEST TIME June–October

AGENCY Hood River Ranger District (Mount Hood National Forest), 541-352-6002, fs.usda.gov/recarea/mthood/recarea/?recid=52776

PERMIT None

Highlights

These three lovely but generally uncrowded mountain lakes are all accessible from the same trailhead off an isolated gravel road southwest of Hood River. They provide a range of difficulty options, from the short and mostly level stroll to scenic North Lake, to a somewhat more difficult hike to Bear Lake, and finally a rugged hike over the view-packed shoulder of Mount Defiance to Warren Lake, a stretch that lets hikers survey some of the damage caused by the Eagle Creek Fire in 2017. (Be sure to stay on the trail and observe all closure signs.) All three lakes are worth visiting, and you won't be disappointed to spend the night at any of them. Which option you choose depends on your time, abilities, and interests.

Getting There

Drive east about 54 miles on I-84, and take Exit 62 (West Hood River/Westcliff Drive). Drive 1.3 miles east on Cascade Avenue, then turn right (south) on 13th Street, and stay on this main road through several turns and intersections for 3.1 miles to a four-way stop. Turn left on Tucker Road, following signs to Odell, go 2 miles, and then veer right at a junction with a sign for Parkdale. Continue another 6.5 miles, and then bear right (downhill) at a sign for Lost Lake and drive 0.2 mile to a junction on the other side of a bridge. Turn right on Punch Bowl Road, drive 0.3 mile to an intersection, and go straight, still on Punch Bowl Road. After 1.1 miles continue straight at another junction, where your route turns to gravel and becomes Forest Service Road 2820. Proceed 7.8 miles on this bumpy but reasonably good gravel road to a T-junction. Turn left to stay on FS 2820, and then drive 2.1 miles to the Upper Mount Defiance Trailhead, with parking for 6–8 cars on the left side of the road. The trail sign on your right is easy to miss, so watch carefully.

GPS COORDINATES N45° 38.172' W121° 44.550'

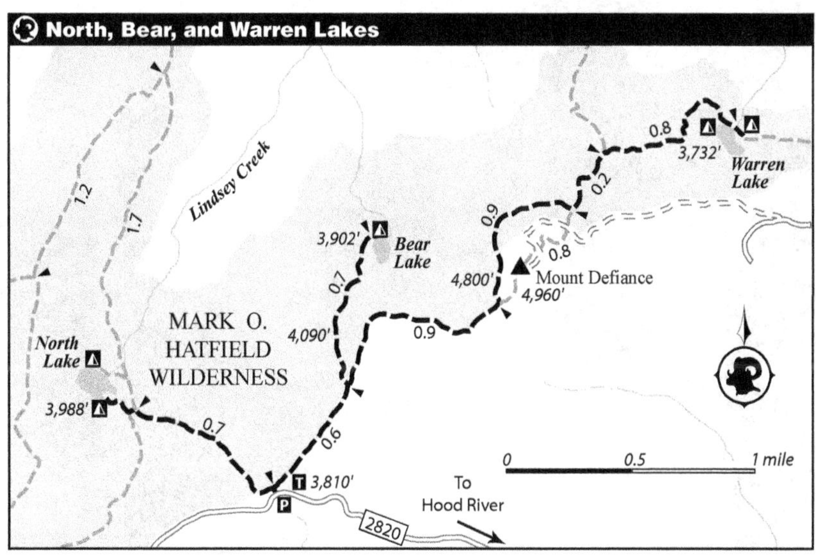

Hiking It

The trail goes south in a forest of firs and hemlocks, with an abundance of beargrass and huckleberries covering the forest floor. After just 20 yards a signboard marks where the trail splits.

To reach North Lake—a great choice for backpackers with younger kids—turn left at the junction and gradually ascend through an open and attractive mid-elevation forest. After 0.7 mile of gentle and easy hiking, you come to a fork. Turn left on North Lake Trail, walk 25 yards, and then turn right at a second junction. In 0.1 mile this path leads to a fine camp at the south end of North Lake. This scenic pool is backed by a rockslide on the ridge that rises above the east shore and supports a healthy population of brook trout. There are additional good camps on the north and east shores.

If you are heading for either Bear or Warren Lake, turn right at the junction near the trailhead onto the Mount Defiance Trail and make your way gently uphill through a forest of western and mountain hemlocks, Douglas firs, Pacific silver firs, and lodgepole pines. The trail's grade gradually increases as you steadily ascend northeast, making your way up the ridge toward Mount Defiance. At 0.6 mile is an obvious but usually unsigned junction.

To reach Bear Lake—another good destination for a family overnighter—veer left at the junction and hike mostly on the level through an attractive and relatively open forest. (Though it skirts the Eagle Creek burn area, you can hike this trail in total blissful ignorance of the fire—there's no sign of it, and it's not until you hike the Mount Defiance Trail that you see the burn scars just over the ridge.) At 0.4 mile from the Mount Defiance Trail, you pass through a small

Bear Lake, like neighboring Warren and North Lakes, offers some lovely campsites.

rocky area where the trail is marked with cairns, and then steeply descend 200 feet in 0.3 mile to a comfortable campsite at the north end of scenic Bear Lake. The talus fields and rounded summit of Mount Defiance rise above the east side of this forest-rimmed lake, providing nice views. Sadly, that view is marred by the presence of radio, microwave, and cell phone towers cluttering the summit of the peak. The shallow lake has brook trout for the angler, but the rocky bottom makes swimming rather unenticing.

The most challenging destination of the trio is Warren Lake. To reach that goal, go straight at the Bear Lake turnoff and continue climbing through forest to a prominent ridgecrest where you can look down to Bear Lake and northeast to distant Mount Adams. The trail turns right (east) here, following the ridge and continuing its ascent, often steeply, to a junction in the middle of a large rockslide. If you want to visit the top of Mount Defiance, the highest point in the Columbia River Gorge at 4,960 feet, veer right and climb 0.2 mile to the summit area with its cluster of towers and a rough dirt road. (The hike to Mount Defiance from the river-level Starvation Creek Trailhead is one of the toughest in the Gorge, but approaching it from this side cuts out a lot of the elevation gain.)

To reach Warren Lake, go left at the junction below the summit of Mount Defiance and gradually descend as you round the open, rocky, west side of the peak. The views to the west are superb: Bear Lake, Green Point Mountain, and numerous other high points and landmarks of the Gorge. Turn left at the junction on the northeast side of Mount Defiance and wind steeply downhill through open forest 0.2 mile to another junction. Turn right and descend partly in forest and partly on an open slope, with fine views of the basin holding Warren Lake. Upon arriving at the north shore of that lovely lake, you will discover a good campsite. Another good site lies along the east side of the lake. Much of the lakeshore is brushy, but there are plenty of places to reach the water. The swimming here is good and the scenery is excellent, as the lake is backed by an impressive talus slope rising above its west shore.

31 Lower Deschutes River Canyon

RATINGS	Scenery **7** Difficulty **1–4** Solitude **4**
ROUND-TRIP DISTANCE	5.5 miles to first campsite; 7.3 miles to Gordon Canyon, with Ferry Springs loop
ELEVATION GAIN	250' to first campsite; 820' to Gordon Canyon with Ferry Springs loop
OPTIONAL MAPS	USGS *Emerson* and *Wishram*
USUALLY OPEN	All year
BEST TIME	March–May; October
AGENCY	Deschutes River State Recreation Area (Oregon State Parks), 541-739-2322, oregonstateparks.org
PERMIT	None. Overnight-parking pass required ($7).

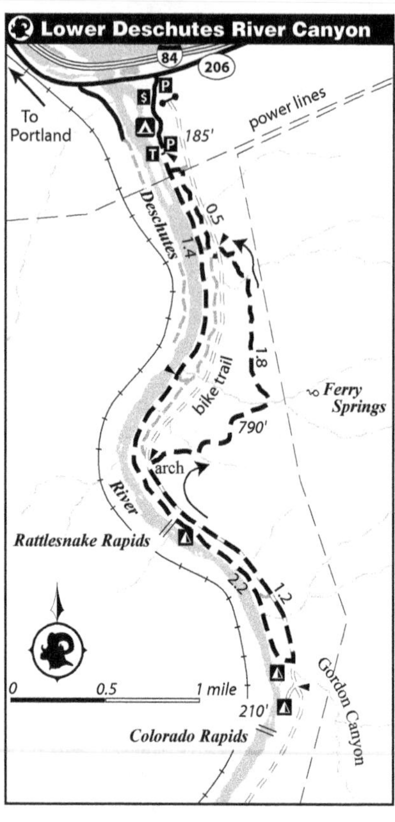

Highlights

Central Oregon's Deschutes River is nationally famous among anglers who come to catch its salmon, steelhead, and record-setting rainbow trout. Its rollicking rapids and beautiful scenery make it a favorite of whitewater rafting enthusiasts, as well as campers, picnickers, photographers, hunters, and many others. Hikers know it as one of the few year-round options in the area, and it's an excellent early-season training hike for more-challenging backpacking trips, as the terrain is relatively flat.

The desert setting of north-central Oregon provides welcome sunshine to water-logged Portlanders looking to escape the clouds and mud of the west side. The steeply sloping canyon walls provide dramatic and unusual canyon scenery. And wildlife is abundant and much easier to see here than it is amid the dense forests west of the Cascades.

Although every season on the river offers something interesting—wildflowers from March to May, nesting songbirds in May and June, scarlet leaves of nonpoisonous sumac bushes in October—it is best to avoid this area in July and August when temperatures are usually over 100°F. All campfires must be in fire pans, and dogs must be leashed along this trail.

Getting There

From Portland, drive about 90 miles east on I-84, through The Dalles, and take Exit 97. Drive east on OR 206, following signs to Deschutes River State Recreation Area, and go 3.1 miles to a junction just after the bridge over the Deschutes River. Turn right and drive 0.3 mile to the trailhead parking lot at the far (south) end of the park's campground. A $7-per-vehicle overnight-parking fee is charged here. Purchase your permit at the self-service fee station near the park entrance.

GPS COORDINATES N45° 37.761' W120° 54.466'

Hiking It

Walk 0.1 mile south from the parking lot along the river to a signboard and junction at the end of a mowed grassy area. If you take the recommended loop on the return, you will come back on the Upper Trail that goes left. For now, go straight on the Atiyeh River Trail, which is named for Victor Atiyeh, a former Oregon governor who worked hard to protect the lower 18 miles of the scenic Deschutes River.

The nearly level, hiker-only trail meanders lazily upstream in the narrow zone between the dense riparian vegetation near the water and the scattered sage, hackberry, and rabbitbrush of the desert. This diverse habitat supports a surprisingly abundant mix of wildlife. Look for kingfishers, great blue herons, Canada geese, minks, and river otters near the river; animals like coyotes, chukars, and prairie falcons can be seen on or flying above the dry canyon walls. Songbirds of all types nest in the riparian shrubs, and both rattlesnakes (watch your step!) and lizards sun themselves on rocks. Mule deer may be seen anywhere.

At 0.5 mile you reach a fenced tower and a junction with a connector trail that goes left to meet the Upper Trail. Go straight; the lower trail continues gently up and down, staying near the water and passing several inviting spots where you can fish, watch wildlife, or just admire the scenery. Although the trail is charming and very scenic, it is not a wilderness experience; you frequently encounter signs of civilization in the form of wooden benches, power lines, and telephone wires visible on the ridge above, as well as trains going by on the other side of the river. A hard-to-see bike trail follows the grade of an old railroad bed on the hillside on your left.

At 1.4 miles you go straight at a signed junction with another connector path to the Upper Trail. Above this junction the River Trail is less heavily used, as it soon becomes more rocky and rough, with steep little ups and downs on the slopes above the water. About 100 yards after the trail rounds the end of a wide bend in the river, look up to the left and locate a small rock arch. Although you can't tell from this angle, this arch is just below the parallel bike trail, and you will pass right next to it

The Lower Deschutes Trail is another great early- and late-season option.

on the way back. Keep an eye out as well for lizards in this area. You'll usually spot them doing nervous pushups while they warily eye your approach, and then rapidly scampering away between rocks when you get too close.

About 0.2 mile past the arch, you pass the roaring cascade of Rattlesnake Rapids. Just above this rapid is the first good campsite, near a pretty little rocky beach next to the river. At 3 miles an unsigned trail angles left toward the bike trail. Go straight on the winding trail near the river and continue to the mouth of Gordon Canyon at 3.6 miles. This side canyon presents a deep gash in the main canyon walls and supports a small creek that flows throughout the spring and early summer. There is a very nice camp near the river just before you reach Gordon Canyon.

Your trail angles left to meet the wide gravel bike trail/road, where you turn right (upstream) and immediately cross the intermittent creek coming out of Gordon Canyon. The road splits just after this crossing. The main trail forks left (uphill) and heads up the Deschutes River, eventually leading to the trailhead at Macks Canyon, 23 miles from where you started. To reach the best campsites, however, bear right at the road fork, and walk 0.1 mile to a large camping area near the river, complete with a modern outhouse. Colorado Rapids rumbles along just upstream from the camp.

For variety on the return route, walk back along the bike trail, as it follows the course of an old railroad grade along a virtually level closed road. About 1.2 miles from Gordon Canyon you reach the rock arch, located a bit below the trail on the left, and a junction. The easiest way to return is to go straight on the bike trail. For better scenery, however, turn right on a possibly unsigned but obvious foot trail that steadily climbs over dry, open slopes. These slopes have fine views, and from late March to early May support a surprising array of colorful wildflowers, such as lupine, lomatium, and prairie star. After 0.5 mile you reach a view-packed high point where you enjoy fine vistas over the canyon walls and down to both the Deschutes and Columbia Rivers.

The trail crosses a fenceline at this viewpoint, then contours briefly to cross the gully holding the permanent creek that flows out of nearby Ferry Springs. From here you descend gradually 0.9 mile to a junction with the bike trail. Turn left (*up* the canyon), go 8 yards, and then turn right on an unsigned foot trail that drops briefly to a junction with the Upper Trail. Turn right and follow this meandering up-and-down trail past ancient sagebrush bushes that are 10–12 feet tall back to the junction just 0.1 mile from the trailhead. Turn right to return to your car.

Spring wildflowers grace the Lower Deschutes River Trail.

Mount Hood and Vicinity

Easily the most recognizable feature on Portland's skyline, Mount Hood towers 11,237 feet (plus or minus a few feet; sources disagree) above the forest-covered ridges of the Cascade Mountains 45 miles east of the city. Its prominent position and considerable beauty draw outdoors lovers like a magnet. They come for the mountain's excellent scenery, abundant wildflowers, and fine hiking trails. Backpacking on the mountain is a joy, with all the usual alpine pleasures in almost embarrassing abundance. The most scenic paths are those high on the mountain's slopes, but the surrounding forests, hills, and basins hide a wealth of additional attractions worth checking out, and usually with far fewer fellow admirers to encroach upon your wilderness experience. So come to Mount Hood to hike the famous, high-elevation Timberline Trail, where the views of glaciers and the smell of wildflowers will absolutely overwhelm you, but hang around for a while and discover hidden lakes, deep river canyons, and view-packed ridges where you may have the wilderness all to yourself.

One thing to note: Blackflies have become a major nuisance here in early and midsummer. They're usually gone by mid- to late August, but it's worth checking trip reports to make sure.

Ramona Falls (Trip 33, page 125) is one of the highlights of hiking Mount Hood.

32 Cairn Basin and Elk Cove

RATINGS Scenery **10** Difficulty **8** Solitude **4**

ROUND-TRIP DISTANCE 8.4 miles to Cairn Basin; 13.6 miles to Elk Cove

ELEVATION GAIN 2,000' to Cairn Basin; 2,450' to Elk Cove

OPTIONAL MAPS Green Trails *Government Camp (No. 461)* and *Mount Hood (No. 462)*

USUALLY OPEN Mid-July–October

BEST TIME Late July–mid-August

AGENCY Hood River Ranger District (Mount Hood National Forest), 541-352-6002, fs.usda.gov/recarea/mthood/recreation/hiking/recarea/?recid=52776&actid=51

PERMIT Required; free at wilderness boundary. Northwest Forest Pass required.

Highlights

Mountain scenery doesn't get much better than what you find on the north side of Mount Hood. This hike, which traverses almost the entire length of this alpine wonderland, is bound to be spectacular. Wildflowers crowd mountain meadows, creeks come tumbling down from massive glaciers, views extend to distant peaks and up to the cliffs and ramparts of Mount Hood, and wildly scenic camps invite overnight stays. Bring your camera, pack along a flower identification guide, and savor a mountain wilderness at its finest.

Getting There

From Portland, take I-84 about 13 miles east, take Exit 16, and turn right onto 238th Drive. Go 1 mile and continue straight, now on 242nd Drive. In 1.8 miles turn left onto Burnside Road, which shortly becomes US 26. Take US 26 about 27 miles to the town of Zigzag, and turn left (north) on East Lolo Pass Road. After 4.3 miles turn right on Forest Service Road 1825 (Muddy Fork Road). Follow this road 0.7 mile, and then go straight at a junction where Muddy Fork Road goes right and crosses a bridge. Now on single-lane paved FS 1828, drive 5.8 miles, bear right onto gravel FS 118, and proceed 1.5 miles to the Top Spur Trailhead.

GPS COORDINATES N45° 24.462' W121° 47.152'

Hiking It

The heavily traveled trail slowly climbs through a forest of Douglas firs, western hemlocks, and true firs with an understory of huckleberries, Pacific rhododendrons, and various low-growing flowering plants. Look especially for bunchberry, beargrass, twisted stalk, groundsel, vanilla leaf, and pearly everlasting. At 0.6 mile you come to a junction with the Pacific Crest Trail, where you go right and 50 yards later pass a dry campsite just before a multiway junction.

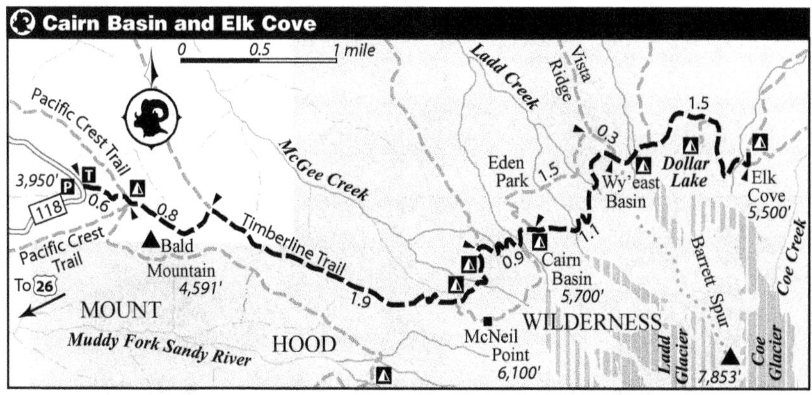

Turn left here on the Timberline Trail and make a mostly level, woodsy, 0.8-mile stroll to a junction with McGee Creek Trail and a wilderness permit station. After obtaining your free permit, go east (right), ascending through a forest of mountain hemlocks and subalpine firs on a root-studded trail that generally stays near the top of a small ridge, taking you toward the still-unseen northwest shoulder of Mount Hood.

Finally, at 2.3 miles, you break out of the forest and enter the first of several ridgetop meadows. These meadows provide great views of Muddy Fork Sandy River Canyon and Yocum Ridge to the south and straight ahead to towering Mount Hood. Heavily crevassed Sandy Glacier covers much of this side of the peak in a mantle of ice. Wildflowers abound in these scenic meadows, including paintbrush, lupine, yarrow, aster, and wallflower, but the dominant plant is beargrass, which carpets the open areas and blooms profusely in mid-July of favorable years. There is also an unusual abundance of ground-hugging junipers in this area.

After the meadows end, the trail angles a little to the left, leaving the ridge and climbing four quick switchbacks to an extremely lush little meadow that is a riot of color in late July. In addition to the previously mentioned wildflower species, look for valerian, spirea, avalanche lily, false hellebore, glacier lily, bistort, groundsel, and countless others. Just after the fourth switchback, you come to an unsigned junction with a use trail that goes right. Keep left on the Timberline Trail and wander in a daze of enchantment through lovely forests and meadows. The meadows are filled with pink heather in July and early August, which give way to goldenrod and blue gentian in late August and September. At 2.8 miles you cross a clear creek, which tumbles in a cascading falls over moss-covered boulders.

At 3 miles you splash across a second little creek, pass a single-tent campsite on the left, and then climb a pair of short switchbacks to a small meadowy plateau with two shallow ponds. These ponds feature an abundance of wildflowers and exceptionally photogenic views of Mount Hood. Camping is not allowed in the meadows here, but you can find some decent campsites in the forest west of the ponds.

The trail climbs to the right of the second pond and goes 200 yards to another small meadow and a junction. Go straight, still on the Timberline Trail, and hike

Mountain scenery doesn't get much better than what you'll find on the Cairn Basin and Elk Cove trip. *photo by Douglas Lorain*

through more of this delightful alpine terrain, which now features excellent distant views of Mounts Rainier, Adams, and St. Helens, as well as closer looks at Barrett Spur and the steep north face of Mount Hood. You ascend a pair of switchbacks to the top of a wooded ridge, and then come to still another meadow and a junction with a signed side trail to McNeil Point, where you go straight (unless you want to add a fairly substantial but scenic side trip to McNeil Point). A little more up and down takes you to the bridgeless but usually easy crossing of a silt-laden branch of Ladd Creek before you reach Cairn Basin at 4.2 miles. The 2011 Dollar Lake Fire scorched parts of Cairn Basin, destroying some of the old campsites; there are still plenty of snags around, but most of the dangerous trees have blown down by now, the undergrowth in the meadow is thick and healthy, and wildflowers thrive. This scenic basin has an interesting old stone shelter and some excellent camps, but if you want to spend the night here, it is better to do so before mid-August because the trickling creek that flows through this meadow usually dries up in late summer.

There is a junction at Cairn Basin. The trail to the left is a possible alternate route that goes down to the wildflower gardens of Eden Park before returning to the Timberline Trail on the Vista Ridge Trail (1.8 miles total). A more direct and slightly shorter route, however, is to go straight on the Timberline Trail and, after 0.2 mile, come to a boulder-strewn ravine and another bridgeless crossing of Ladd Creek. By midsummer this crossing is usually a simple rock-hop, but on a hot afternoon in early summer it can be a dangerously raging torrent carrying meltwater runoff from Ladd Glacier. As with other glacial streams, it is better to cross in the cool of the morning. If you want to use this creek for water, you should first let it sit in a pot for about 20 minutes to allow the silt to settle, and then filter and drink the water as usual.

After crossing Ladd Creek, you ascend a couple of switchbacks to the top of yet another wooded ridge, and then cross a few flower-choked meadows before briefly dropping to a junction with the Vista Ridge Trail in Wy'east Basin. Go straight, soon pass a faint use path that goes right on its way up to Barrett Spur, and then pass two mediocre camps at the east side of the basin. The lovely little creeks in this basin are lined with monkey flower, lupine, aster, wild carrot, and a host of other colorful wildflowers.

Shortly after Wy'east Basin, go straight at a junction with Pinnacle Ridge Trail, and then go up and down 0.4 mile to a small cairn marking the 0.2-mile side trip to Dollar Lake. Although not officially maintained, the steep path is easy to follow, and the views and excellent camps beside this minuscule lake make the side trip worth the effort. (Tip: For even better views, continue up the trail and set up camp at one of a handful of sites just above the lake.)

From the Dollar Lake turnoff, the Timberline Trail goes around the end of a spur ridge and then at 6.8 miles makes a downhill traverse into spectacular Elk Cove, one of the classic beauty spots on Mount Hood. With a bubbling creek, acres of wildflowers, scenic tree islands, and excellent views of Mount Hood and Coe Glacier, this place is easy to love. Please don't be a part of loving it to death, however, by camping in the fragile meadows. Camping and fires are prohibited in the tree islands of the Cove. Instead, set up your tent at one of the designated sites along the Elk Cove Trail, which drops to the left at a junction 100 yards after you cross the creek. Unless you are continuing around the mountain, Elk Cove is the place to spend the night before heading back the way you came.

33 Ramona Falls and Yocum Ridge

RATINGS Scenery **9** Difficulty **4–9** Solitude **4–7**

ROUND-TRIP DISTANCE 7 miles for Ramona Falls loop; 18.6 miles to Yocum Ridge

ELEVATION GAIN 1,100' for Ramona Falls loop; 4,500' to Yocum Ridge

OPTIONAL MAPS Green Trails *Government Camp (No. 461)* and *Mount Hood (No. 462)*

USUALLY OPEN Late April–November for Ramona Falls; Late July–mid-October for Yocum Ridge

BEST TIME Anytime it's open

AGENCY Zigzag Ranger District (Mount Hood National Forest), 503-622-3191, fs.usda.gov/recarea/mthood/recarea/?recid=52778

PERMIT Required; free at the trailhead. Northwest Forest Pass required.

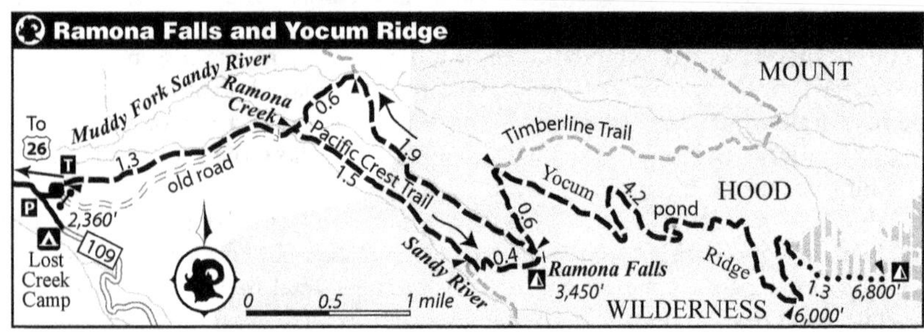

Highlights

Yocum Ridge, an alpine wonderland that extends west from the slopes of Mount Hood, enjoys an unequaled position in the long list of scenic treasures around Oregon's highest peak. The views are absolutely incredible, not only of the towering mountain, but also of huge glaciers, distant peaks, and even (with binoculars) the buildings of downtown Portland. Wildflowers grow in incredible abundance, adding color and an intoxicating aroma to the gentle breezes that waft over the ridge. It is a land of excitement and great scenic beauty, but it is rather difficult to reach. The trail here gains over 4,000 feet, so hikers must be prepared to sweat to enjoy the ridge's many rewards. Those with less energy can settle for the much easier loop to extremely popular Ramona Falls, which offers few flowers or mountain views but boasts easy walking through a fascinating mixture of moss-floored, sandy, rocky, and woodsy terrain and one of the most beautiful veil-like waterfalls in the Pacific Northwest. (The only catch is a sometimes sketchy crossing of the Sandy River.)

Getting There

From Portland, take I-84 about 13 miles east, take Exit 16, and turn right onto 238th Drive. Go 1 mile and continue straight, now on 242nd Drive. In 1.8 miles turn left onto Burnside Road, which shortly becomes US 26. Take US 26 about 27 miles to the town of Zigzag, about 40 miles east of Portland, and turn left (north) on East Lolo Pass Road. After 4.3 miles, turn right on paved Forest Service Road 1825 (Muddy Fork Road), and drive 0.7 mile to a junction. Turn right, immediately cross a bridge, and drive 0.9 mile to a fork. Bear left, still on FS 1825, go 1.5 miles, and then bear left at a junction and quickly arrive at the large parking area for the Ramona Falls Trail.

GPS COORDINATES N45° 23.215' W121° 49.929'

Hiking It

The sandy trail departs from the northeast end of the parking lot and travels up the wide valley of the Sandy River. After 0.6 mile the trail meets a closed road and parallels it all the way to an abandoned upper trailhead. You then reach the Sandy River, the only challenge on the Ramona Falls section of the hike; the original bridge across was washed out years ago, and the Forest Service has decided not to replace it. Usually there are plenty of logs across the river near the original crossing point, so you can either walk or scoot across one of these. Looking up the river valley, there's a nice view of Mount Hood peeking out, if it's not hidden in clouds.

WARNING The river is glacial and always fast-moving, so exercise caution; if the water level is extremely high or there's been a recent storm, you might have to turn around.

For the shorter approach to the falls, turn right at a fork after the crossing, onto the Pacific Crest Trail, and walk an up-and-down path through the wide and attractively desolate glacial valley of the Sandy River.

At 2.8 miles is a junction with the Timberline Trail, where you bear left, make two quick switchbacks, and go 0.4 mile through open forest to a designated camping area on the right. If you are spending the night, do so here because

Beautiful Ramona Falls is an understandably popular destination.

camping and fires are prohibited within 500 feet of the falls. Just beyond the camping area, seeming to appear out of nowhere, is lovely Ramona Falls, which cascades over a basalt cliff in an impressive veil of water. It's no surprise this hike is one of the most popular on the mountain.

Immediately after crossing a bridge just below the falls, you come to a junction. If you are doing the Ramona Falls Loop, go straight on the signposted return trail, and gradually descend beside clear Ramona Creek 1.9 miles to a junction. Turn left and walk 0.6 mile through open forest back to the close of the loop at the Sandy River crossing.

Those headed for Yocum Ridge should bear right (uphill) at the junction beside Ramona Falls and follow the Timberline Trail as it gradually ascends beneath moss- and fern-draped cliffs. At the top of the ridge, you meet the Yocum Ridge Trail and turn right.

This path goes up the south side of the wooded ridge, often traveling through jungles of Pacific rhododendron, where spiders put up thousands of webs for the first hiker of the day to break through. You pass a rocky slope and then switchback up to the wide summit of the ridge. Another long switchback, this one with occasional steeper sections, takes you past a tiny shallow pond, after which the forest gradually becomes more open and the meadows more attractive as you continue gaining elevation. In early summer, the meadows here come alive with masses of yellow glacier lilies and white avalanche lilies.

All around you now is some of the most beautiful country in Oregon. The trail passes through gorgeous sloping meadows, with scattered subalpine firs and mountain hemlocks adding scenic contrast. Flowers abound, including bistort, columbine, beargrass, lupine, paintbrush, wallflower, larkspur, and countless others. The most awe-inspiring scenery starts at 8 miles when you come to a stunning overlook above the steep-walled Sandy River Canyon. From here you can crane your neck upward to look at the craggy ice sheet of Reid Glacier.

The main trail switchbacks to the left at this viewpoint, traveling uphill beneath a cluster of towering rock formations to the top of a ridge. From here, the trail turns right and ascends the spine of the ridge. You soon climb above timberline and wander through alpine terrain that features unrestricted views, ranging from Mount Rainier in the north to Mount Jefferson in the south.

The diminishing trail ends at 8.8 miles near the base of a rocky cliff. To reach the top of the cliff, simply trudge up one of the semipermanent snowfields or scramble up the steep rocks. On top is a glorious alpine plateau that you can happily explore for as long as you like. Ambitious types can follow the ridge all the way to the base of Sandy and Reid Glaciers, but just sitting back and enjoying the incredible views is more than enough for most hikers. On hot afternoons, don't be surprised if you hear loud cracking sounds coming from the moving ice of the glaciers.

You can camp almost anywhere in this alpine wonderland, but keep in mind that the area is extremely fragile, so set up your tent on rocks or snow rather than atop delicate flowers and grasses. The only available water is from snowfields. Sunsets from up here are otherworldly, and you can even see the lights of Portland far below. The ridge is very exposed, so do not camp here in bad weather.

34 Burnt Lake

RATINGS Scenery **7** Difficulty **5** Solitude **3**
ROUND-TRIP DISTANCE 5.4 miles
ELEVATION GAIN 1,500'
OPTIONAL MAP Green Trails *Government Camp (No. 461)*
USUALLY OPEN Late June–October
BEST TIME Late June–July; late August–early September
AGENCY Zigzag Ranger District (Mount Hood National Forest), 503-622-3191, fs.usda.gov/recarea/mthood/recarea/?recid=52778
PERMIT Required; free at the trailhead. Northwest Forest Pass required.

Highlights

Given that it's one of only a handful of lakes in the heavily traveled Mount Hood Wilderness, it's not surprising that Burnt Lake is popular. But even if there were hundreds of other lakes to choose from, this lovely mountain pool would probably attract crowds. Not only does this lake have a fine view of the wilderness' glacier-clad namesake, but it is also a nice spot for a swim or to fish for brook trout. As with other popular destinations, it is better if you visit in the middle of the week and try to get an early start.

Burnt Lake offers good swimming and fine views of Mount Hood.

Getting There

From Portland, take I-84 about 13 miles east, take Exit 16, and turn right onto 238th Drive. Go 1 mile and continue straight, now on 242nd Drive. In 1.8 miles turn left onto Burnside Road, which shortly becomes US 26. Take US 26 about 27 miles to the town of Zigzag, and turn left (north) on East Lolo Pass Road. After 4.3 miles, turn right on paved Forest Service Road 1825, and drive 0.7 mile to a junction. Turn right, immediately cross a bridge, and drive 0.45 mile to a fork. Bear left, still on FS 1825, go 1.3 miles, and then go straight at a second fork, now on FS 109. You soon pass McNeil Campground on the left and Lost Creek

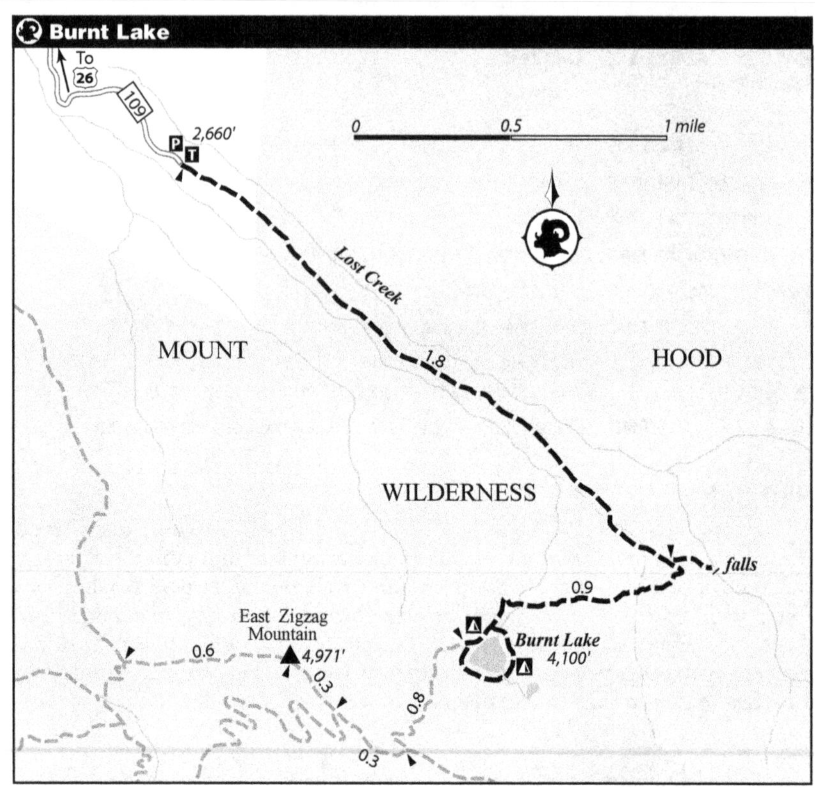

Campground on the right; the pavement ends, and you go another 0.4 mile to an unsigned junction. Go right and stay with this narrow, winding dirt road another 0.9 mile to the road-end Burnt Lake Trailhead.

GPS COORDINATES N45° 22.324' W121° 49.348'

Hiking It

The trail heads gradually uphill through a relatively open, mostly coniferous forest with only limited undergrowth. For the first 1.8 miles, the path traces a route between two parallel creeks in a narrow valley. Even though there are no views along this section, the hiking is pleasant, shady, and relatively easy. At the end of this gentle hike, the trail crosses a small creek and soon comes to a junction with a 0.1-mile spur trail that goes left to a small waterfall on Lost Creek.

The main trail keeps right at the junction, soon makes a switchback, and then begins a lengthy uphill traverse on a shady hillside covered with a dense canopy of firs and hemlocks. At the top of the traverse, you cross Burnt Lake's outlet creek and soon come to the northwest shore of your destination. A sometimes brushy trail circles the 8-acre lake, passing several designated campsites along the way. Please avoid trampling the fragile shoreline vegetation, and don't camp too close to the lake. The best camps are near the northeast shore, but the best views of Mount Hood—and they are really outstanding—are from the lake's southwest side (or, on a warm day, from the middle of the lake). The swimming is good anywhere, but it is especially excellent off a group of rocks on the lake's east shore. Campfires are prohibited within 0.5 mile of the lake.

If you are looking for a bit more exercise, consider climbing to the viewpoint atop East Zigzag Mountain. The trail departs from the southwest shore of Burnt Lake, climbing gently through forest openings, then switchbacking up a steep, north-facing slope to a ridgetop junction. Turn right, climb a little to a second junction, and then go straight and steeply ascend 0.3 mile to the open summit of East Zigzag Mountain. A garden of tiny alpine wildflowers provides a colorful foreground for the excellent views both down to Burnt Lake and up to towering Mount Hood. The scene easily makes the 1.4-mile one-way climb from the lake worth the effort. (Be aware that if there's any snow lingering here, the trail can sometimes be difficult to find.)

35 Cast Lake and Zigzag Mountain Loop

RATINGS	Scenery **7** Difficulty **6** Solitude **6**
ROUND-TRIP DISTANCE	10.6 miles
ELEVATION GAIN	2,600'
OPTIONAL MAP	Green Trails *Government Camp (No. 461)*
USUALLY OPEN	Late June–October
BEST TIME	Early–mid-July; late August–early September
AGENCY	Zigzag Ranger District (Mount Hood National Forest), 503-622-3191, fs.usda.gov/recarea/mthood/recarea/?recid=52778
PERMIT	Required; free at the trailhead

Highlights

Huckleberries (delicious in late August and providing plenty of color in mid-October), beargrass (blooming profusely with tall white blossoms in mid-July), and views (especially of nearby Mount Hood) are the main attractions of this enjoyable loop trip. Relative solitude is another bonus because difficult road access keeps the crowds to a minimum. Although Cast Lake features no mountain views, the surrounding area is so beautiful you will have no complaints about the scenery.

Getting There

From Portland, take I-84 about 13 miles east, take Exit 16, and turn right onto 238th Drive. Go 1 mile and continue straight, now on 242nd Drive. In 1.8 miles turn left onto Burnside Road, which shortly becomes US 26. Take US 26 about 30 miles to a poorly signed junction 1.5 miles east of Rhododendron, where you turn

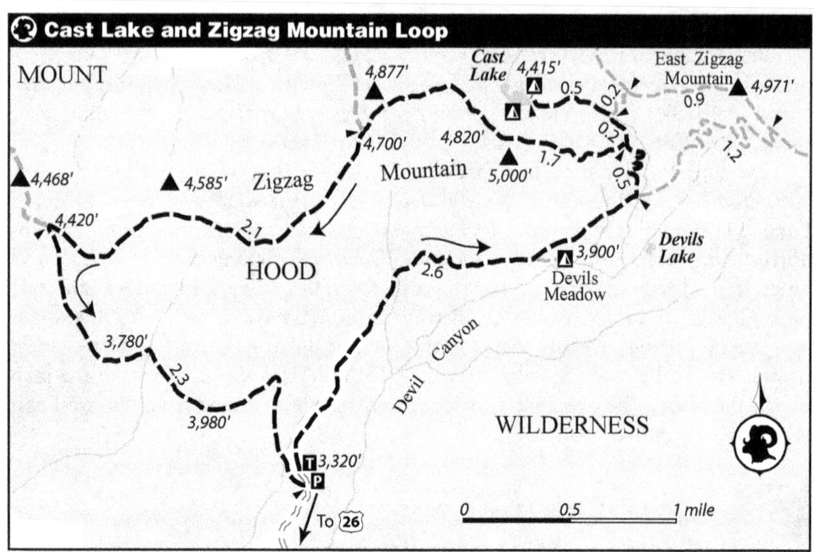

left (north) onto single-lane paved Forest Service Road 27 (aka Zigzag Mountain Road). After 0.6 mile this narrow road makes a sharp switchback to the left and turns to rough gravel and dirt. Slowly climb this miserably rutted road 4.6 miles, doing your best to avoid potholes and rocks along the way, to the road-end trailhead parking area.

GPS COORDINATES N45° 19.444' W121° 51.437'

Hiking It

The wide and gently graded trail begins as a long-abandoned jeep road that goes north from the trailhead, gradually climbing in dense forest. Throughout the summer, a wide array of forest birds will serenade your passage, including red-breasted nuthatches, mountain chickadees, golden-crowned kinglets, dark-eyed juncos, hairy woodpeckers, and various warblers and thrushes. The dense forest providing habitat for this feathered menagerie is nearly as attractive as the birdsong, featuring a canopy of western hemlock, western red cedar, and red alder towering over a thick covering of Pacific rhododendron, bracken fern, salal, and a profusion of wildflowers. Common blossoms here include larkspur, lupine, paintbrush, beargrass, arnica, spirea, bistort, and valerian.

At 1.8 miles the forest opens up somewhat as you go through an area of brushy meadows before coming to a fork. The dead-end path to the right leads to the long-abandoned Devils Meadow Campground, but you keep left, now on a narrower foot trail that gradually climbs through forest on the north side of lush Devils Meadow. After crossing a trickling creek, you arrive at a junction with the Devils Tie Trail at 2.6 miles. Going straight will take you to East Zigzag Mountain and Burnt Lake (see Trip 34, page 129). For this trip, you turn left and ascend six moderately steep switchbacks through dense forest where beargrass and huckleberries increasingly dominate the forest floor.

At 3.1 miles you come to a junction with the Zigzag Mountain Trail. The recommended return loop goes left here, but to reach the camps at Cast Lake, go straight, and walk 0.2 mile past an exceptionally pretty wildflower meadow rimmed with lodgepole pines and mountain hemlocks to a junction with the Cast Lake Trail. Turn left and gain about 150 feet in 0.3 mile before dropping to Cast Lake. This lake has no great views but is still quite pretty, backed by a mostly forested ridge. The shore is a mix of brush and meadows, and the lake is deep enough for swimming. A rough, up-and-down angler's path circles the lake, taking you past good campsites both on a little rise above the north shore and in a grove of trees near the south shore.

For the recommended loop, return to the junction of the Devils Tie and Zigzag Mountain Trails and turn right (west). This trail climbs a wide, woodsy ridge and then traverses the north side of a nameless high point through an area filled with tangled Sitka alders. Near the west end of this traverse you enjoy your first good views down to Cast Lake and up to Mount Hood, which rises majestically about 6 miles to the northeast. In the distance to the north you can also spot Washington's Mount Rainier and Mount Adams.

After rounding the unnamed peak, the trail curves left, generally staying near the top of a scenic up-and-down ridge and passing through acres of huckleberries, which provide a treat for the palate in late August and a fall-color treat for the eyes in late September and early October. In mid-July this area is also justly famous for its fields of blooming beargrass. Shortly after the trail passes below a rocky high point is a junction with the Horseshoe Ridge Trail; go left. You will pass through terrain that is increasingly forested, with fewer views; nonetheless, the hiking remains fun as you go up and down another 2 miles to a junction. Turn left on West Zigzag Mountain Trail, and steadily descend a shady slope to a crossing of an intermittent creek. You then regain almost 200 feet of that recently lost elevation to the top of a broad spur ridge before dropping moderately steeply for the next 0.8 mile. At the bottom of this descent you make an easy hop-over crossing of a small creek and then go uphill a final 0.1 mile to the road just 50 yards below the trailhead and your car.

Expect fantastic views of Mount Hood from Zigzag Mountain.
photo by Douglas Lorain

36 Paradise Park

RATINGS	Scenery **7** Difficulty **6** Solitude **3**
ROUND-TRIP DISTANCE	10.1 miles
ELEVATION GAIN	2,100'
OPTIONAL MAP	Green Trails *Mount Hood (No. 462)*
USUALLY OPEN	Mid-July–October
BEST TIME	Late July–early August
AGENCY	Zigzag Ranger District (Mount Hood National Forest), 503-622-3191, fs.usda.gov/recarea/mthood/recarea/?recid=52778
PERMIT	Required; free at the trailhead

Highlights

Situated just below timberline on the gently sloping southwest side of Mount Hood, Paradise Park is famous for its wildflowers and mountain views. The truth is that both of these features, although excellent at Paradise Park, are actually better at places like Elk Cove (Trip 32, page 122) or Yocum Ridge (Trip 33, page 125), but those locations are also harder for the average backpacker to reach. Because this hike begins at nearly 6,000 feet at Timberline Lodge, your car has already accomplished much of the elevation gain before you start the hike. Paradise Park is extremely popular, so be prepared for plenty of company, and try to visit in midweek or in September, after Labor Day, to avoid the worst of the crowds.

Getting There

From Portland, take I-84 about 13 miles east, take Exit 16, and turn right onto 238th Drive. Go 1 mile and continue straight, now on 242nd Drive. In 1.8 miles turn left onto Burnside Road, which shortly becomes US 26. Take US 26 about 38 miles to the junction with Timberline Lodge Road (OR 173) just east of Government Camp. Turn left (north), and climb this winding paved road 5.5 miles to the historic lodge with its acres of parking.

GPS COORDINATES N45° 19.799' W121° 42.503'

Hiking It

From the back of Timberline Lodge, you pick up a paved footpath marked with a small sign saying TIMBERLINE TRAIL. This route climbs 0.1 mile amid midsummer wildflowers to a junction with the Pacific Crest Trail (PCT). Turn left, go under a ski lift, and then gradually wander at a slight downhill grade through open timberline meadows with good views of Mount Jefferson and the Three Sisters in the distance to the south. Go straight at a four-way junction with the Mountaineer Trail, and soon reach the lip of the small canyon holding Little Zigzag River. The trail descends a little to this "river" (nothing more than a small creek), crosses it on rocks, and then climbs out of the canyon. From here you travel in open

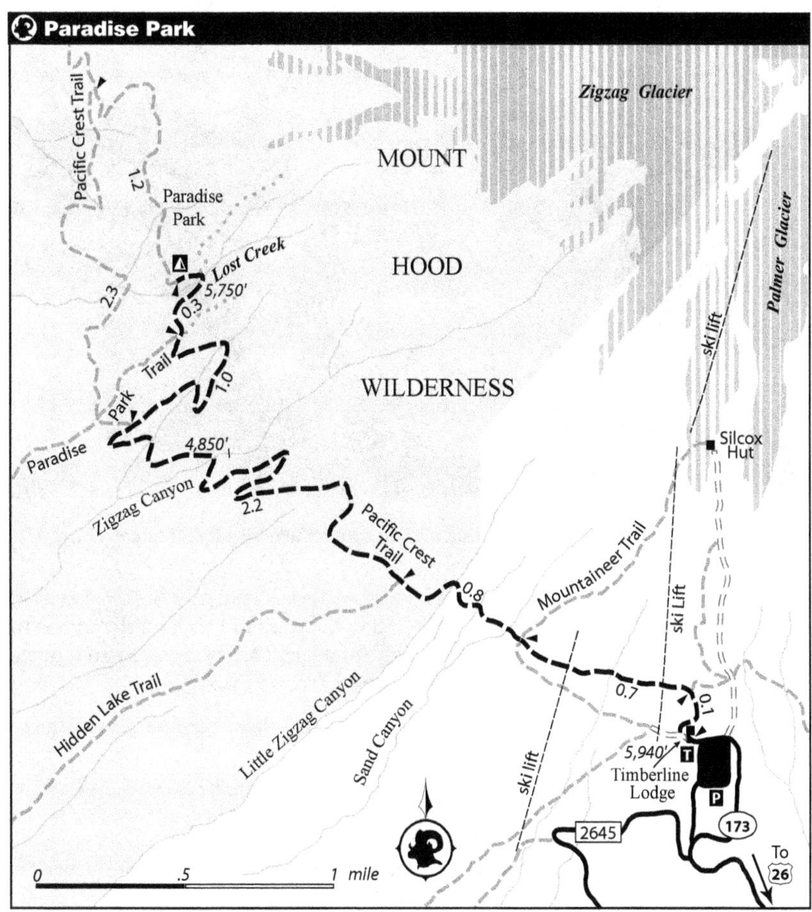

subalpine forests to a junction with the little-used Hidden Lake Trail. Go straight on the PCT and gradually lose elevation, first in forest and then across open meadowy slopes where the soil is loose and sandy. After a couple of short zigs and zags, you reach a stunning viewpoint on the lip of deep Zigzag Canyon. Mount Hood towers above the scene on your right, while below you the rocky canyon slopes plunge all the way down to the rushing waters of the river.

The path briefly follows the edge of the canyon, ducks into the trees, and then makes three long switchbacks down a cool, forested slope. There are several small creeks and springs on this segment that provide habitat for water-loving plants, including both yellow monkey flower and pink Lewis' monkey flower. At the bottom of the 1,000-foot descent is a bridgeless crossing of the silt-laden Zigzag River. In early summer this ford can be wet and a little tricky, but by mid-August it's a fairly simple rock-hop. Less than 0.1 mile upstream from the crossing is an impressive waterfall, which is visible from the trail and can be reached by those

The meadows above Paradise Park provide a prime spot for admiring Mount Hood.
photo by Douglas Lorain

willing to scramble over the loose rocks beside the stream. Once on the opposite bank, follow the PCT as it climbs in and out of a small tributary gully to a junction at 3.8 miles with the equestrian bypass trail around Paradise Park.

NOTE After the crossing of the Zigzag River, you might run into some fairly substantial obstructions in the form of blown-down trees. The Forest Service is actively working to clear the trail, and the problem is primarily concentrated on Paradise Park Trail 778 to the east, but consider calling ahead to check conditions, and be ready to do some zigzagging of your own.

The hiker's trail goes right and continues uphill as you regain all the elevation you lost in reaching the Zigzag River. At first this route ascends through trees, but then it crosses open slopes and switchbacks up a wide ravine with pleasant scenery but very little shade. Shortly after you reach the top of the canyon, you reach a junction with the Paradise Park Trail. If you want to do some exploring, consider following a use trail up the flower-covered meadow slopes to your right to some fine views of Mount Hood.

After finishing your exploring, go north on the Paradise Park Loop Trail to a crossing of clear Lost Creek in a gully that positively bursts with wildflowers, and soon reach the camp area at Paradise Park. Since this place is extremely popular, it is crucial that you camp only in official sites that have been used for years and can handle the stress. Fires are prohibited.

Once you've set up camp, take some time for a bit of exploring. The most rewarding option is to go cross-country around a bluff northeast of Paradise Park and wander up sloping meadows toward the rocks and glaciers on Mount Hood's higher slopes. A somewhat easier option continues north on the PCT 0.5 mile to some great above-timberline meadows with lots of delicate heather and views of the wide bulk of Mount Hood's southwest flank.

37 Elk Meadows Loop

RATINGS Scenery **7** Difficulty **4–7** Solitude **5**

ROUND-TRIP DISTANCE 6 miles to Elk Meadows; 13.1 miles as a loop

ELEVATION GAIN 1,250' to Elk Meadows; 2,700' as a loop

OPTIONAL MAP Green Trails *Mount Hood (No. 462)*

USUALLY OPEN July–October

BEST TIME July–October

AGENCY Hood River Ranger District (Mount Hood National Forest), 541-352-6002, fs.usda.gov/recarea/mthood/recreation/hiking/recarea/?recid=52776&actid=51

PERMIT Required; free at the trailhead. Northwest Forest Pass required.

Highlights

Elk Meadows is a generally flat, grassy expanse at the headwaters of Cold Springs Creek that boasts a picture-postcard view of the east face of Mount Hood. In midsummer the wildflower display here is quite impressive, adding greatly to the already fine scenery. As you might expect, these qualities make Elk Meadows a popular destination, so try to visit during midweek. But even if you can only visit on a weekend, the beauty is more than adequate compensation for the crowds. By turning this hike into a long loop, you can visit several additional worthwhile locations, including sliding Umbrella Falls, numerous excellent viewpoints, and some interesting locations where you can treasure-hunt for items lost during the ski season at Mount Hood Meadows.

Getting There

From Portland, take I-84 about 13 miles east, take Exit 16, and turn right onto 238th Drive. Go 1 mile and continue straight, now on 242nd Drive. In 1.8 miles turn left onto Burnside Road, which shortly becomes US 26. Take US 26 about 41 miles to the junction with OR 35 east of Government Camp. Go north on OR 35 toward Hood River, drive 7.8 miles, then turn left and quickly left again, following a sign for the Elk Meadows Trailhead. Drive 0.3 mile and park on the right, at a sign for the Elk Meadows and Sahalie Falls Trailhead.

GPS COORDINATES N45° 19.344' W121° 38.015'

Hiking It

From the trailhead, go north on Elk Meadows Trail through huckleberry fields, passing on your left a sign for the Mount Hood Nordic Center and then a signed junction with the Umbrella Falls Trail. Continue another 0.2 mile to reach a junction and the start of the recommended loop.

At the junction, you continue straight; almost immediately cross the silty, glacial torrent of Clark Creek on a footbridge; and wind your way very gradually uphill 0.6 mile to another junction. Go straight, and soon reach the crossing of

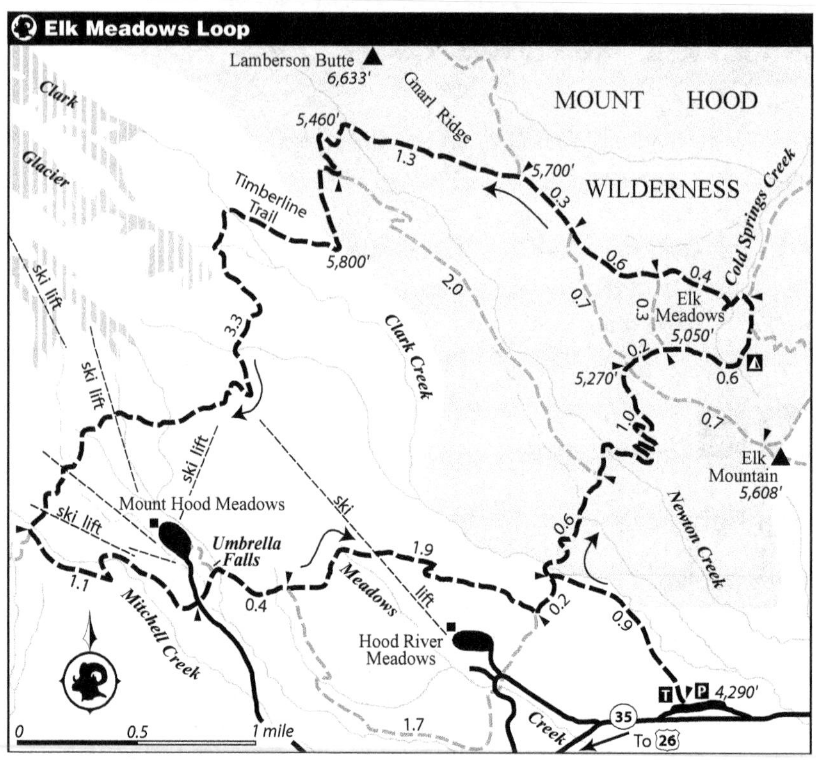

Newton Creek, an even larger glacial stream than Clark Creek. The trail crosses this rock-lined stream on a log, and then ascends eight long switchbacks to a four-way junction at the top of a ridge. Go straight, walk very gradually downhill 0.2 mile, and then turn right on the Elk Meadows Perimeter Trail. As it loops through the forest bordering the south and east sides of Elk Meadows, this trail passes several campsites. If you're planning to stay the night here, camp at one of these established sites—setting up your tent in the meadow itself or the tree islands within it is prohibited.

After passing a junction with a little-used trail that goes uphill to the right, you soon reach a junction beside clear-flowing Cold Springs Creek. Turn left and walk about 100 feet to a crossing of the creek and a fork in the trail. To reach the best picnic spot, go straight and walk 150 yards to an old wooden shelter. The views from here across the waving grasses of Elk Meadows up to Mount Hood are superb. If you eat lunch here, you should expect gray jays to come around asking for a handout (or simply stealing anything left unguarded).

To do the loop, return 150 yards to the fork and go left, back on the Perimeter Trail, as it loops around the north side of Elk Meadows to a junction. Go right and ascend in open forest 0.6 mile to another junction where you go straight and climb along the partly forested top of scenic Gnarl Ridge. There are some decent but partially obstructed views here of Mount Hood. At 4.6 miles is a junction with the Timberline Trail. You turn left and traverse a steep hillside as you work your way down to the crossing of Newton Creek. By late summer, hikers have often placed a helpful log across this roaring stream, but if not, you should expect a tricky and cold ford.

The trail now climbs to a junction at a minor ridgecrest, where you go straight, still on the Timberline Trail, and make your way out to a switchback atop a higher ridge with some nice views to the east. You now traverse to a crossing of Clark Creek (much easier than Newton Creek), and then begin an extended section of gradual ups and downs in open forests and small meadows. The trail goes in and out of small ravines and over minor ridges as it makes its way slowly south and west. After topping a somewhat taller ridge, you cross beneath several ski lifts radiating from the resort at Mount Hood Meadows. Frequently, there is good hunting here for items left behind by skiers and snowboarders in the winter. At 9.2 miles you come to a junction in a small meadow with a nice view of Mount Hood.

Turn left at the junction, leaving the Timberline Trail and descending through meadows and increasingly dense forests for 1.1 miles to the paved access road serving Mount Hood Meadows. Cross the road, pick up the trail on the other side, and follow it 0.1 mile to Umbrella Falls. This long, sloping falls is a real treat and well worth a rest stop to appreciate its charms. After crossing the creek just below the falls, the trail wanders mostly on the level for 0.3 mile to a junction. Go straight and hike gradually downhill 1.9 miles, passing under at least one more ski lift as you enjoy occasional views down to the developed area around lush Hood River Meadows. At 12.6 miles you come to a junction. Turn right to complete the loop and return to the trailhead.

A rare footbridge lies near the beginning of the Elk Meadows Loop. *photo by Paul Gerald*

38 Salmon River Trail

RATINGS	Scenery **6** Difficulty **1–6** Solitude **6**
ROUND-TRIP DISTANCE	4 miles to Rolling Riffle Camp; 14.3 miles total (point-to-point)
ELEVATION GAIN	250' to Rolling Riffle Camp; 2,700' total
OPTIONAL MAPS	Green Trails *Government Camp (No. 461)* and *High Rock (No. 493)*
USUALLY OPEN	March–November to Rolling Riffle Camp; late May–late October for entire trail
BEST TIME	Anytime it's open
AGENCY	Zigzag Ranger District (Mount Hood National Forest), 503-622-3191, fs.usda.gov/recarea/mthood/recarea/?recid=52778
PERMIT	Required; free at the trailhead. Northwest Forest Pass required.

Highlights

As the scenic highlight of the Salmon-Huckleberry Wilderness, Salmon River Canyon has been a popular hiking destination for decades. Starting in a magnificent old-growth forest, the trail eventually climbs to forested hillsides above the water, passes a spectacular viewpoint on an open slope, and then travels past a series of impressive but virtually unreachable waterfalls. The eastern part of the canyon is less dramatic but still very attractive, with lovely forests and scattered spots along the river that are ideal for quiet contemplation. The biggest advantage of the eastern section of the trail is that it sees few visitors because day hikers rarely travel that far.

There are several excellent camps along the river, providing options for overnight hikes of almost any length. If you are doing the entire trail, it is better to

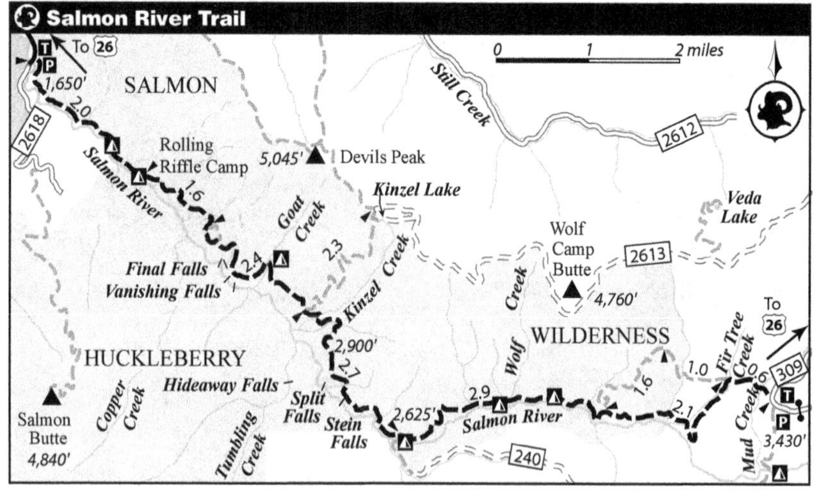

start at the east trailhead and hike downhill. Unfortunately, even though the west trailhead is usually accessible year-round, the east trailhead is closed by snow until at least late May. In addition, many people, especially hikers with children, prefer to start at the bottom and make a shorter hike to one of the lower campsites in the western section, instead of tackling the entire trail. To accommodate this, the trail will be described starting from the lower, west trailhead.

Getting There

From Portland, take I-84 about 13 miles east, take Exit 16, and turn right onto 238th Drive. Go 1 mile and continue straight, now on 242nd Drive. In 1.8 miles turn left onto Burnside Road, which shortly becomes US 26. Take US 26 about 27 miles to the town of Zigzag.

To reach the west trailhead, turn right (south) on East Salmon River Road (following signs to Green Canyon Campground), which becomes Forest Service Road 2618, and follow this paved route 5 miles to the large parking area on the left, just before a bridge over the Salmon River.

To reach the east trailhead, continue 12 miles east from Zigzag on US 26 to a junction 1.8 miles past Government Camp. Turn right (south), following signs to Trillium Lake, and follow paved FS 2656 for 1.7 miles to a junction at the southeast corner of the lake (keep straight/right as you pass the entrance to the campground on the right at about 1.3 miles). Bear left, staying on FS 2656, and after 1.1 miles come to a fork where you bear left. (Pass by the narrow, gated dirt road marked 903—you don't want that one, and, trust me, it's difficult to turn around if you accidentally take it.) The pavement ends as you continue on a good gravel road 0.7 mile to another fork. Bear right, now on FS 309, and drive a final 2 miles to the Salmon River/Jackpot Meadows Trailhead.

GPS COORDINATES N45° 16.669' W121° 56.387' (west trailhead)
N45° 13.584' W121° 46.408' (east trailhead)

Hiking It

The western section of the trail begins beside a prominent signboard and heads upstream on the Douglas fir–covered slopes above the water. After curving down to a viewpoint above a large, deep pool in the river, you wander lazily uphill through an exceptionally impressive old-growth forest of massive Douglas firs, western red cedars, and western hemlocks. Moss hangs from the limbs and covers the trunks of these old giants, while ferns and new young trees grow out of downed nurse logs. Nearly as impressive as the forest is the river, which glides along in a series of delightful glassy pools, small rapids, and quiet riffles. At 1.6 miles you pass a nice camp, and then at 2 miles reach Rolling Riffle Camp, below the trail on the right. This is a good goal for hikers with children. (Be aware, though, that it can fill up early on a summer weekend.)

Just past Rolling Riffle Camp the trail pulls away from the water and climbs steadily but not steeply up a forested hillside. You cross several small creeks along the way, so water remains plentiful even though you are now well above the river. At 3.6 miles, shortly after climbing out of a good-sized side canyon, the trail splits. For the best scenery keep right, and almost immediately leave the forest for an open slope with outstanding canyon views. The river cascades through a

The west end of the Salmon River Trail meanders gently through old-growth forest.

cliff-walled chasm almost 600 feet below, while delicate wildflowers add color to the foreground. This is the best canyon viewpoint of the trip. Unfortunately, these views are short-lived, as the narrow, pebble-strewn path soon leaves the open hillside and makes a short, steep climb back up to a junction with the main trail.

Over the next 0.6 mile you pass several unsigned use paths that drop very steeply to the right. These lead to stunning overlooks down into the canyon and especially of towering Final and Frustration Falls.

WARNING *Be very careful* because the loose rocks on these steep paths make for extremely dangerous footing, and it is a very long way down to the rocks at the bottom of the canyon. People have fallen and died from these heights, so please take these warnings seriously.

Few day hikers go beyond this point, but backpackers can continue their journey, enjoying the solitude of the upper trail. The route stays in attractive forest nearly the entire way, always on the hillside north of the river. For the next several miles you will not see the river or any of the several impressive waterfalls along it.

That may be frustrating, but reaching those remote falls requires dangerous scrambling and sometimes technical equipment, so don't even think about it. The trail stays mostly level until it reaches a campsite at the crossing of Goat Creek at 5.4 miles, after which you gradually ascend to a junction with the Kinzel Lake Trail.

Go straight, descend a little to cross small Kinzel Creek, and then ascend to a minor ridgecrest before beginning a pattern of zigzags that go into little gullies and out to small ridges, always on the heavily forested hillside well above the Salmon River. Over the next couple of miles, the trail gradually works closer to the river, until it finally comes to a fork at 8.7 miles. To visit the river, bear right on the Linney Creek Trail and walk 50 yards downhill to the water. An excellent campsite beneath some large cedar and fir trees is located just upstream from the river crossing, on your side of the river.

To continue your upstream tour, return to the main trail, which soon climbs away from the river onto the steep slopes above. The trail then descends once again, reaching a fine campsite just before you splash across small Wolf Creek. Another 0.6 mile of mostly gentle walking takes you to a final excellent campsite right beside the river.

The trail continues going gradually upstream, generally through viewless but attractive forest. The river remains unseen in the canyon on your right, but its river music is constantly heard. Go straight at an unsigned and easy-to-miss junction with an old trail that goes steeply uphill to the left, and then go up and down through forest and past the base of a large talus slope to the crossings of several small creeks, the last of which is Fir Tree Creek.

The trail now makes a long uphill switchback on an increasingly open slope with nice views across the forested Salmon River Canyon. At the top of the climb you cross Fir Tree Creek again, just above a small marsh, and then go gradually uphill to a junction with Dry Lake Trail, which is still signed, even though it is now officially abandoned. Turn right, immediately cross Fir Tree Creek a final time, and then climb through forest over a little ridge and down to a dilapidated but functional log footbridge over misnamed Mud Creek. From here a short but steep uphill takes you to the upper, eastern trailhead and the end of your hike.

39 Veda Lake

RATINGS Scenery **5** Difficulty **3** Solitude **8**

ROUND-TRIP DISTANCE 2.8 miles

ELEVATION GAIN 750'

OPTIONAL MAPS Green Trails *Government Camp (No. 461)* and *High Rock (No. 493)*

USUALLY OPEN Mid-June–October

BEST TIME July; late August

AGENCY Zigzag Ranger District (Mount Hood National Forest), 503-622-3191, fs.usda.gov/recarea/mthood/recarea/?recid=52778

PERMIT None

Highlights

In 1917 two local outdoorsmen named Vern Rogers and Dave Donaldson packed in a load of trout to a small, unnamed lake south of Government Camp, probably hoping to create a private fishing hole. Much to their surprise, their efforts garnered them a sort of immortality. To honor their achievement, the local forest ranger named the lake by combining the first two letters of each man's first name. The offspring of the original fish can still be caught today. On the way to the lake's shores, hikers can also enjoy fine views of nearby Mount Hood. All in all, this short hike is well worth having to endure the lousy road access to the trailhead.

Getting There

From Portland, take I-84 about 13 miles east, take Exit 16, and turn right onto 238th Drive. Go 1 mile and continue straight, now on 242nd Drive. In 1.8 miles turn left onto Burnside Road, which shortly becomes US 26. Take US 26 about 39 miles to a junction about 0.7 mile east of Government Camp, and then turn right (south) on the road to Still Creek Campground (Forest Service Road 2650). Proceed 0.7 mile through the campground, and then keep straight at a junction where the campground loop road goes left. Following signs for Trillium Lake, drive south on a pothole-plagued gravel road 0.4 mile to a junction where you turn right onto East Chimney Rock Road (FS 126). This road goes past several private cabins 0.5 mile to a four-way junction. Go straight on Forest Service Road 2613 (Sherar Burn Road) and slow down because this soon becomes a bumpy dirt road. (It has recently been graded, but high-clearance vehicles are still recommended.) After 3.6 carefully negotiated miles, pull into the parking area on the right (north) side of the road, just opposite the Fir Tree/Veda Lake Trailhead sign.

GPS COORDINATES
N45° 14.878' W121° 47.260'

Hiking It

The trail starts on the north side of the road next to a small brown sign, climbing through a forest of Pacific silver fir and mountain hemlock. Tall red huckleberry bushes crowd the forest floor, providing a treat for the taste buds when the berries ripen in late August. After gaining about 250 feet, you top a viewless ridge and then begin a gradual descent.

Try fishing for brook trout at Veda Lake.
photo by Douglas Lorain

About 200 yards later, you reach an excellent viewpoint of Mount Hood, nicely framed by the forested valley of Still Creek and with round Veda Lake sparkling in the basin below.

You switchback down past three more good viewpoints, each occupying an opening in the forest where plentiful sunshine allows for fine displays of July wildflowers such as lupine, paintbrush, beargrass, arnica, and showy Washington lily. You make the final descent in one long switchback across a partly forested hillside to a campsite on the north shore of 3-acre Veda Lake. Ever since Vern and Dave stocked this lake, it has produced catchable brook trout. If fishing isn't your goal, the lake is also a good place to swim or just relax and enjoy a peaceful mountain setting.

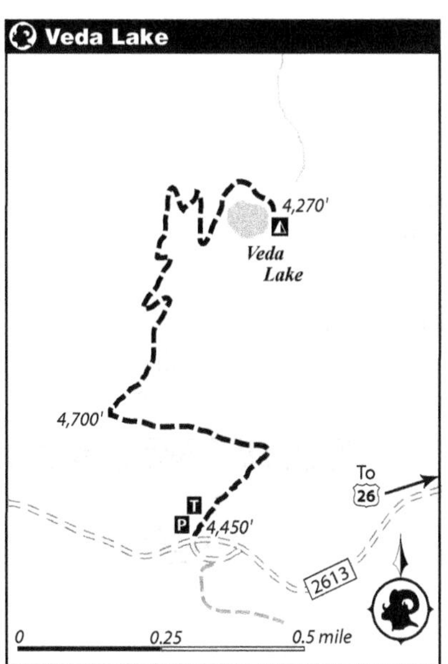

40 Twin Lakes Loop

RATINGS	Scenery **5** Difficulty **2–5** Solitude **3**
ROUND-TRIP DISTANCE	4 miles to Lower Twin Lake; 9 miles for the full loop
ELEVATION GAIN	700' to Lower Twin Lake; 1,500' for the loop
OPTIONAL MAPS	Green Trails *Mount Hood (No. 462)* and *Mount Wilson (No. 494)*
USUALLY OPEN	June–October
BEST TIME	Mid- to late August
AGENCY	Zigzag Ranger District (Mount Hood National Forest), 503-622-3191, fs.usda.gov/recarea/mthood/recarea/?recid=52778
PERMIT	None. Northwest Forest Pass required.

Highlights

Two sparkling lakes with easy trail access, pretty settings beneath forested ridges, plenty of fish, good swimming, and fine camps make this pleasant overnighter an ideal way to introduce kids or beginners to the best parts of backpacking. The lakes are popular, so midweek is better, but they are worth a visit anytime. Upper Twin Lake is less crowded, so camp there if you prefer solitude. By adding a loop through the scenic country north of the lakes, you can enjoy some excellent viewpoints of Mount Hood and less crowded hiking.

Getting There

From Portland, take I-84 about 13 miles east, take Exit 16, and turn right onto 238th Drive. Go 1 mile and continue straight, now on 242nd Drive. In 1.8 miles turn left onto Burnside Road, which shortly becomes US 26. Take US 26 about 40 miles to the junction of US 26 and OR 35 east of Government Camp, go 6 miles southeast on US 26 (toward Bend), and then turn left into the large Frog Lake Sno-Park and Trailhead at Wapinitia Pass.

GPS COORDINATES N45° 13.762' W121° 41.950'

Hiking It

Pick up a signed spur trail at the north end of the parking lot and walk a few feet to a junction with the Pacific Crest Trail (PCT). Turn right on the PCT and, after 120 yards, go straight at the junction, ignoring a trail that heads right (south) to the busy car campground at Frog Lake. The gently graded PCT climbs gradually in one long switchback on a hillside covered with mountain hemlocks and firs. The forest floor is covered with dense thickets of huckleberries, which ripen nicely in late August.

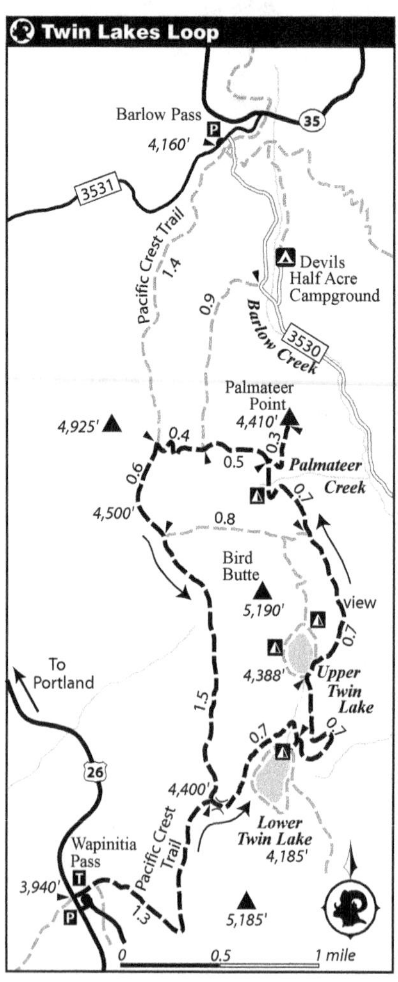

At 1.3 miles is a trail junction at the start of the recommended loop. Leave the PCT here and turn right, following a path that soon crosses a saddle and makes a gradual descent toward Lower Twin Lake, which is visible through the trees on the right. Just after crossing the often-dry inlet creek, a signed trail drops to the right and leads to a spacious camping area at the north end of the lake. The green-tinged 15-acre lake has pleasant views of forested Frog Lakes Buttes to the south and is very deep, so it is excellent for swimming. A fisherman's path goes around the lake, while the trail to Frog Lake Buttes climbs away from the lake's east shore.

To reach Upper Twin Lake, which features a partial view of Mount Hood, return to the main trail and turn right. This trail soon rounds a ridge and then climbs two well-graded switchbacks to the shallow upper lake. This lake also has a shoreline trail, with the best camps above the northeast and west shores.

Since the views from both of the Twin Lakes are limited, you can hike a loop that takes you past two excellent viewpoints. To follow it, turn right (northeast) onto the poorly marked Palmateer View Trail from the east shore of Upper Twin Lake, and hike 0.4 mile to an unmarked viewpoint atop a rock outcropping just a few feet to the right of the trail. From here you enjoy an outstanding view of the Barlow Creek Valley and Mount Hood. The trail continues north from here, passing a junction after another 0.3 mile and then descending to a campsite at the crossing of small Palmateer Creek. Although it is less scenic than the camps at the Twin Lakes, this site provides considerably more solitude.

Shortly beyond the crossing of Palmateer Creek, you come to a signed junction with the 0.3-mile spur trail to Palmateer Point. This is worth a visit, even though the view is not as good as the trailside one above Upper Twin Lake.

To complete the recommended loop, take the trail going west from the Palmateer Point turnoff and hike mostly uphill through an unusually varied and interesting forest for 0.9 mile, passing one easily missed junction along the way, to a junction with the PCT. Turn left (south) and hike gradually up and down through forest for 1.5 miles back to the junction with the trail to Lower Twin Lake and the close of the loop. Go straight to return to the trailhead.

The sparkling Twin Lakes make an excellent introduction to backpacking.

41 Boulder Lake

RATINGS	Scenery **6** Difficulty **1–4** Solitude **7**
ROUND-TRIP DISTANCE	0.6 mile to lake; 4 miles with side trip to Bonney Meadows
ELEVATION GAIN	200' to lake; 950' to Bonney Meadows
OPTIONAL MAP	Green Trails *Mount Hood (No. 462)*
USUALLY OPEN	Late June–October
BEST TIME	July (for the best wildflowers in Bonney Meadows)
AGENCY	Barlow Ranger District (Mount Hood National Forest), 541-467-2291, fs.usda.gov/recarea/mthood/recarea/?recid=52772
PERMIT	None

Highlights

There are two approach trails to Boulder Lake, a scenic pool set beneath a line of impressive cliffs and talus slopes in a small roadless area southeast of Mount Hood. In the past, most hikers started from Bonney Meadows and descended from this wildflower haven to the shores of the lake. The downside to this plan is that the approach road has gone from awful to pretty much impassable for all but high-clearance four-wheel-drive vehicles, and the hike, while scenic, requires plenty of uphill on the return trip. What relatively few people realize is that there is another option that is very short, never crowded, suitable for backpackers of any age, and has a good gravel access road. The recommended itinerary, therefore, is to take the shorter trail, saving wear and tear on both your car and your knees, then set up camp at Boulder Lake and make the trip to Bonney Meadows as a scenic day hike.

Getting There

From Portland, take I-84 about 13 miles east, take Exit 16, and turn right onto 238th Drive. Go 1 mile and continue straight, now on 242nd Drive. In 1.8 miles turn left onto Burnside Road, which shortly becomes US 26. Take US 26 about 40 miles to the junction with OR 35 east of Government Camp, then

Plan to camp beside scenic Boulder Lake.

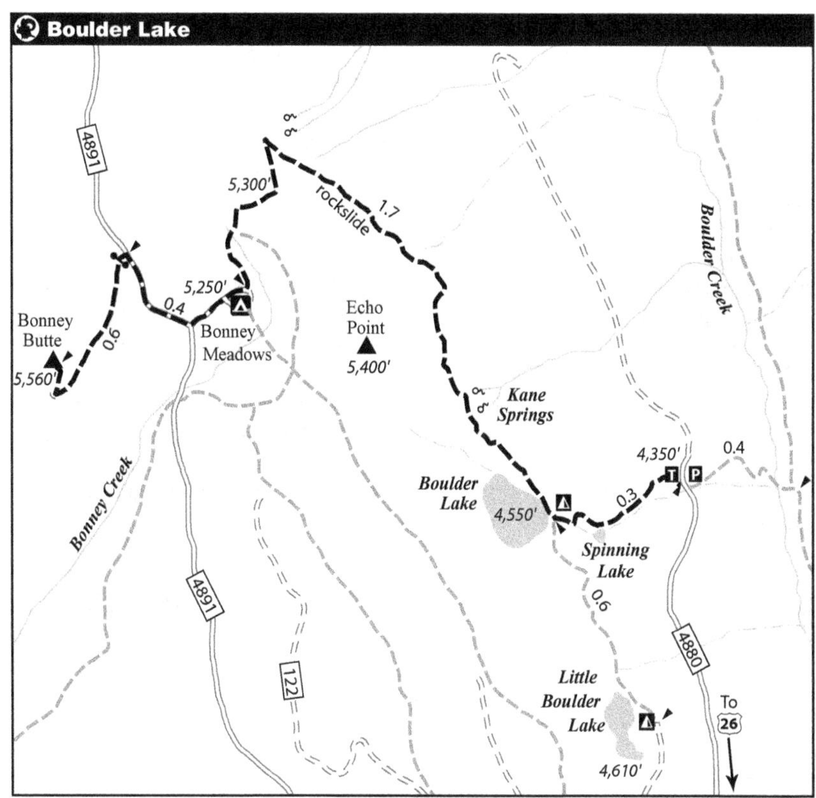

take OR 35 (toward Hood River), another 4.5 miles to a junction with paved FS 48. Turn right, following signs to Wamic, and drive 14.4 miles. Turn left on one-lane, paved FS 4880, following signs to Boulder Lake Trail, and proceed 2.4 miles to a fork. Veer right to stay on FS 4880, and drive another 4.2 miles to reach the trailhead pullout on the left.

GPS COORDINATES N45° 15.507' W121° 33.564'

Hiking It

The trail goes west, steadily climbing through a forest of mixed conifers beside a tiny seasonal creek. After 0.2 mile you pass shallow Spinning Lake, actually little more than a pond, and 0.1 mile later reach a junction beside the east shore of much larger and prettier Boulder Lake. There are two nice campsites near this junction, each with its own picnic table. In addition to its fine scenery, the 11-acre lake supports a healthy population of small brook trout and a few larger rainbow trout.

To reach the beautiful rolling expanse of Bonney Meadows, take the trail that goes north along the east shore of Boulder Lake, and follow it up a forested hillside. After 0.2 mile you pass bubbling Kane Springs (easy to miss in dry years), and then climb one long switchback to the top of a ridge. Here the trail levels out and goes southwest through forest 0.1 mile to a junction at the north end of the wildflower-covered expanse of Bonney Meadows. This end of the meadow has only limited mountain views, but it is still extremely lovely, with a meandering creek, waving grasses, and plenty of wildflowers. The trail to the left loops through the forest around the edge of the meadows; going straight will take you across a small portion of the meadows to primitive Bonney Meadows Campground, the alternate trailhead.

You can turn around at the meadows, well satisfied with your side trip, but we strongly recommend a side trip to Bonney Butte. It's a bit of a trudge, but the views are well worth the effort. To reach it, walk down the dirt access road to Bonney Meadows Campground to its junction with FS 4891, turn right, and walk uphill 0.2 mile to the junction with a gated jeep road going left. Turn onto this road and climb increasingly open slopes 0.6 mile to the summit. The view of Mount Hood from this high point makes the extra sweat worthwhile. In October, Bonney Butte is an important "hawk watch" site where migrating birds of prey are counted as they move south. Bring your binoculars and keep an eye out for golden eagles, prairie falcons, merlins, and various hawks.

42 Lookout Mountain and Oval Lake

RATINGS	Scenery **7** Difficulty **7** Solitude **6**
ROUND-TRIP DISTANCE	6.4 miles (including side trip to Palisade Point)
ELEVATION GAIN	2,050' (including side trip)
OPTIONAL MAPS	Green Trails *Flag Point (No. 463)* and *Mount Hood (No. 462)*
USUALLY OPEN	Late June–October
BEST TIME	July
AGENCY	Barlow Ranger District (Mount Hood National Forest), 541-467-2291, fs.usda.gov/recarea/mthood/recarea/?recid=52772
PERMIT	None. Northwest Forest Pass required.

Highlights

Rising like a green wall east of Mount Hood, Surveyors Ridge is the last major outpost in the Cascade Range before those mountains slope down to the arid grasslands of north-central Oregon. The highest point along that ridge is Lookout Mountain, and, not surprisingly, it provides one of the best views anywhere of Oregon's highest mountain, just 6 miles west.

A short trail reaches this fine viewpoint, but backpackers can turn this into a longer and more satisfying hike by going east on the Divide Trail, a scenic route that passes a string of impressive cliff-edge viewpoints, wildflower meadows, and dramatic rock outcroppings. The overnight destination is Oval Lake, a tiny but attractive pool that is almost never crowded.

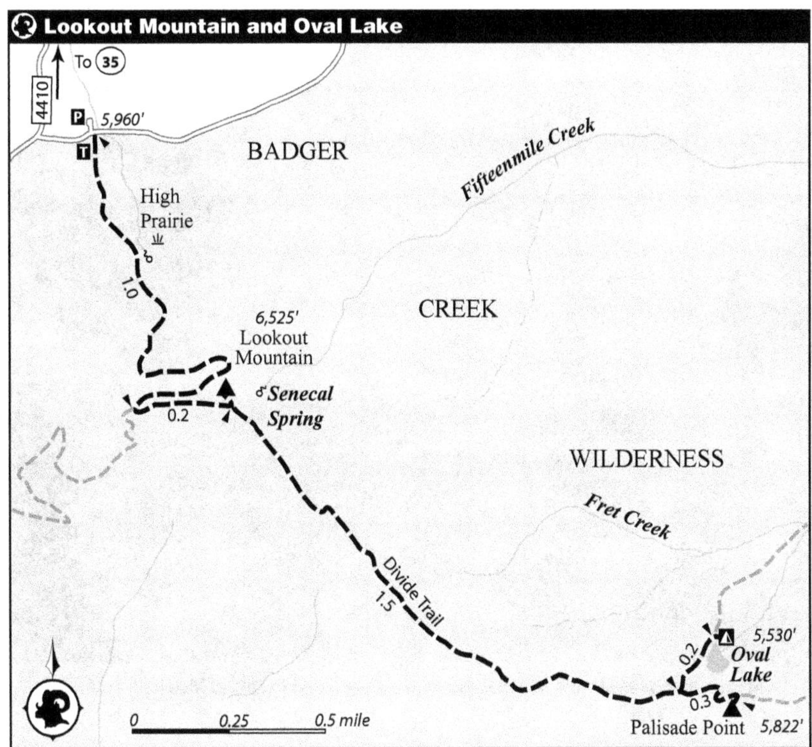

Getting There

Drive OR 35 either north 13 miles from its junction with US 26, east of Government Camp, or south 25 miles from Hood River to a junction between mileposts 70 and 71. Turn east onto Forest Service Road 44, following signs to Dufur, and proceed 3.8 miles to a junction just after you top a ridge. Turn right onto gravel FS 4410, drive 4.6 miles to a junction, and then turn left to reach the signed trailhead in about 0.1 mile.

GPS COORDINATES N45° 21.137' W121° 31.868'

Hiking It

The well-developed trail goes south following a long-abandoned jeep road that makes a very gradual climb beside a large meadow called High Prairie. In July this meadow is a riot of wildflowers, with false hellebore, bistort, aster, valerian, dandelion, and a host of other blossoms putting on a grand display of color. After passing a small spring at 0.4 mile, you leave the meadow for a forest of subalpine firs and mountain hemlocks as the trail, or old road, gradually ascends a couple of lazy switchbacks to a ridgetop junction. Turn left on the main route and cross increasingly open and rocky slopes to a fork just below the summit of Lookout Mountain. If you want to visit the summit, simply veer left and walk uphill for the

Twisted whitebark pines frame Mount Hood on the aptly named Lookout Mountain Trail.

final 75 yards. The view from this old fire lookout site is outstanding, including distant snow-covered peaks from Mount Rainier in the north to the Three Sisters in the south, east to the dry wheat fields and grasslands of eastern Oregon, and especially west to the towering summit of Mount Hood.

To reach Oval Lake, return to the junction just below the summit and go east, leaving the old road and following the Divide Trail. This footpath steeply descends a flower-covered slope that hosts such beautiful varieties as cliff penstemon, stonecrop, buckwheat, and skyrocket gilia. Once at the bottom of this slope, the trail traces a course along a scenic ridgeline going in and out of forest, frequently passing silvery old snags and wildflower meadows along the way. At several points it is possible to follow short side trails that go right (south) to rock outcroppings with terrific views south over Badger Lake and the Badger Creek Wilderness to distant Mount Jefferson. The trail has at least four knee-crushingly steep downhill segments interspersed with more gentle sections. (As steep as they seem on the way down, they somehow become even steeper on the way back.)

At 2.7 miles you reach a prominent junction signed for Fret Creek. Turn left and wander downhill through a dense forest of mountain hemlocks 0.2 mile to tiny and shallow Oval Lake. The best camps are on the other side of the outlet creek above the north shore. Although a welcome permanent source of water, this lake has only marginal swimming because it is very shallow and rather muddy.

The lake has no fish. There are some decent views south over the water to the crags of Palisade Point.

If you have the time and energy, it is worth taking a side trip to Palisade Point. To reach it, return to the Divide Trail and turn left (east), climbing a few short but steep and occasionally slippery switchbacks. After 0.3 mile, you leave the trail and walk south about 50 yards to the dramatic clifftop viewpoint atop Palisade Point—an excellent place for a picnic lunch. After exploring the unusual terrain up here and admiring the views, especially to the south of Mount Jefferson, return the way you came.

43 Badger Creek

RATINGS Scenery **5** Difficulty **2** Solitude **7**

ROUND-TRIP DISTANCE 5.8 miles (with many shorter and longer options)

ELEVATION GAIN 450'

OPTIONAL MAP Green Trails *Flag Point (No. 463)*

USUALLY OPEN March–November

BEST TIME May; late October

AGENCY Barlow Ranger District (Mount Hood National Forest), 541-467-2291, fs.usda.gov/recarea/mthood/recarea/?recid=52772

PERMIT None

Highlights

Although it has none of the spectacular mountain scenery found on some of the other trails in this book, this uncrowded hike up charming Badger Creek has plenty to recommend it. The trail is easy and fun for backpackers of any age. The creek is very pretty and a constant joy to walk beside. The forest is exceptionally attractive and, due to its eastside location, features an interesting and unusual mix of trees, shrubs, and flowers found both in the high mountains and in the dry semidesert lands of eastern Oregon. Finally, there are dozens of possible campsites along the way, so hikers can travel whatever distance suits their abilities and interests.

Getting There

From Portland, take I-84 about 13 miles east, take Exit 16, and turn right onto 238th Drive. Go 1 mile and continue straight, now on 242nd Drive. In 1.8 miles turn left onto Burnside Road, which shortly becomes US 26. Take US 26 about 40 miles to the junction with OR 35 east of Government Camp. Continue southeast on US 26 for 11.1 miles, then turn left onto paved Forest Service Road 43, following signs to Rock Creek Reservoir. Drive 6 miles, turn right on paved FS 48, and proceed 15.5 miles to an unsigned junction just as the main road makes a sweeping turn to the right. Turn left on FS 4810, go 0.2 mile to a fork, and then bear right, still on one-lane, paved FS 4810. After another 2 miles turn right on

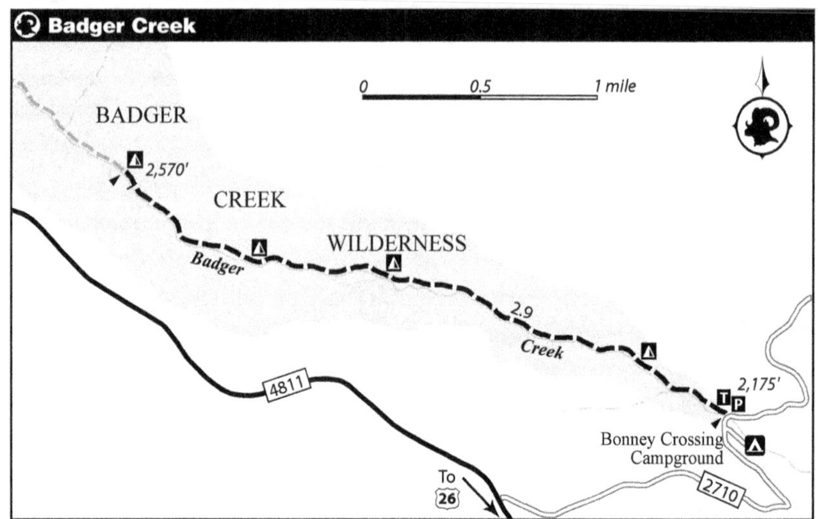

FS 4811, following signs to Bonney Crossing Campground, drive 1.3 miles, and then turn right on gravel FS 2710. Proceed steeply downhill 1.7 miles, pass the campground entrance, and come to the tiny trailhead parking area on the left immediately after a bridge over Badger Creek.

GPS COORDINATES N45° 15.451' W121° 23.562'

Hiking It

The gentle creekside Badger Creek Trail heads upstream in an open and exceptionally attractive forest of grand firs, Douglas firs, western red cedars, ponderosa pines, and Oregon white oaks. The dappled sunshine coming through this forest provides enough light for many low shrubs, dominated by snowberry and wild rose. Along the creek are willows and other water-loving plants. The forest here is particularly beautiful in May, when wildflowers are abundant, and in mid- to late October, when the fall colors from the oaks, Douglas maples, willows, and red alders are quite showy. Clear-flowing Badger Creek is a constant and welcome companion, adding its beauty to the mix as it tumbles over boulders in a narrow streambed on your left.

The first of many inviting campsites comes at 0.4 mile, and above that point the generally flat ground at the bottom of this steep-walled canyon ensures that you could set up camp at dozens of additional locations over the next few miles. The trail avoids most of the ups and downs that usually plague creekside paths, remaining either level or at a very gentle uphill slope for almost its entire length. At 1.7 miles, immediately after one of the few brief downhill sections, you'll find an exceptionally nice campsite on your left. At 2.2 miles is yet another fine camp, and then at 2.9 miles you'll come to a lovely little spot where the creek chutes over a tiny waterfall between two large, moss-covered boulders into a deep wading pool. Just 30 yards past this scenic little falls is a fine campsite, the recommended spot for you to spend the night, especially if you are hiking with children.

Keep in mind that equestrian use is fairly high on this trail, so try to camp well away from the trail so horses aren't frightened by your children running around or making noise. One other note: We spotted lots of skunks along this trail, so keep dogs on a leash and make sure kids know to give the critters a wide berth; they're cute, but if you startle one, everybody in your party will know it.

Hardy hikers have the option to continue upstream, as the trail follows the creek all the way to its source at artificially dammed Badger Lake, 10.7 miles from the trailhead. The creekside scenery is attractive throughout, and by the time you reach Badger Lake you will have been treated to an abundance of western larch, which pepper the hillsides with gold in the latter part of October.

For most of the year, you're likely to have the Badger Creek Trail and its campsites all to yourself.

Clackamas River Country

The strikingly beautiful Clackamas River flows clear and cold through a scenic, twisting canyon cut into a contorted landscape of forest-covered ridges. There are relatively few options for backpackers to hike directly beside the river, but the surrounding mountains hide countless treasures to explore. Although there are no glacier-clad peaks, you will discover dozens of mostly small but unusually pretty mountain lakes, each surrounded by lush forests and often backed by scenic talus slopes and ridges. There are also view-packed ridges, old-growth forests, and wildflower-filled meadows, all accessible by trails that generally receive only a fraction of the pedestrian traffic tramping the more famous paths around Mount Hood or in the Columbia River Gorge. So if you are willing to forgo the alpine scenery of the high volcanic peaks, the Clackamas River country has plenty to offer the weekend backpacker.

The Shellrock and Serene Lakes Loop (Trip 46, page 163) hike is a Clackamas River classic.

44 High Lake

RATINGS	Scenery **6** Difficulty **7** Solitude **9**
ROUND-TRIP DISTANCE	6.6 miles
ELEVATION GAIN	2,300'
OPTIONAL MAP	Green Trails *Fish Creek Mountain (No. 492);* new trail alignment not shown
USUALLY OPEN	Mid-June–October
BEST TIME	Late June–early October
AGENCY	Clackamas River Ranger District (Mount Hood National Forest), 503-630-6861, fs.usda.gov/recarea/mthood/recarea/?recid=52774
PERMIT	None

Highlights

The once popular trail to Fish Creek Mountain and High Lake fell off the radar screens of most local hikers when the massive floods of February 1996 permanently closed the western access roads to this scenic area. In recent years, however, a group of dedicated volunteers has reopened a rugged older route that approaches the area from the east, once again allowing hikers and backpackers to enjoy the many charms of this region. And those charms are indeed many, including outstanding views, excellent wildflower displays, interesting rock formations, and a fine camp at scenic High Lake tucked beneath the hulking east face of Fish Creek Mountain. Although it is improving over time, the new access trail is still rough, steep in places, and mostly unsigned, so hikers must be prepared to work for their rewards.

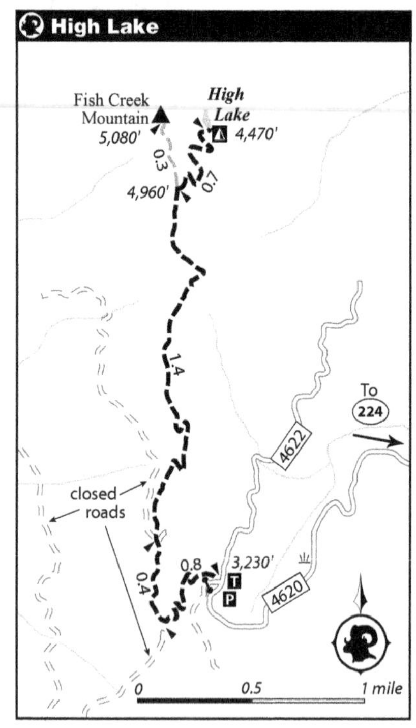

Getting There

From Estacada, drive 22 miles southeast on OR 224 to the junction with Forest Service Road 4620 (aka Sandstone Road) just before a bridge over the Clackamas River. Turn right, soon pass Indian Henry Campground, and drive 4.6 miles to the end of the pavement. Continue on gravel for another

Reaching High Lake is the reward for tackling a trail that requires some effort.

2.7 miles, and park where an unsigned road, which is blocked by large boulders, goes left. (There's a small wooden sign for FS 4622 if you were to continue straight. If you need a landmark, this road is exactly 0.4 mile after you pass a side road, also going left, that is a strange reddish-pink color.)

GPS COORDINATES N45° 03.036' W122° 07.211'

Hiking It

The unsigned trail angles uphill to the right on the north side of the blocked road, traveling through a mixed forest of western hemlock, Douglas fir, and various deciduous trees with a thick understory of Pacific rhododendrons and a variety of smaller shrubs. After 100 yards the trail veers right and begins climbing, sometimes steeply, through dense forest. The trail here feels new and appealingly primitive and obviously took a lot of work to build; it's sort of hacked into the hillside but is clearly the trail, and finding the way is no problem.

The trail makes several short switchbacks and then tops a wooded ridge at 0.8 mile before dropping briefly to a junction with an old road. The surface is now almost totally overgrown with grasses, shrubs, and other vegetation. Turn right (north) on the abandoned road, which was covered with jumbles of rocks and berms after the road was closed in 1996. After 0.4 mile the road forks and you take an obvious but steep and narrow trail that goes up the rocky rib directly between the two forks. (There's a sign identifying this trail just a few yards up.)

The trail, which is now in good shape, generally remains near the top of the ridge using a few irregularly spaced switchbacks to gradually gain elevation. Most of the way is in forest, but occasional breaks in the tree cover open up good views of pointed Mount Jefferson to the southwest. A few tiny meadows provide enough sunshine for late-June-blooming larkspur, columbine, arnica, and phlox to put on a nice show. Another highlight along the way is a pair of impressive rock formations that jut up from the ridgetop, hosting their own array of colorful wildflowers.

The path remains loyal to the ridgetop, sometimes ambling along with almost no elevation gain, to a junction at 2.6 miles. For a worthwhile side trip, take the trail that goes straight ahead for 0.3 mile to the old lookout site atop Fish Creek Mountain. The views here remain excellent, even though fast-growing trees are rapidly getting in the way.

To reach High Lake, turn right at the ridgetop junction and switchback downhill, losing 500 feet in 0.7 mile to the lake. This scenic 2.5-acre pool is backed by a talus slope and features excellent views of nearby Fish Creek Mountain. Anglers can try their luck at catching brook trout, and, by late summer, swimmers will enjoy the clear 10-foot-deep water. The best campsite is above the lake's south shore.

45 Shining Lake

RATINGS Scenery **7** Difficulty **3** Solitude **7**

ROUND-TRIP DISTANCE 8.8 miles

ELEVATION GAIN 800'

OPTIONAL MAPS Green Trails *Fish Creek Mountain (No. 492)* and *High Rock (No. 493)*

USUALLY OPEN Late June–October

BEST TIME Late August–mid-October

AGENCY Clackamas River Ranger District (Mount Hood National Forest), 503-630-6861, fs.usda.gov/recarea/mthood/recarea/?recid=52774

PERMIT None

Highlights

If your car can handle the rough road to the trailhead, the hike into Shining Lake is a relatively easy route that leads to that rarest of phenomena, a scenic mountain lake that is almost never crowded. As with most lakes in our mountains, you should expect plenty of mosquitoes in July. Due to the bugs, it is usually more enjoyable to make this hike either at huckleberry time in late August or fall-color time in October.

Getting There

Go 26 miles southeast of Estacada on OR 224 to a junction immediately after a bridge over the Oak Grove Fork of the Clackamas River. Turn left on paved Forest Service Road 57, proceed 7.5 miles, and then turn left (north) on FS 58. Stay on this single-lane, paved road 7.1 miles to a ridgetop junction, and then turn left on paved FS 4610. Drive 1.3 miles, and then, where the road makes a turn to the right, bear slightly left onto FS 240, a rocky dirt track. Slowly drive 4.3 miles on this very rough road to a fork, veer right (uphill), and then go 0.1 mile and park in the primitive Frazier Fork Campground at the Frazier Turnaround Trailhead.

GPS COORDINATES N45° 09.017' W121° 58.052'

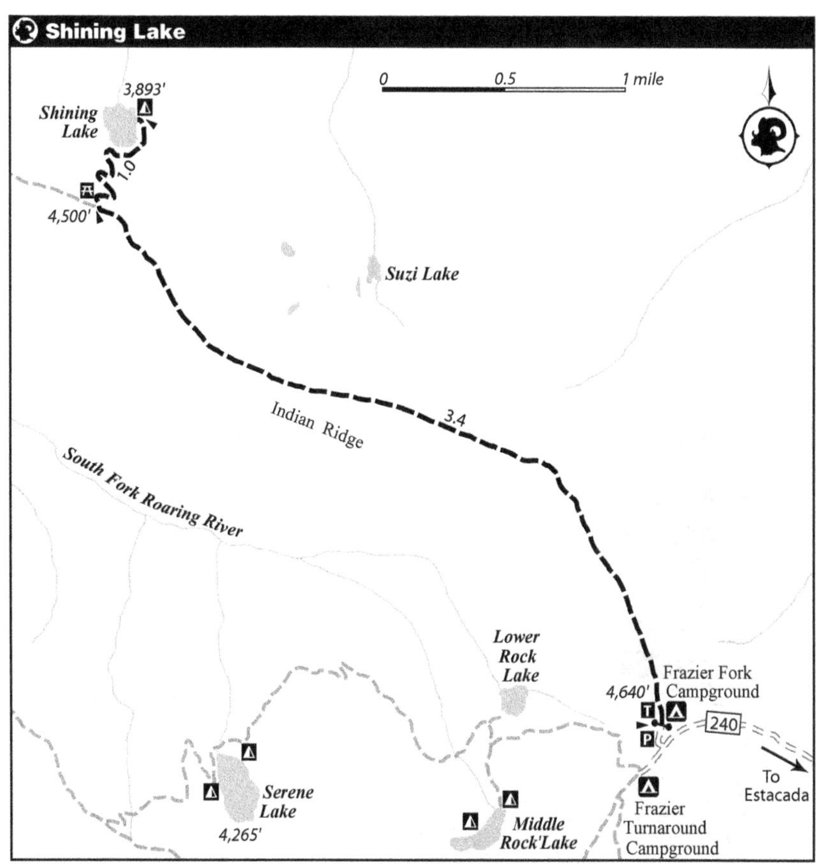

NOTE If you're not sure your car is up to the task, you can include this hike as a side trip from the Shellrock and Serene Lakes Loop hike (Trip 46, page 163), which passes right through the Frazier Fork campground and parking area. (Or just start this hike from the Shellrock Lake Trailhead, which adds 2.2 miles; its GPS coordinates are N45° 07.626' W121° 58.230'.)

Hiking It

The trail begins as an abandoned jeep road that goes northwest from the campground. The first 0.3 mile includes several obstacles such as large boulders, holes, and berms that are designed to keep out motor vehicles while allowing access for hikers, horses, and mountain bikers. The trail stays near the top of Indian Ridge, mostly in a forest of small western and mountain hemlocks, noble firs, and Douglas firs, but with several small openings that provide fine views to the northeast of the rugged Signal Buttes and distant Mount Hood. The entire route is lined with huckleberries (delicious in late August), as well as beargrass and Pacific rhododendrons, both of which bloom in early July. The hiking is easy because the ridgetop route is never steep, with only gradual ups and downs.

Stay on the main route at a couple of indistinct intersections until you come to a major unsigned fork at 3.4 miles. Go right and walk 100 yards to an old campsite complete with a broken-down picnic table. To reach Shining Lake, look for an obvious foot trail that departs from the north side of the old campsite, and follow it down a partially open north-facing slope with nice views of Mount Hood. In 1 mile this well-graded trail uses five switchbacks to descend 600 feet to a lovely and spacious campsite above the northeast shore of 12-acre Shining Lake. This scenic and nearly circular pool sits in an old glacial cirque and is backed by forests and talus slopes. With beautifully clear water and a maximum depth of 24 feet, this lake is ideal for both fishing and swimming.

Surprisingly, scenic Shining Lake is almost never crowded. *photo by Douglas Lorain*

46 Shellrock and Serene Lakes Loop

RATINGS	Scenery **7** Difficulty **1–6** Solitude **4**
ROUND-TRIP DISTANCE	1.4 miles to Shellrock Lake; 6 miles to Middle Rock Lake; 12 miles as a loop
ELEVATION GAIN	200' to Shellrock Lake; 1,250' to Middle Rock Lake; 2,050' as a loop
OPTIONAL MAPS	Green Trails *Fish Creek Mountain (No. 492)* and *High Rock (No. 493)*
USUALLY OPEN	Late June–October
BEST TIME	Late August–mid-October
AGENCY	Clackamas River Ranger District (Mount Hood National Forest), 503-630-6861, fs.usda.gov/recarea/mthood/recarea/?recid=52774
PERMIT	None

Highlights

This outstandingly scenic hike has a little of everything. Among other things, the trail passes several scenic lakes, a wildflower-covered mountain meadow, fine high-elevation forests, viewpoints to distant snowcapped peaks, and fields of tasty huckleberries. There are three different backpacking options, so hikers can select among a very short and easy outing to scenic Shellrock Lake, a longer but still fairly easy trip to Middle Rock Lake, or a more strenuous loop past Serene Lake and Cache Meadow.

Although early summer is beautiful here, with an abundance of wildflowers, that is also when the mosquitoes outnumber the wildflowers by about 10,000 to one (at least by this author's rough estimate). Try late summer for a more enjoyable experience.

Getting There

Go 26 miles southeast of Estacada on OR 224 to a junction immediately after a bridge over the Oak Grove Fork of the Clackamas River. Turn left on paved Forest Service Road 57, proceed 7.3 miles, and then turn left (north) on FS 58. Stay on this single-lane, paved road 2.9 miles, and then turn left on gravel FS 5830. Drive this good gravel road 4.9 miles to a junction with the turnoff to Hideaway Lake Campground, go straight, and continue 0.3 mile to the signed trailhead on the right.

GPS COORDINATES N45° 07.624′ W121° 58.223′

Hiking It

Your route goes north from the trailhead, initially gaining a little elevation and then contouring across an open slope through a recovering clear-cut. Huckleberries and wildflowers are common here, as they are for most of this hike. After 0.5 mile you enter an old-growth forest shortly before the path takes you through a broken-down wooden gate, crosses a little creek, and comes to the south shore of

Shellrock Lake. This fairly large but shallow lake is very scenic, with a talus slope to the west and attractive forests on all sides. There are several good campsites along the east shore near the trail. The lake makes a good overnight destination for hikers with young children.

To continue the trip, hike to the northeast corner of Shellrock Lake and follow the trail as it climbs steeply on a sometimes rough trail (full of ankle-twisting rocks and resembling a dry creekbed) through forest about 1 mile to a junction with an abandoned jeep road, now used as a trail. This junction marks the start of the recommended loop.

Turn right and descend 200 yards to a trailhead at primitive and waterless Frazier Turnaround Campsite, which is little more than a wide spot at the end of a miserable dirt road. Pick up the continuation of the loop from the north end of the camp area, and descend in lazy turns through a lovely forest 0.9 mile to a junction. To reach Middle Rock Lake, turn left and hike uphill 0.2 mile on a trail lined with tall huckleberry bushes to an excellent camp at the northwest end of this 15-acre gem. Frazier Mountain rises in impressive cliffs above the east shore of this deep lake, providing fine scenery. There is another good campsite about 0.1 mile along the west shore, reached by a brushy, unmaintained path. This lake makes a good intermediate destination if you don't want to do the full loop.

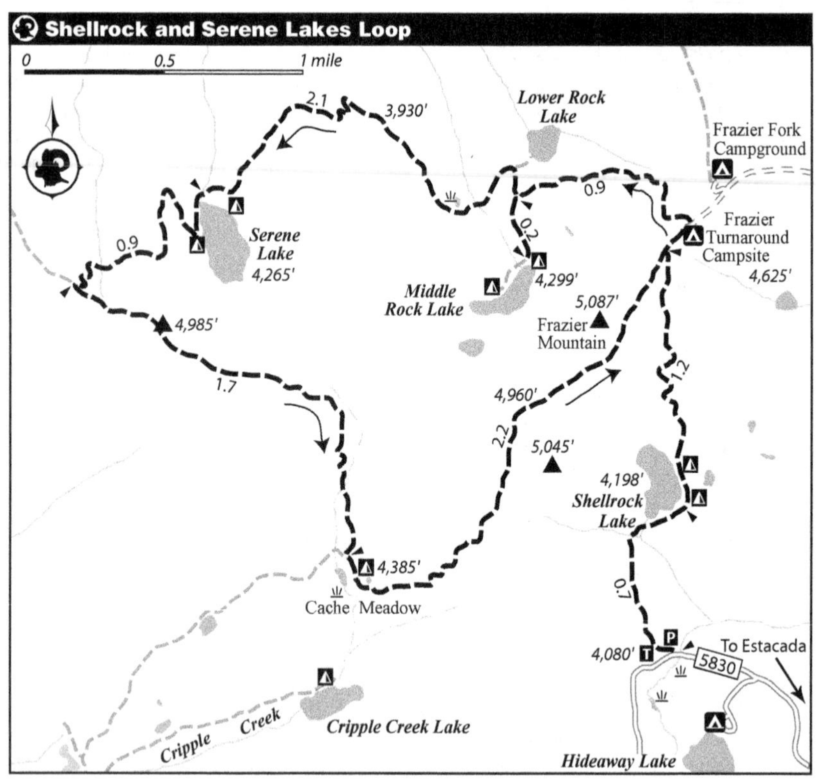

Tree-shaded campsites beckon at Serene Lake.

If you are tackling the entire loop, return to the main trail, and go down a forested hillside 0.1 mile to a junction with the spur trail to Lower Rock Lake, which is neither as large nor as scenic as Middle Rock Lake. Turn left, still on the main trail, soon pass a small marshy area, and then go up and down across a hillside, where you enjoy occasional views north over the deep canyon of Roaring River. The trail then climbs a series of short but steep switchbacks before going up and down once again to initially unseen Serene Lake. Unsigned use paths go left to possible campsites (the first of these, however, goes to a viewpoint, not a campsite). After crossing the lake's outlet creek, the trail turns left and follows the shore to a large and popular camp area, complete with picnic tables, along the west side of this 20-acre, very deep, and invitingly swimmable lake.

The loop trail departs from this camp, climbing the forested hillside to the northwest and then ascending a series of long switchbacks and traverses to a ridgetop junction. Turn left and continue uphill in forest 0.3 mile on a trail lined with tall rhododendron bushes to a clifftop viewpoint with a fine view down to Serene Lake and northeast to distant Mount Hood. The trail now descends, gradually at first but then rather steeply, losing almost 600 feet before finally leveling off as it passes a narrow little meadow along a seasonal creek.

After following this creek about 0.2 mile, you go left at a junction and skirt Cache Meadow, where there is a shallow pond and a fine campsite. Just after the snowmelt in June, this meadow comes alive with the showy white blossoms of marsh marigolds. Later in the summer, the meadow dries out and sports a mat of pink shooting stars.

Just beyond the campsite, the trail passes to the right of a seasonal pond and then goes steeply uphill in forest almost 1 mile before leveling out on a forested plateau. Here the route follows a long-abandoned jeep road that soon leaves the forest and crosses a rocky hillside with fine views to the south of pointed Mount Jefferson. Shortly after the trail returns to forest, you close the loop back at the junction near Frazier Turnaround Campsite. Turn sharply right, and return past Shellrock Lake the way you came.

47 Pechuck Lookout

RATINGS Scenery **6** Difficulty **8** Solitude **8**

ROUND-TRIP DISTANCE 7.2 miles (including 1.2-mile side trip to Rooster Rock)

ELEVATION GAIN 2,200' (including 350' on side trip to Rooster Rock)

OPTIONAL MAP USGS *Rooster Rock*

USUALLY OPEN June–November

BEST TIME Mid- to late June

AGENCY Northwest Oregon District, Bureau of Land Management, 503-375-5646, blm.gov/office/northwest-oregon-district-office

PERMIT None

Highlights

This hike takes you to a beautifully restored fire lookout in a little-known section of the western Cascades. The historic lookout, which is open to campers on a first-come, first-serve basis, provides a cozy shelter, wooden sleeping platforms, and wonderful views. On the downside, the trail is very steep, and you will have to carry plenty of water, as there is no convenient source near the lookout. This hike is particularly beautiful in the latter part of June, when blooming beargrass and rhododendrons bring color to the forest.

Pechuck Lookout is the only remaining stone lookout in Oregon. *photo by Douglas Lorain*

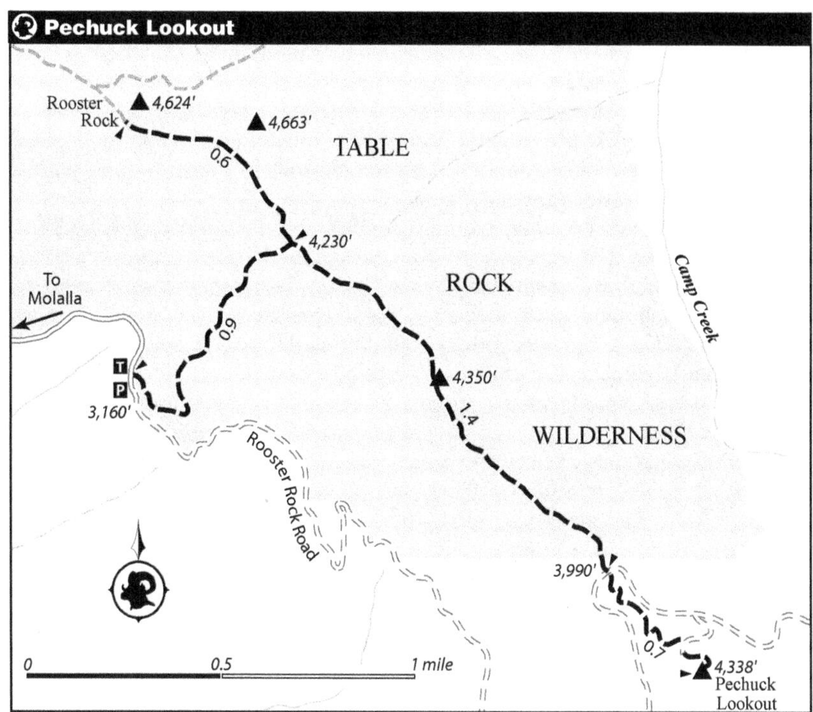

Getting There

From Exit 10 off I-205 in Oregon City, go 13 miles south on OR 213 to the junction with OR 211. Turn left (east), drive 2.1 miles through the town of Molalla, then turn right (south) on South Mathias Road. After 0.3 mile turn left on South Feyrer Park Road, drive 1.7 miles, and then turn right at a T-junction onto South Dickey Prairie Road. Stay on this winding, paved road 5.4 miles, through several minor intersections, and then turn right at a small brown sign for Molalla River Recreation Corridor. This single-lane, paved road immediately crosses a bridge and then follows a scenic, winding course along the river for 13.1 miles to a junction. Bear right on the main road, which immediately crosses a bridge over the Table Rock Fork Molalla River, passes the Old Bridge Trailhead, and turns into gravel Rooster Rock Road. After 0.6 mile bear left to stay on narrow, unsigned Rooster Rock Road for 2.8 miles, bear left at a junction, then continue driving another 3.5 miles to the road's end and a signed trailhead on the right.

GPS COORDINATES N44° 56.494' W122° 19.439'

Hiking It

Walk back down the road about 15 yards from the pullout and look for an obscure trail going up the road cut to the east. The brushy trail almost immediately enters the Table Rock Wilderness and then climbs quite steeply in a dense forest of red alders, western hemlocks, and Douglas firs, with a tangle of Pacific rhododendrons and vine maples below. The uphill abates briefly where the trail makes a turn to the left but then becomes steep once again and remains unrelentingly so all the way to an unsigned ridgetop junction at 0.9 mile.

For an excellent side trip, turn left at this junction and walk gently uphill 0.6 mile to Rooster Rock. For a better look at this rock's numerous jagged spires, leave the trail and scramble uphill through forest about 150 yards to some photogenic locations directly beneath the crags.

To reach Pechuck Lookout, go right (southeast) at the ridgetop junction and hike up and down through viewless forest as you climb over a prominent knoll, and then descend to a junction with a rough road. There is a trailhead signboard here, even though this road is gated and closed to private vehicles about 5.5 miles down the hill. The sometimes sketchy trail crosses the road and ascends a series of short, steep switchbacks before coming to an abandoned jeep road. You turn up this road, follow it 50 yards to its end, and then climb a good trail 0.2 mile to Pechuck Lookout.

Originally built in 1932, this lookout went out of service in 1964 and subsequently deteriorated. Starting in 1989, however, volunteers led by Oregon's parks and recreation department and Bureau of Land Management workers began to restore the structure. The historic building is now the last remaining stone lookout in Oregon and one of only a handful nationwide. Volunteers are responsible for the upkeep of the lookout and welcome overnight use, but visitors are asked to keep the lookout clean and in good condition. Growing trees are rapidly blocking the view, but there is still a good perspective of impressive Table Rock to the northwest.

48 Pansy and Twin Lakes

RATINGS	Scenery **6** Difficulty **1–6** Solitude **5**
ROUND-TRIP DISTANCE	2.2 miles to Pansy Lake; 13.8 miles to Twin Lakes
ELEVATION GAIN	400' to Pansy Lake; 2,950' to Twin Lakes
OPTIONAL MAP	Green Trails *Battle Ax (No. 524)*
USUALLY OPEN	Mid-June–early November
BEST TIME	Late August and September
AGENCY	Clackamas River Ranger District (Mount Hood National Forest), 503-630-6861, fs.usda.gov/recarea/mthood/recarea/?recid=52774
PERMIT	None (just sign the trail register)

Highlights

The Bull of the Woods Wilderness protects a lovely subalpine landscape of small lakes, rolling forests, and rugged peaks and ridges far from the more famous hiking areas around Mount Hood, Mount Jefferson, or the Columbia River Gorge. Although not as spectacularly scenic as those better-known areas, this wilderness offers plenty of beauty, fine lakes for swimming and fishing, and a good chance for solitude. The trip described here takes you into the heart of this remote preserve and provides an excellent sampling of everything the wilderness has to offer.

NOTE The trails in this description are identified by number rather than name because almost all the signs at junctions in this wilderness use only the number without any names or destinations listed.

Getting There

From Estacada, drive 25.4 miles southeast on OR 224 to Ripplebrook Guard Station, and then continue south 4.1 miles on the main road (now Forest Service Road 46) to a junction with FS 63. Turn right, following signs to Bagby Hot Springs, and proceed 3.7 miles to a fork. Go straight, still on FS 63, drive 2.1 miles, and then turn right (uphill) on gravel FS 6340. Stay on the main road at several minor intersections for 8 miles to a fork, bear right onto FS 6341, and go 3.6 miles to the Pansy Lake Trailhead.

GPS COORDINATES N44° 53.995' W122° 06.982'

Hiking It

Pansy Lake Trail #551 heads south through a lichen-draped forest of western hemlocks and Douglas firs, towering over the usual western-Cascades understory of sword ferns, vine maples, Oregon grapes, huckleberries, Pacific rhododendrons, and various forest wildflowers. The well-graded path steadily ascends 0.8 mile, crossing several tiny creeks along the way, to a junction with Trail #549. Go right on the main trail, which goes up and down 0.2 mile to a poorly signed junction with the 120-yard spur trail to popular Pansy Lake. To visit or camp here, turn right and walk down the path to the scenic but marshy lake, which is backed by the steep slopes and ridges radiating off of Pansy Mountain. The best camps are above the northwest shore. Hikers with children will want to stop here.

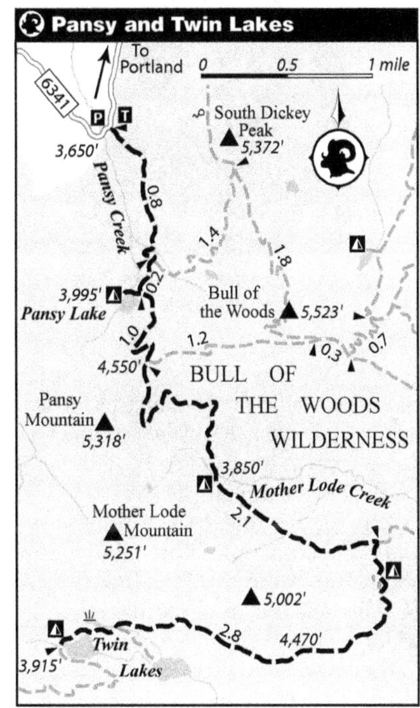

If you are continuing to the Twin Lakes, bear left on the main trail at the Pansy Lake junction, and make two switchbacks up rocky slopes and through open forest for 1 mile to a junction atop a wooded ridge. Go straight and descend Trail #558, mostly in forest but with occasional glimpses through the trees of pointed Mount Jefferson to the southeast. A few irregularly spaced switchbacks take you down to a low point at a

Upper Twin Lake is usually comfortable enough for swimming from about late July to mid-September. *photo by Douglas Lorain*

campsite beside the trickling headwaters of Mother Lode Creek. Unfortunately, this creek is often dry by late summer and cannot be relied upon for water. Beyond this campsite, it's another 1.1 miles of up-and-down hiking to the next junction.

Bear right (uphill) on Trail #573 and gradually climb, still in forest, for 0.4 mile to a good and scenic campsite on a small knoll above a pair of pretty, lily pad–covered ponds. More climbing follows before you level off and then lose about 500 feet to the Twin Lakes, 6.6 miles from the trailhead. An unsigned but obvious side trail goes sharply left to Lower Twin Lake. To reach the upper lake, which is more scenic and has better campsites, stick with the main trail 0.3 mile to the fine camps at that lake's west end. A rocky but delightful little swimming beach is nearby, with easy access to the deep, clear water.

49 Big Slide Lake

RATINGS Scenery **7** Difficulty **5** Solitude **7**
ROUND-TRIP DISTANCE 10.8 miles
ELEVATION GAIN 2,325'
OPTIONAL MAP Green Trails *Battle Ax (No. 524)*
USUALLY OPEN June–November
BEST TIME Mid-June–late October
AGENCY Clackamas River Ranger District (Mount Hood National Forest), 503-630-6861, fs.usda.gov/recarea/mthood/recarea/?recid=52774
PERMIT None (just sign the trail register)

Highlights

Nestled in a deep, mostly forested bowl, Big Slide Lake is a wonderfully scenic destination in the generally overlooked Bull of the Woods Wilderness. The approach trail is attractive throughout, with plenty of old-growth forests, a clear stream, some good viewpoints, and a pretty little marshy meadow where wildlife is common. But it's the destination that will really enchant you. With its reflections of nearby peaks, small island, fine swimming, and good fishing, this place has everything a backpacker could want from a mountain lake.

Getting There

From Estacada, drive 25.4 miles southeast on OR 224 to Ripplebrook Guard Station, and then continue south 4.1 miles on the main road (now Forest Service Road 46) to a junction with FS 63. Turn right, following signs to Bagby Hot Springs, and proceed 3.7 miles to a fork. Go straight, still on FS 63; drive 2.1 miles; and then turn right (uphill) on gravel FS 6340, following signs to Bull of the Woods Wilderness. Drive 2.9 miles, turn left on narrow FS 140 at a sign for Dickey Creek Trail, and go 1.6 miles to the road-end trailhead.

GPS COORDINATES N44° 56.727' W122° 02.907'

Hiking It

In a dense forest of Douglas fir and western hemlock, the trail begins by descending gradually 0.1 mile along an overgrown old road. Once this abandoned road ends, the trail turns left, crosses a ravine on a log, and then does a brief bit of up and down before winding downhill at an irregular but often steep grade into the canyon of Dickey Creek. After losing 350 feet, and shortly before reaching the creek, the trail turns right and heads up the canyon.

The forest in this canyon is impressive, with lots of stately old-growth western hemlocks, Douglas firs, and western red cedars. Below these giants is an assortment of vine maples, Pacific rhododendrons, Pacific yews, Oregon grapes, and various other understory species, all surviving on what little light makes it through the canopy. The climb is irregular but easy, leading to a pretty little meadow at

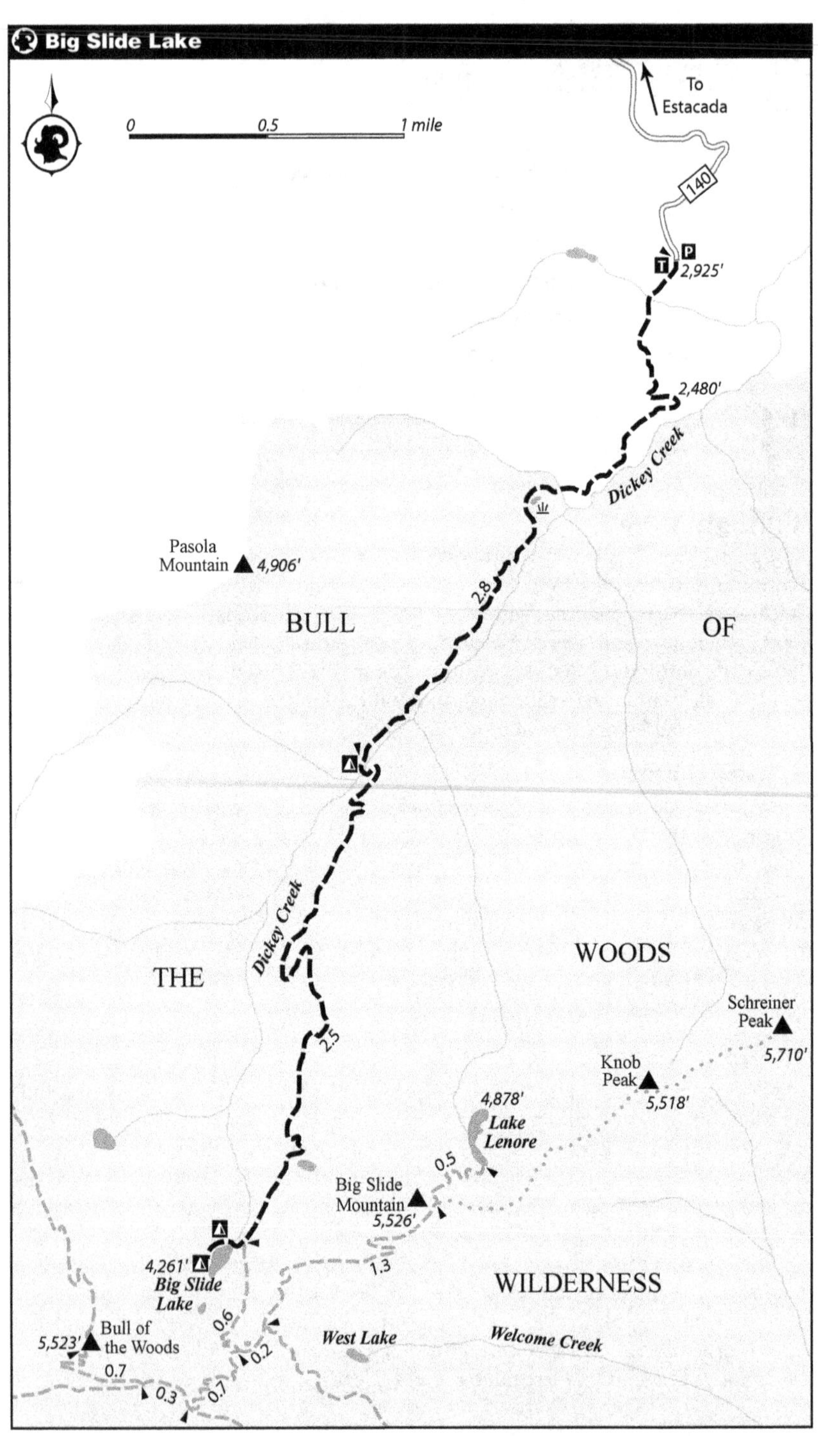
Big Slide Lake
0
0.5
1 mile
To Estacada
140
2,925'
2,480'
Dickey Creek
Pasola Mountain
4,906'
2.8
BULL
OF
Dickey Creek
THE
WOODS
2.5
Schreiner Peak
5,710'
Knob Peak
5,518'
4,878'
Lake Lenore
0.5
Big Slide Mountain
5,526'
4,261'
Big Slide Lake
1.3
WILDERNESS
0.6
Bull of the Woods
5,523'
West Lake
Welcome Creek
0.2
0.7
0.3
0.7

1.4 miles, with a shallow pond that is choked with grasses and water lilies. Look for deer and beaver here, especially early in the morning. There is a nice view southeast over the pond to Schreiner Peak. After rounding the meadow, the trail continues its irregular uphill course, reaching a pleasant campsite immediately before a bridgeless crossing of Dickey Creek at 2.8 miles. In June you'll get wet at this crossing, but by early–mid-July it is usually an easy rock-hop.

The trail now climbs at a steady grade, soon pulling away from Dickey Creek in a series of long traverses and switchbacks. The hillside here supports an unusual abundance of Pacific rhododendrons that are covered with pink blossoms from late June to mid-July. Most of the way is in forest, but at 4.2 miles you come to a rocky opening with a fine view of the Dickey Creek Valley and the surrounding craggy summits of Big Slide Mountain, North and South Dickey Peaks, and Pasola Mountain.

Pond along Dickey Creek Trail, Bull of the Woods Wilderness
photo by Douglas Lorain

At 5.3 miles, shortly after you cross a large rockslide, is an unsigned junction. The main trail goes straight (uphill), but to reach Big Slide Lake, you turn right and steeply descend 0.1 mile to an excellent campsite on the northeast shore of the 4-acre lake. This watery jewel is surrounded by forest-covered, craggy peaks; has a scenic little island; supports a population of hungry brook trout; and is the ideal depth for swimming. What more could a wilderness-loving backpacker want? Well, how about plenty of nearby exploring to such worthwhile destinations as Bull of the Woods Lookout, Schreiner Peak, and Lake Lenore? An easily followed angler's path continues 150 yards past the first campsite to another good campsite on the west shore of Big Slide Lake.

50 Olallie Lake Scenic Area Loop

RATINGS Scenery **7** Difficulty **3** Solitude **5**

ROUND-TRIP DISTANCE 9.1 miles (including side trips to Fish Lake viewpoint, Sheep Lake, and Upper Lake), with many shorter options

ELEVATION GAIN 1,200' (including side trips)

OPTIONAL MAP Green Trails *Breitenbush (No. 525)*

USUALLY OPEN Late June–October

BEST TIME Late August; early–mid-October

AGENCY Clackamas River Ranger District (Mount Hood National Forest), 503-630-6861, fs.usda.gov/recarea/mthood/recarea/?recid=52774

PERMIT None

Highlights

The Olallie Lake Scenic Area is a gentle subalpine landscape full of lakes, meadows, and joyous campsites that is an ideal destination for families with children. Every lake is attractive; provides good fishing; and is a fun place for kids to splash in the water, swim, and explore. In July, the wildflowers are outstanding, but the mosquitoes will drive you to distraction, so plan to visit in either late August, when the huckleberries are ripe and the water temperature is more comfortable for swimming, or mid-October for solitude and superb fall color.

Getting There

From Estacada, drive 25.4 miles southeast on OR 224 to Ripplebrook Guard Station, and then continue 22.7 miles on the main road (now Forest Service Road 46) to a junction with FS 4690. Turn left (east), following signs to Olallie Lake, and proceed 8.3 miles on this paved then good gravel road to a T-junction. Turn right on FS 4220, drive 4.7 miles, and then turn right into the Lower Lake Campground. The trailhead is at the west end of the campground loop road.

GPS COORDINATES N44° 49.397' W121° 47.882'

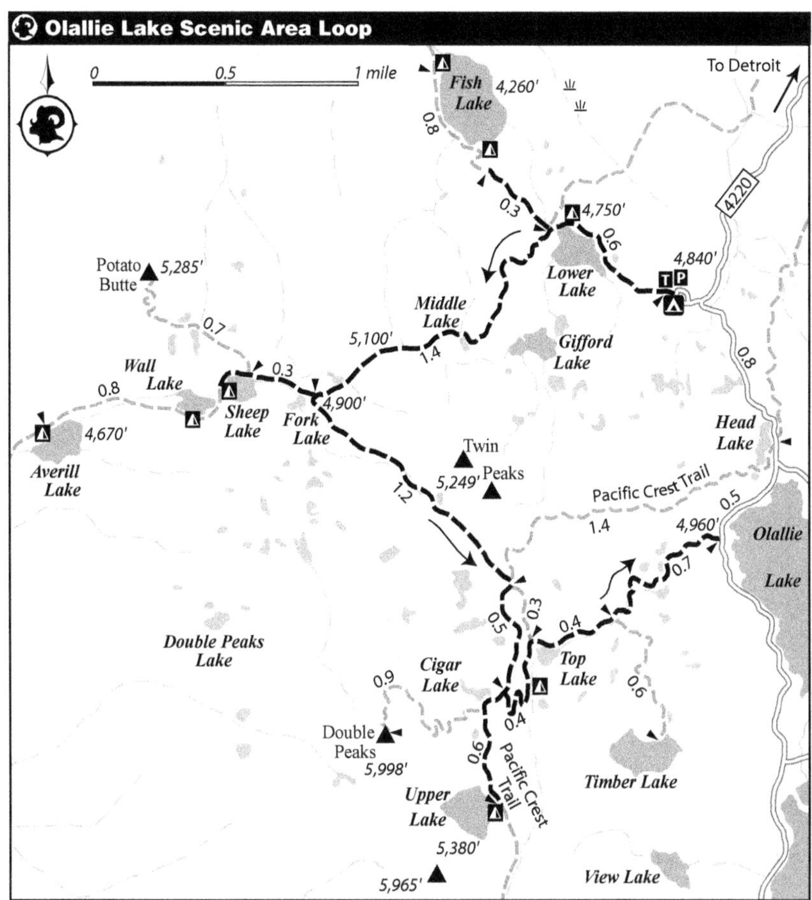

Hiking It

The trail goes west, staying nearly level as it wanders through a forest of Pacific silver firs, lodgepole pines, western white pines, and mountain hemlocks. The forest floor is covered with grouse whortleberries, pinemat manzanitas, and abundant huckleberries. After less than 0.5 mile, you reach sparkling Lower Lake, a 15-acre body of water with good campsites near its northwest shore and fine views to the east of pyramid-shaped Olallie Butte.

Near the outlet creek at the northwest corner of Lower Lake is a four-way junction. The main loop route veers slightly left, but for a worthwhile side trip, take the trail that goes a little to the right (not sharply right), and follow it 0.3 mile to a fine viewpoint atop the rounded bowl holding large and deep Fish Lake. After returning to the junction beside Lower Lake, turn right (southwest) and wander uphill on an often rocky trail through open forest and huckleberry-fringed meadow openings. These small meadows often feature wildflowers and shallow ponds, which add to their beauty. After gaining 300 feet, you come to Middle Lake, which is really nothing more than a pond but features a pleasant view of rugged Twin Peaks to the south.

The trail now descends to a junction at 2 miles (excluding the side trip to the Fish Lake viewpoint). Another excellent side trip begins here. To take it, go straight; you'll soon pass shallow, meadow-rimmed Fork Lake, and then come to a junction on the north shore of larger and deeper Sheep Lake. The trail to the right goes 0.7 mile to the viewpoint atop Potato Butte (another worthwhile destination), but the recommended goal is just ahead at the west end of Sheep Lake. Here you will find a delightful campsite with a fine view of Olallie Butte to the east. For even more exploring, you can continue west on a gradually descending trail that takes you to Wall and Averill Lakes, both of which have good campsites.

Back at the junction just east of Fork Lake, turn right (south) and climb steadily for 1.2 miles past several small ponds to a four-way junction with the Pacific Crest Trail (PCT). Turn right (southbound) on the PCT and, 0.5 mile later, come to a usually unsigned junction. The recommended return route goes left here, but before going that way, keep right (uphill) on the PCT and almost immediately reach narrow, rock-lined Cigar Lake. This scenic lake has nice campsites and a good view of Double Peaks rising above its west shore. About 50 yards along the east shore of Cigar Lake, the PCT passes a junction with the trail up Double Peaks, which is marked only with a low cairn.

Stick with the PCT as it goes gradually uphill 0.5 mile through pretty little meadows and open forest to Upper Lake. This extremely beautiful lake has fine campsites along its east shore and excellent views of Double Peaks to the northwest and a scenic talus slope on Peak 5965 to the south.

To complete the loop, return to the unsigned junction just below Cigar Lake and turn right (southeast). This trail switchbacks downhill to a small meadow with an excellent campsite and then comes to a junction at the northwest corner of Top Lake. Turn right and, 0.4 mile later, bear left at a junction with the side trail to Timber Lake, yet another good side trip. The trail ends at a gravel road beside Olallie Lake. It's an easy 1.3-mile stroll north along this road back to Lower Lake Campground and your car.

The Olallie Lake Scenic Area is an ideal destination for families with children.
photo by Paul Gerald

Mount Jefferson and Vicinity

There are those who convincingly argue that Oregon's second-highest peak, glacier-draped Mount Jefferson, is even more beautiful than Mount Hood, its taller and more famous cousin to the north. Jefferson's pointed summit and changing profile from every angle support this claim, as do the dozens of lakes at its base that reflect the mountain's glory, unlike any of the tiny and less numerous ponds on the slopes of Mount Hood. The trails around Mount Jefferson also receive higher use than those on Mount Hood, despite being farther from major cities. More people means more restrictions, so be prepared for camping limits at overused locations and rules prohibiting fires in others. You'll need advance reservations to enter certain especially fragile areas.

Stretching to the south of Mount Jefferson is a somewhat less visited wilderness with plenty of attractions in its own right, especially Three Fingered Jack, the distinctively spiky remnants of an old volcano. For even more solitude, go a bit farther south to Mount Washington, a pointed spire that presides over a little-visited but scenic land of lava and forests.

The southwest slopes of Three Fingered Jack (Trip 56, page 193) on the Pacific Crest Trail *photo by Douglas Lorain*

51 Firecamp Lakes

RATINGS Scenery **6** Difficulty **2** Solitude **4**
ROUND-TRIP DISTANCE 2.4 miles to Crown Lake
ELEVATION GAIN 640'
OPTIONAL MAP Green Trails *Breitenbush (No. 525)*
USUALLY OPEN Mid-June–October
BEST TIME July (for the best flowers, but expect bugs)
AGENCY Detroit Ranger District (Willamette National Forest), 503-854-3366, fs.usda.gov/recarea/willamette/recarea/?recid=4207
PERMIT Required; free at the trailhead

Highlights

Three sparkling lakes, surrounded by forest and with partial views of a glacier-clad volcano, are the destination of this easy and enjoyable trip. Although the lakes are fairly popular, they are not as crowded as some other destinations in the Mount Jefferson Wilderness. In fact, if you spend the night at the more secluded camps at Sheep Lake or Claggett Lake, you may have things all to yourself. In late June and early July of favorable years, the show of blooming beargrass along the lower trail is quite impressive. Sadly, mosquitoes can be a significant problem at that time, so you have to decide if it is worth it. By mid-August the lakes are nearly bug-free.

Getting There

From Salem, drive 50 miles east on OR 22 to a junction immediately after a bridge over an arm of Detroit Reservoir and just before you enter the small town of Detroit. Turn left (northeast) on paved Forest Service Road 46, following signs

Beargrass lines the trail to Firecamp Lakes. *photo by Douglas Lorain*

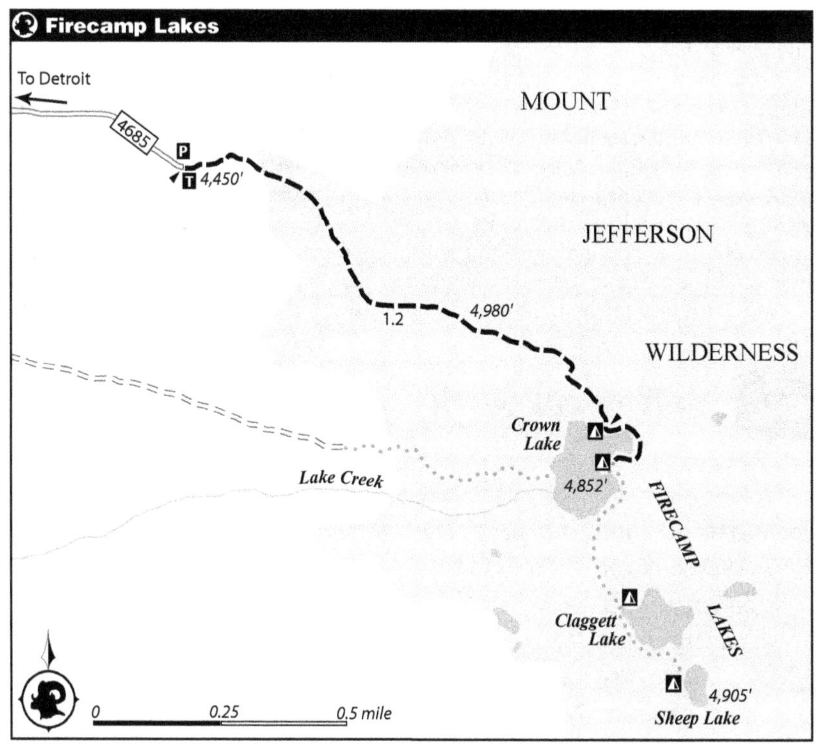

to Breitenbush; go 11.9 miles; and then turn right on gravel FS 4685. Stay on the main road 7.5 miles to a fork. Go straight, still on FS 4685, and proceed 1.1 miles to the road-end parking area and trailhead.

GPS COORDINATES N44° 45.680' W121° 53.262'

Hiking It

From its start in an old and mostly recovered clear-cut, the initially rocky trail ascends rapidly past young noble firs, mountain hemlocks, and lodgepole and western white pines. In late June of favorable years, this mostly open area is carpeted with an impressive display of thousands of tall beargrass blossoms. After 0.3 mile the steep uphill ends when you leave the clear-cut, enter the Mount Jefferson Wilderness, and begin to climb at a much gentler grade. Huckleberries line the path, providing a tasty treat in late summer.

As it nears the top of a minor ridge, the trail twice emerges from the forest to nice viewpoints where you can look down to the sparkling Firecamp Lakes and see southeast to the towering summit of glacier-clad Mount Jefferson.

The trail's last 0.3 mile is a gradual downhill across rocky, mostly open slopes. At 1.2 miles you reach a spacious campsite on the north shore of Crown Lake, the largest in the Firecamp Lakes chain. This shallow but lovely lake is surrounded by forest and has a view of the top third of Mount Jefferson. The trail continues left, working around the north and east sides of the lake to another good campsite on the east shore.

From Crown Lake, a sometimes sketchy boot path continues southeast to Claggett and Sheep Lakes, the two smaller and slightly higher lakes in the chain. The trail beyond Crown Lake is not maintained and is often faint, so be prepared to navigate with a map and compass to reach these lakes.

All the Firecamp Lakes are attractive and support either rainbow or brook trout. Unfortunately, Crown Lake is so shallow it is prone to freezing nearly to its bottom, thus killing almost all the fish. As a result, Crown Lake is no longer stocked. Claggett Lake is deeper and more reliable for both fishing and swimming. Sheep Lake is also fairly shallow and a bit brushy, but it has some really big trout.

52 Jefferson Park

RATINGS	Scenery **10** Difficulty **5–8** Solitude **2**
ROUND-TRIP DISTANCE	11.8 miles via Whitewater Trail; 13 miles via PCT from the north
ELEVATION GAIN	1,900' via Whitewater Trail; 2,700' via PCT
OPTIONAL MAPS	Green Trails *Breitenbush (No. 525)* and *Mount Jefferson (No. 557)*
USUALLY OPEN	Mid-July–October
BEST TIME	Late July–mid-August
AGENCY	Detroit Ranger District (Willamette National Forest), 503-854-3366, fs.usda.gov/recarea/willamette/recarea/?recid=4207, and Clackamas River Ranger District (Mount Hood National Forest), 503-630-6861, fs.usda.gov/recarea/mthood/recarea/?recid=52774
PERMIT	Required; free at the trailhead. Northwest Forest Pass required.

Highlights

Many seasoned backpackers contend that Jefferson Park is Oregon's most outstanding backcountry location. Certainly this alpine wonderland, with its wildflowers, tree islands, small lakes, and drop-dead-gorgeous views of nearby Mount Jefferson, has few, if any, equals. But if you visit here, do not expect to be alone because lots of other folks have heard about Jefferson Park as well. To protect this fragile area, the Forest Service initiated a permit-and-reservation system in 2016, but it didn't seem to work—people camped outside the designated areas anyway—so the reservation system was abandoned. For now, you must use sites that are designated by wooden posts if you're camping within 250 feet of any of the lakes. And no campfires are allowed within Jefferson Park. If possible, you should time your visit for midweek.

The most popular access route is from the west along the Whitewater Trail, but a wildfire in 2017 means it's less scenic than it used to be. If you don't mind a bumpy drive, the hike is much more scenic if you start along the Pacific Crest Trail (PCT) from the north. The view along the way from the top of Park Ridge

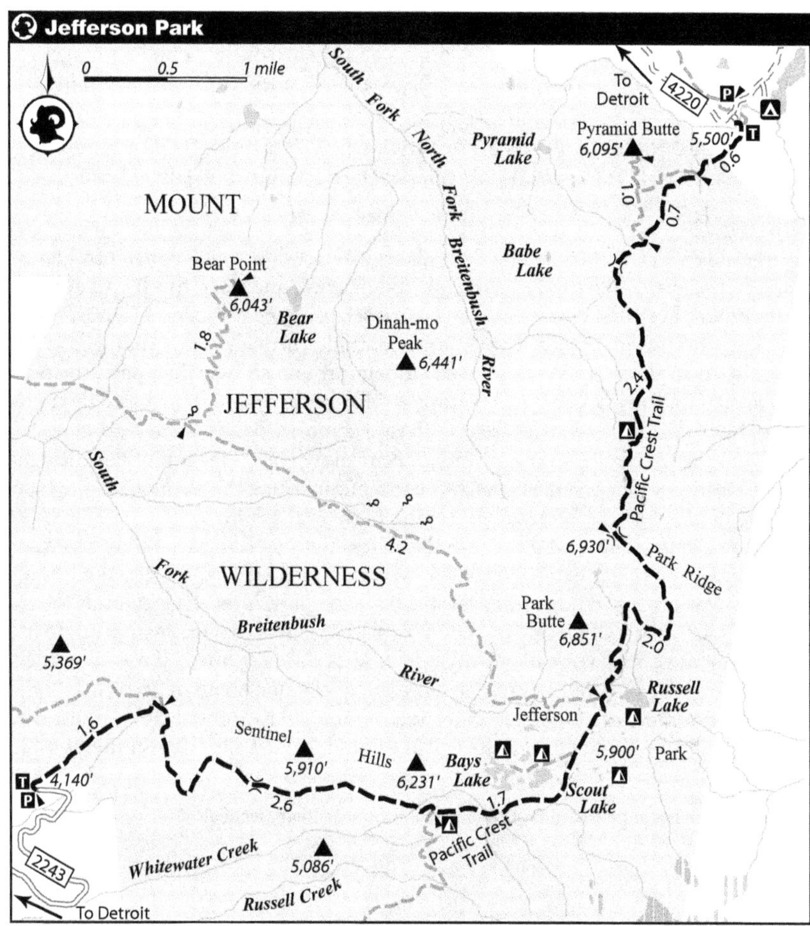

may be the finest viewpoint in the state of Oregon. (Just remember to allow a lot more driving time than you think you'll need.)

Getting There

From Salem, drive 50 miles east on OR 22 to a junction immediately after a bridge over an arm of Detroit Reservoir and just before you enter the small town of Detroit.

To reach the PCT Trailhead, turn left (northeast) onto paved Forest Service Road 46, following signs to Breitenbush, and drive 16.9 miles to a ridgetop junction with FS 4220. Turn right (east) and drive 1 mile to a gate, where the gravel road changes to dirt. From here, the road is bumpy and rough, but it remains passable if you drive slowly. (The worst part is a rocky section right before you reach Breitenbush Lake, but it's a short stretch, and you're almost there.) The signed red-dirt spur road to the PCT trailhead is on the right, 5.5 miles from the gate.

If you are planning to take the Whitewater Trail from the west, continue on OR 22 from Detroit another 10.4 miles, and then fork left onto wide, gravel Whitewater Road (FS 2243). Follow this road 7.4 miles to the large parking lot at a road-end clear-cut.

GPS COORDINATES N44° 45.924' W121° 47.186' (northern [PCT] trailhead); N44° 42.403' W121° 52.505' (western [Whitewater] trailhead)

Hiking It

Northern (PCT) Option: The PCT winds its way south through a delightful landscape of meadows filled with heather, huckleberries, and open forests dominated by mountain hemlocks. To the west you can see prominent Pyramid Butte. At 0.6 mile keep left at an unsigned fork, and continue through forest that gradually opens up to wildflower meadows. After going through an indistinct pass, the trail wanders south, slowly gaining elevation as the terrain becomes increasingly dominated by rocks and snow patches. You pass a campsite beside a small pond at 2.7 miles and then ascend a large, semipermanent snowfield to the top of Park Ridge. (Look for the vintage wooden sign at the summit marking the Skyline Trail, which was the name of the Oregon section of the PCT until 1968.)

On a clear day, the view from here surpasses anything I could possibly describe. In the foreground, almost 900 feet below you, is the flat expanse of lake-dotted Jefferson Park, while rising impressively above the park is towering Mount Jefferson, with its mantle of glaciers. You have to see this place to really appreciate it.

Once you've had your fill of this view, walk 2 miles down the well-graded trail in two long switchbacks to Russell Lake at the north end of Jefferson Park. Designated campsites are scattered around this and all the other lakes in the park, but the most scenic ones are those at Russell and Scout Lakes. If you prefer a bit

Jefferson Park might be Oregon's most outstanding backcountry location.
photo by Paul Gerald

of solitude, try exploring the trailless eastern part of the park. This area has lesser views of the mountain but plenty of wildflowers and some lovely little ponds.

Western (Whitewater Trail) Option: In the wake of the 2017 Whitewater Fire, this trail is bound to look a little different. The trailhead is in an old clear-cut, but the trail soon climbs out of this rather unattractive area and makes a steady, moderately graded climb in Douglas fir forest 1.6 miles to a ridgetop junction. Go right on the main trail and continue uphill, although now less steeply, winding your way south and east through a high-elevation forest of true firs and mountain hemlocks. After passing through a minor saddle, the trail levels out and crosses a partly open hillside on the south side of the ridge containing the Sentinel Hills. The openings along this scenic section provide outstanding views of Mount Jefferson, with the shimmering masses of Russell and Jefferson Park Glaciers on its flanks.

At 4.1 miles you cross Whitewater Creek in the middle of a small, wildflower-covered meadow and soon reach a junction with the PCT. There is a nice campsite near this junction. You turn left (northbound) on the PCT and gradually climb through forest and small meadows, crossing Whitewater Creek a second time before leveling out as you enter the southwest part of Jefferson Park. The trail soon passes unsigned side trails that go left to Scout Lake and explore all the other wonders of this alpine paradise.

53 Pamelia and Shale Lakes Loop

RATINGS Scenery **8** Difficulty **3–8** Solitude **3**

ROUND-TRIP DISTANCE 4.4 miles to Pamelia Lake; 17.7 miles for Shale Lake Loop

ELEVATION GAIN 800' to Pamelia Lake; 3,000' for Shale Lake Loop

OPTIONAL MAP Green Trails *Mount Jefferson (No. 557)*

USUALLY OPEN Late May–late October to Pamelia Lake; mid-July–October for Shale Lake loop

BEST TIME Late July–mid-August

AGENCY Detroit Ranger District (Willamette National Forest), 503-854-3366, fs.usda.gov/recarea/willamette/recarea/?recid=4207

PERMIT Required. Reservations are advised. Northwest Forest Pass required. The Forest Service has imposed a limited-entry permit system to protect the overused Pamelia Lake basin. Between the Friday of Memorial Day weekend and October 31, all hikers entering this area (except those day hiking on the Pacific Crest Trail) must obtain a limited-entry permit. Advance permits are available starting May 1 each year, online at recreation.gov or by calling 877-444-6777. Permits are free, but there's a $6 nonrefundable reservation fee. If space is available, day-of-trip permits are available from the Detroit Ranger Station (a $6 processing fee applies). Weekends in July and August are the most popular, so try to reserve as early as possible.

Highlights

Although there is a better view of Mount Jefferson over Jefferson Park (Trip 52, page 182), the view from Shale Lake comes in a solid second place. That alone would make a visit here worthwhile, but this hike offers many other benefits. First, there is deservedly popular Pamelia Lake, a large, lower-elevation gem that is accessible from May to November. Next, there are the stupendous views of Mount Jefferson from the trail on the ridge south of Hunts Cove, as well as fine views of both the Cathedral Rocks and jagged Goat Peak. Finally, there are plenty of wildflower-covered meadows and lovely forests along the route. Overall, this is one of the better mountain loop hikes in our area.

Getting There

From Salem, drive 60 miles east on OR 22 to a junction between mileposts 62 and 63. Turn left (east) on single-lane, paved Pamelia Creek Road (Forest Service Road 2246) and drive about 3.6 miles to the trailhead.

GPS COORDINATES N44° 39.611' W121° 53.492'

Hiking It

The wide trail's first 2.2 miles are a pleasant walk through a shady, old-growth forest of western red cedars, western hemlocks, and Douglas firs. Adding to the ambience is cascading Pamelia Creek, which is always nearby to soothe hikers with its "river music." This gentle hike ends at a four-way junction immediately

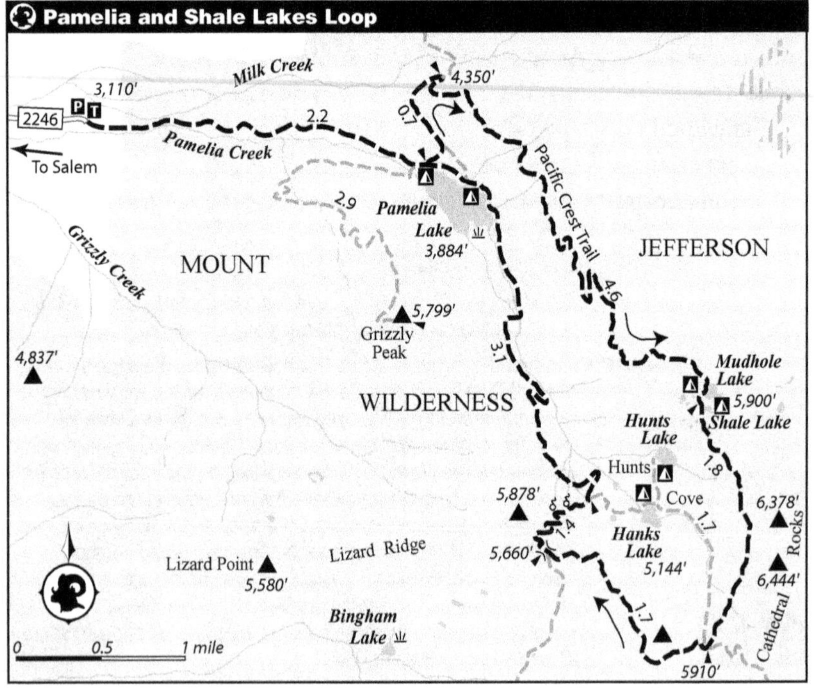

Enjoy top-notch views of Mount Jefferson from the Pamelia and Shale Lakes Loop.
photo by Paul Gerald

before you reach the northwest tip of Pamelia Lake. There are fine camps along the north shore of this 45-acre lake, although the water level often drops 10–20 feet by late summer, making the lake less attractive. *Note:* If you're camping within 250 feet of Pamelia Lake, you must use designated sites.

If you are doing the loop, turn left at the junction and climb away from the lake 0.1 mile to a second junction. Go left again and ascend in a long curve through forest 0.6 mile to a junction with the Pacific Crest Trail (PCT). Turn right (southbound) and make a long, gradual, switchbacking ascent through forest and past a couple of open areas where you can look down to Pamelia Lake. Eventually you enter more interesting high-elevation terrain with open forests and small wildflower-covered meadows. At 7.5 miles you reach shallow Mudhole Lake and, just beyond, deeper but smaller Shale Lake. There are superb views north across these lakes to pointed Mount Jefferson. You can also look east to ruggedly scenic Goat Peak. Camps are plentiful and very popular, especially with thru-hikers on the PCT. The best sites are along the west side of Mudhole Lake and on a low rise between the two lakes.

From Shale Lake, the southbound PCT passes a couple of small ponds, visits a fine clifftop viewpoint over Hunts Cove, and then cuts across the west side of the rugged Cathedral Rocks. At 9.3 miles you come to a junction at a wide saddle, with a terrific view looking north to Mount Jefferson over an area of red cinders. An old and now unmaintained trail goes north down the gully containing the red cinders on its way to Hanks Lake. This is a somewhat shorter but less scenic alternative to the recommended loop.

The recommended route turns right (west) at the junction and loops around the south side of a little butte before coming out on the northeast side of a ridge and traversing an open slope with stupendous views to the north of Mount Jefferson. After an all-too-short 0.5 mile, the trail crosses back over the ridge and drops to a junction in a saddle. You turn right and descend a series of relatively short switchbacks for 1.4 miles to a junction with the spur trail into Hunts Cove. If you have the time, this side trail is worth taking to visit popular Hanks and Hunts Lakes, both of which feature fine campsites but no views of Mount Jefferson.

To complete the loop, take the trail that goes left (north) from the junction with the Hunts Cove Trail, and drop steadily in long traverses and switchbacks to a crossing of Hunts Creek. You then gradually descend to Pamelia Lake, passing fine camps along its north shore, back to the junction at the northwest corner of that large lake. Go straight and return the 2.2 miles to your car.

54 Carl Lake Loop

RATINGS	Scenery **7** Difficulty **4–6** Solitude **5**
ROUND-TRIP DISTANCE	9.8 miles to Carl Lake; 15.6 miles for the loop (plus explorations)
ELEVATION GAIN	1,000' to Carl Lake; 1,900' for the loop
OPTIONAL MAPS	Green Trails *Mount Jefferson (No. 557)*
USUALLY OPEN	Mid-July–October
BEST TIME	Late July–mid-August
AGENCY	Sisters Ranger District (Deschutes National Forest), 541-549-7700, fs.usda.gov/recarea/deschutes/recarea/?recid=81781
PERMIT	Required; free at the trailhead

Highlights

A deep, sparkling jewel set beneath a particularly rugged and scenic stretch of the Cascade Mountains, Carl Lake is a fun destination for an overnight trip in the central Mount Jefferson Wilderness. Adventurous hikers can make this into a semiloop trip by seeking out an unofficial path up to the Pacific Crest Trail (PCT), with the option to do a bit of off-trail exploring. Although never very steep or difficult, the trail into Carl Lake travels through a large burn area from the 2003 B&B Complex Fire that can be hot on summer afternoons.

Getting There

From Santiam Pass, 89 miles east of Salem, go east 7.6 miles on US 20 to the signed junction with paved Jack Lake Road (Forest Service Road 12). Turn left (north), following signs to Mount Jefferson Wilderness Trailheads; drive 4.4 miles; and

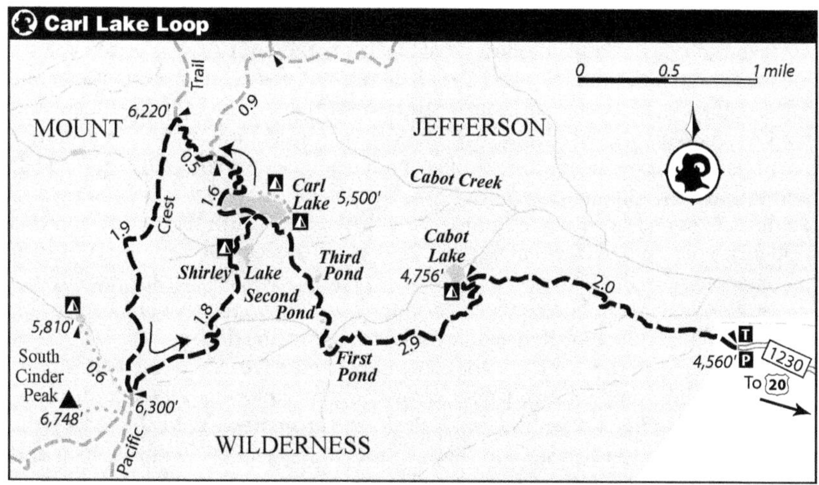

then go left on single-lane, paved FS 1230. Proceed 1.6 miles, and then go right at a junction, staying on FS 1230, which now turns to gravel. Remain on FS 1230 through several minor intersections for 4.9 miles, and then fork left and proceed a final 2 miles to the signed Cabot Lake Trailhead.

GPS COORDINATES N44° 34.427' W121° 43.842'

Hiking It

Starting in a slowly recovering burn area, the often dusty trail wanders intermittently uphill past blackened snags and some brave little lodgepole pines, typically among the first pioneers in a burned area. Without the usual forest cover, the vegetation here consists of shrubs such as deer brush, huckleberries, and red-flowering currant, as well as sun-loving wildflowers like pearly everlasting, beardtongue, and (not surprisingly) fireweed.

At 1.5 miles you leave the burn zone and enter a beautiful, shady forest that features a mix of mountain hemlocks, western white pines, lodgepole pines, Engelmann spruces, and a few ponderosa pines. At 2 miles an obvious but unsigned spur trail goes downhill to the right to forest-and-marsh-rimmed Cabot Lake, a pleasant but viewless pool with decent campsites.

After the Cabot Lake turnoff, the main trail begins a sustained ascent, climbing a mostly forested hillside in 12 well-graded switchbacks. Once the switchbacks end, you continue uphill another 0.5 mile and then meander past a series of small lakelets with the rather unimaginative names of First, Second, and Third Ponds. Finally, at 4.8 miles, you reach the southeast end of Carl Lake. This deep, oval-shaped lake has a rocky shoreline and numerous possible campsites. The most popular sites are near the trail on the south side of the lake, but the most scenic sites are on the east and north shores, where you can look across the water to the crags along the Cascade divide. The east-shore sites are easy to reach along an unsigned but obvious spur trail; those along the north shore require a bit of relatively easy scrambling.

The main trail goes through the forest on the south shore of Carl Lake to a junction with the trail to Shirley Lake. This is the return route of the recommended loop. Since the loop is easier to navigate if you travel counterclockwise, go straight on the main trail as it loops around the west side of Carl Lake and then ascends 20 well-graded switchbacks to a tiny, shallow pond. Immediately past this pond is an unsigned fork. The main trail goes straight, but you turn left and follow a winding and unofficial trail as it steeply ascends 0.5 mile to the top of the divide and an unsigned junction with the PCT. Turn left (south) on this trail as it goes up and down along the ridge, passing excellent viewpoints of such landmarks as South Cinder Peak to the south and pointed Mount Jefferson to the north. In one or two places, you can also look east down to sparkling Carl Lake. After 1.9 miles you come to a saddle and a four-way junction.

The trail back to Carl Lake goes left, but if you have extra time and energy, consider doing some relatively easy cross-country exploring. One excellent option is the scramble up South Cinder Peak, the prominent, reddish cinder cone that rises to the southwest. The route to the view-packed summit is open and easy to negotiate. Another possible destination is a small but scenic unnamed lake at the northern base of South Cinder Peak. To reach it, go northwest from the pass down a steep, forested hillside into a prominent drainage. Once on the bottom, head downstream on a sketchy and intermittent boot path that travels gradually downhill through forests and flower-covered meadows 0.5 mile to the meadow-rimmed little lake. There is a good campsite at the lake's west end, which provides a less crowded alternative to spending the night at popular Carl Lake.

Once you've had your fill of exploring, head northeast from the four-way junction at the pass, and descend a good trail that crosses a mostly open hillside with good views of Mount Jefferson and the nearby crags of the Cascade divide. After 1.4 miles you pass irregularly shaped Shirley Lake, which has decent campsites, and return to Carl Lake. Turn right and retrace your steps back to the trailhead.

South Cinder Peak overlooks this small but scenic pond. *photo by Douglas Lorain*

55 Duffy and Santiam Lakes

RATINGS Scenery **8** Difficulty **3–5** Solitude **5**

ROUND-TRIP DISTANCE 7 miles to Duffy Lake; 9.6 miles to Santiam Lake

ELEVATION GAIN 800' to Duffy Lake; 1,200' to Santiam Lake

OPTIONAL MAP USFS *Mount Jefferson Wilderness*

USUALLY OPEN Mid-June–October

BEST TIME July (but be prepared for mosquitoes)

AGENCY Detroit Ranger District (Willamette National Forest), 503-854-3366, fs.usda.gov/recarea/willamette/recarea/?recid=4207

PERMIT Required; free at the trailhead. Northwest Forest Pass required.

Highlights

The forested terrain of the southern Mount Jefferson Wilderness is dominated by two outstanding features, the rugged crags of Three Fingered Jack and the tranquil beauty of dozens of mountain lakes. Both features are included in this relatively easy hike that visits two of the most attractive and popular lakes in this area. Forest-rimmed Duffy Lake has no good view of Three Fingered Jack but features fine camps and a nice view of pointed Duffy Butte. Santiam Lake, on the other hand, sits in a meadow basin and has a great view of Three Fingered Jack, in fact one of the best anywhere of this impressive mountain. Although huge fires swept through this area in 2003, most of the damage occurred north and east of the trails described here. Only a few places along this route display evidence of the fire, and most are recovering well, so the hiking remains scenic and the forests green.

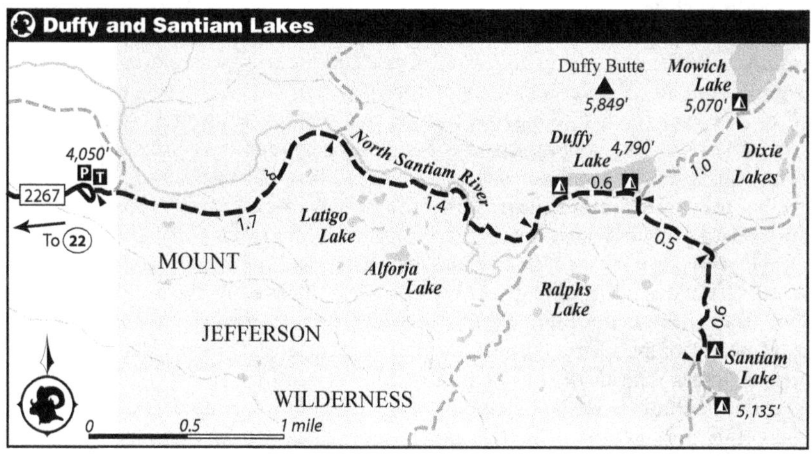

This lovely wildflower meadow lies below Duffy Butte.

Getting There

From Salem, drive east on OR 22 about 72 miles to milepost 76, then turn left (east) onto one-lane, paved Big Meadows Road (Forest Service Road 2267). Stay on this road 3.1 miles to the Duffy Lake Trailhead.

GPS COORDINATES N44° 29.466' W121° 57.003'

Hiking It

The trail goes east at a gentle grade through forest, soon meeting an equestrian trail that starts at a different trailhead. Go straight and continue with your gradual uphill, passing a spring at 1.1 miles and coming to a junction with the Turpentine Trail at 1.7 miles. Go straight and soon level off as you proceed through a lovely mix of forest and meadows along the sluggish headwaters of the North Santiam River. After making an easy but unbridged crossing of the tiny "river," you proceed through more meadows to a junction at 3.1 miles.

Go straight on the more heavily used trail, and walk another 0.4 mile, mostly on the level, to a junction near the southwest corner of long, clear Duffy Lake. There is a good campsite not far to the left here, plus more sites on the north and southeast shores. The ridge north of Duffy Lake, which is dominated by the pyramid-shaped summit of rocky Duffy Butte, is still covered with blackened snags from the huge 2003 B&B Complex Fire. Fortunately, although there is spotty fire damage nearer the trail, the south side of Duffy Lake generally escaped the flames.

After making a bridged crossing of Duffy Lake's often-dry outlet creek, you come to a junction. The trail going straight leads to Mowich Lake and the fire-ravaged Eight Lakes Basin. To reach Santiam Lake, turn right and soon come to a second junction. Turn left and gradually ascend to a junction in a lovely meadow that in July is covered with a beautiful display of pink shooting stars.

Turn right at the junction, and climb on a steep and badly eroded trail 0.6 mile to spectacular, meadow-rimmed Santiam Lake. There are several excellent camps near this lake, all of which provide outstanding views across the water to jagged Three Fingered Jack. In July the scene is particularly beautiful, with lots of wildflowers in the foreground and plenty of snow still on the peak. Unfortunately, that is also mosquito time, and the nasty little vampires are abundant. By mid-August most of the bugs are gone, but so are the flowers. Take your pick.

56 Three Fingered Jack Loop

RATINGS Scenery **9** Difficulty **8** Solitude **5**

ROUND-TRIP DISTANCE 20.5 miles

ELEVATION GAIN 3,300'

OPTIONAL MAP USFS *Mount Jefferson Wilderness*

USUALLY OPEN Mid-July–October

BEST TIME Late July

AGENCY Detroit Ranger District (Willamette National Forest), 503-854-3366, fs.usda.gov/recarea/willamette/recarea/?recid=4207, and Sisters Ranger District (Deschutes National Forest), 541-549-7700, fs.usda.gov/recarea/deschutes/recarea/?recid=81781

PERMIT Required; free at the trailhead. Northwest Forest Pass required.

Highlights

A jagged sentinel for much of the Central Oregon Cascades, Three Fingered Jack is all that remains of an extinct volcano that has eroded away, leaving only the hard central plug of lava. Scenic trails go almost all the way around the mountain, offering excellent views, passing small lakes, and taking the hiker through some of the best wildflower fields in Oregon. Part of the recommended loop involves some easy cross-country travel, but that should not deter experienced hikers. Literalists beware, however, because despite the mountain's name, even after walking the entire loop and seeing the peak from every angle, it is hard to identify the three "fingers." One theory is that the name refers to an early trapper with somewhat fewer than the usual number of digits.

Getting There

From Salem, drive 83 miles east on OR 22 to where it merges with US 20, and continue east another 6 miles to a signed junction with the spur road to the Pacific Crest Trailhead just west of Santiam Pass. Turn left and proceed 0.2 mile to the large trailhead parking lot.

GPS COORDINATES N44° 25.537' W121° 50.958'

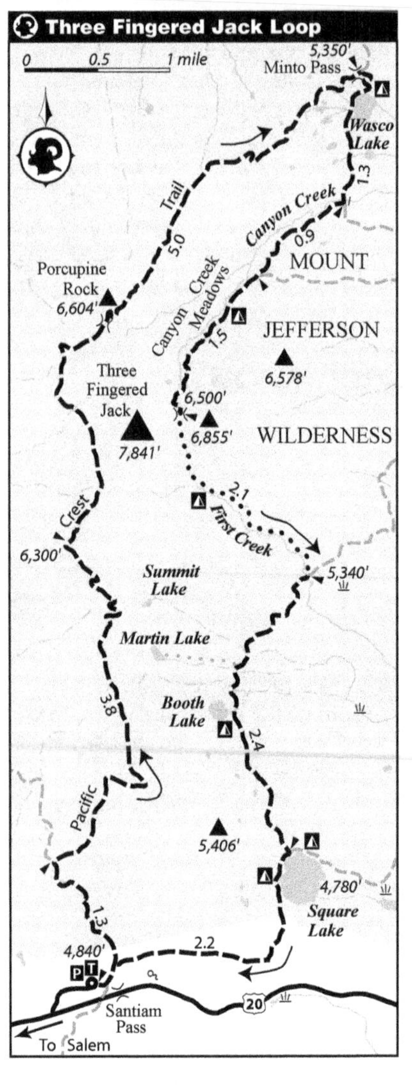

Hiking It

From the parking lot, you follow a short spur trail that goes east to a junction with the Pacific Crest Trail (PCT), and then turn left (north). This wide trail winds gradually uphill through what used to be an open forest of lodgepole pines and true firs, with an abundance of beargrass covering the forest floor. After the huge B&B Complex Fire swept through this area in 2003, however, many of the trees became blackened snags. In gray or foggy weather these tree skeletons create a spooky effect, while in summer the lack of vegetation overhead makes for hot, shadeless hiking, but the tradeoff is better views and more life-giving sunshine for wildflowers. You will be going in and out of the fire zone for most of this trip.

After 0.2 mile you pass a poorly signed junction with the trail going right (east) to Square Lake, which will be your return trail if you do the recommended loop. Keep straight on the PCT and continue uphill, mostly through burned areas and past a couple of stagnant, lily pad–covered ponds to a junction at 1.3 miles. Go right, still on the PCT, and keep going steadily but not steeply uphill.

At about 3.8 miles, just as you leave the burn zone, you pass the first nice viewpoint of Three Fingered Jack, which looks like a single tall spire from this angle. Another first-rate viewpoint comes at 4.6 miles when you pass a rocky outcropping on the left (southwest) side of the trail. The view to the south of Mount Washington, the Three Sisters, and for miles beyond is breathtaking. The best view of all, however, comes at 5.1 miles when you round a corner and are suddenly faced with an up-close view of the huge west face of Three Fingered Jack. Snow streaks the slopes of the mountain into August, making this view even more photogenic.

The PCT now contours across the west side of Three Fingered Jack, mostly across rocky slopes. There are views to the west of the forests and burned areas around Santiam Lake. At 6.9 miles you go through a little pass next to Porcupine Rock, and then make a few downhill switchbacks across an open slope. The views here looking south to nearby Three Fingered Jack are outstanding, especially highlighting the dark bands of red and black rock that make up the jagged mountain. From here the trail slowly descends, mostly in forest and areas that show spotty effects of the fires. Finally, you circle around a series of shallow ponds before coming to Minto Pass and a junction at 10.1 miles.

Turn right, leaving the PCT, and descend a fairly steep trail to clear Wasco Lake. The Forest Service requires that overnight visitors use designated campsites located along this lake's north and east sides.

The trail goes south along the west shore of Wasco Lake and then travels through forest to a junction immediately after you cross Canyon Creek. There is a small but attractive waterfall just below this crossing. Turn right at this junction and make your way gradually upstream, passing old beaver ponds along the way, to a junction near the lower end of Canyon Creek Meadows. Turn right and wind your way gradually through these gorgeous meadows that in late July feature incredible displays of lupine, monkey flower, paintbrush, and other wildflowers. The upper parts of the meadows offer terrific views of Three Fingered Jack. After leaving the meadows, the trail climbs through a rocky area and then steeply ascends along the top of an old moraine above a tiny lake to a windswept pass directly beneath the sheer cliffs of Three Fingered Jack.

The trail ends at the pass. To complete the recommended loop, carefully pick your way down the steep, rocky slope on the south side of the pass to a barren,

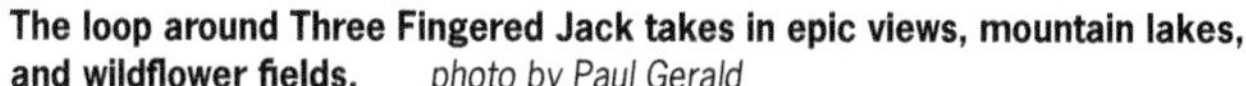
The loop around Three Fingered Jack takes in epic views, mountain lakes, and wildflower fields. *photo by Paul Gerald*

pumice-covered meadow at the head of trickling First Creek. There are excellent and extremely scenic camps in the trees at the edge of this meadow. From here you continue going cross-country, following the creek downstream mostly through large burn areas. Be prepared to hike over or around some deadfall in this area. About 0.5 mile below the first meadow, look for a shallow pond a little northeast of the creek. This pond provides terrific early-morning reflections of Three Fingered Jack. About 0.6 mile below the pond, you intersect a maintained trail.

Turn right on the trail, and go mostly downhill through forest and burn areas, crossing several seasonal creeks along the way to pleasant Booth Lake at 17 miles. This lake has nice campsites and is good for swimming. To close the loop, continue south another 1.3 miles to a junction at large and popular Square Lake (more camps). Turn right and close out the loop with a 2-mile stroll through forest and burn areas back to the junction with the PCT just 0.2 mile from the trailhead. Turn left and return to your car.

57 Washington Ponds and George Lake

RATINGS Scenery **7** Difficulty **5–8** Solitude **7**

ROUND-TRIP DISTANCE 12 miles to Washington Ponds; 17.5 miles to George Lake

ELEVATION GAIN 1,150' to Washington Ponds; 1,600' to George Lake

OPTIONAL MAP USFS *Mount Washington Wilderness*

USUALLY OPEN Mid-June–October

BEST TIME Late June; July

AGENCY McKenzie River Ranger District (Willamette National Forest), 541-822-3381, fs.usda.gov/recarea/willamette/recarea/?recid=4210, and Sisters Ranger District (Deschutes National Forest), fs.usda.gov/recarea/deschutes/recarea/?recid=81781

PERMIT Required; free at the trailhead

Highlights

In its long course from Mexico to Canada, the Pacific Crest Trail (PCT) takes hikers high on the slopes of many of the northwest's famous volcanic peaks, providing fine views and excellent mountain scenery. One of the lesser known of those peaks is Mount Washington, which rises above a land of rolling forests and vast lava flows in the Central Oregon Cascades. But "lesser known" is not the same as less beautiful, as this section of that famous trail amply demonstrates. The views and scenery here are perhaps not as spectacular as those around Mount Jefferson or Mount Hood, but they are still mighty impressive and well worth seeing. The biggest drawback to backpacking this section of the PCT is a lack of water. The only reliable water sources are the two small Washington Ponds and larger and more attractive George Lake. Both of these locations are off the main trail, which makes them harder to find but provides greater solitude.

Getting There

From Salem, drive 83 miles east on OR 22 to where it merges with US 20, and continue east on US 20 another 6 miles to the junction with Big Lake Road at milepost 80, just before Santiam Pass. Turn right (south) on Big Lake Road, drive 1 mile, and veer left at the junction with the road into Hoodoo Ski Area. Drive 2.2 miles and then go left on rough gravel Old Santiam Wagon Road, following signs to Big Lake Youth Camp. After 0.4 mile go straight where the main road turns right, and proceed 0.2 mile on a rough dirt road to the trailhead on the right.

GPS COORDINATES N44° 22.820' W121° 51.392'

Hiking It

The well-graded Pacific Crest Trail (PCT) goes south through a rather monotonous and viewless forest of lodgepole pines and mountain hemlocks. The route is generally either level or very gradually uphill for the first 2 miles until you come to an unsigned but obvious junction with a wide and dusty trail that goes sharply right toward a youth camp. Continue south on the PCT, which remains in forest but now steadily climbs, gaining a little over 400 feet in 1.4 miles, to the small meadow holding Coldwater Spring. There is a camp just beyond the spring on the right (west) side of the trail and a partial view over the meadow of the summit spire of Mount Washington. Unfortunately, the often muddy spring is rather unattractive and overused by climbers, backpackers, and equestrians. By late summer it may dry up.

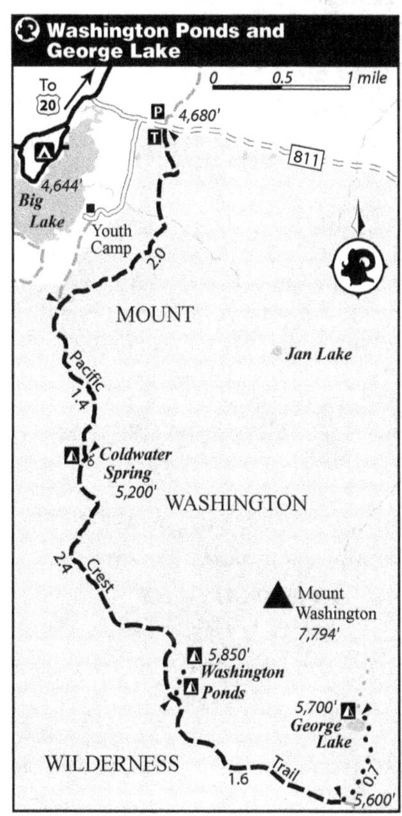

For better scenery and better camping options, continue on the PCT as it gains elevation and at 5 miles crosses the rocky south side of an open ridge. Here you are greeted with the first really good views of the trip. Especially impressive are the vistas to the south over the huge McKenzie lava flows to Belknap Crater, the Three Sisters, and distant Diamond Peak. The hiking is now delightful, as the trail soon leaves the rocky slope and rounds a little basin that features an open forest of mountain hemlocks and subalpine firs and a cinder-covered meadow with outstanding views up to the jagged spire of nearby Mount Washington. About 0.2 mile beyond the end of the meadow is a normally dry gully. Look carefully here for an

Mount Washington towers over Lower Washington Pond. *photo by Douglas Lorain*

unsigned and hard-to-locate route that goes left (north-northeast) about 250 yards to shallow Lower Washington Pond. This pond has a decent view of the top third of Mount Washington and a pleasant camp on flat ground above its west shore. Locating more attractive Upper Washington Pond requires a bit of exploring, as the trail to it is sketchy and often disappears. To find it, go north then northeast up a steep little slope about 0.2 mile, and look for the small basin holding the pond. There is a nice campsite above the northwest shore. Both of the Washington Ponds are more attractive in early summer when the water is high and fresh from new snowmelt.

The hike's best camps and water, however, are at George Lake. To find this lake, continue south on the PCT, descending gradually through forest 1.6 miles, and then leave the trail about 0.4 mile before you round the end of a large lava flow. The route is cross-country, but you may see a faint tread in places or pick out a few orange flags to guide you along the way. The best way to find the lake is to go very gradually uphill, heading north-northeast over a forested ridge until you see the shimmering lake in the basin to the north. Drop down to its welcome waters, and set up camp above the northeast shore. The lake has excellent and reliable water and is fine for swimming. It also features a superb view of the towering summit spire of Mount Washington. For an even better view, scramble to the top of a ridge about 0.4 mile north of George Lake, where you gain a terrific perspective on the impressive east face of Mount Washington.

58 Cache Creek

RATINGS Scenery **7** Difficulty **5** Solitude **9**

ROUND-TRIP DISTANCE 5.5 miles

ELEVATION GAIN 900'

OPTIONAL MAP USGS *Mount Washington*

USUALLY OPEN Late June–October

BEST TIME July

AGENCY Sisters Ranger District (Deschutes National Forest), 541-549-7700, fs.usda.gov/recarea/deschutes/recarea/?recid=81781

PERMIT Required; free at the trailhead

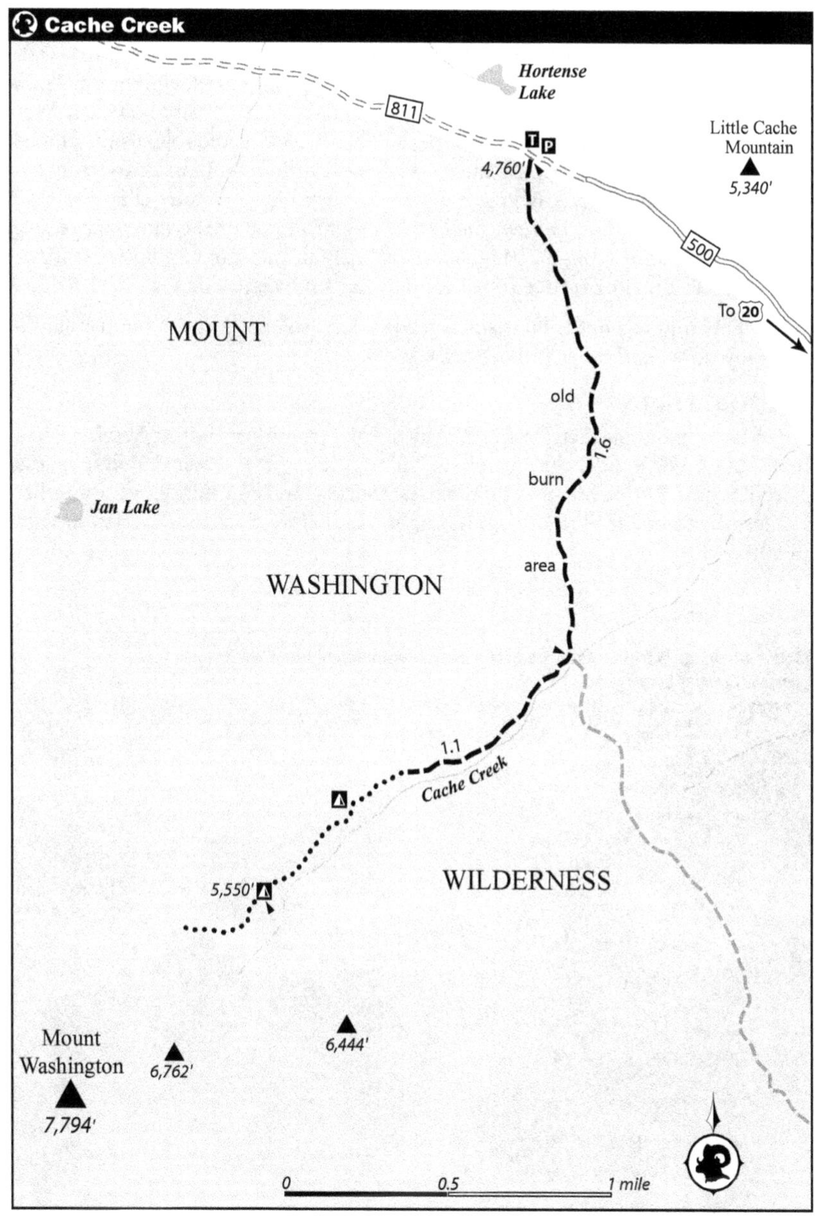
Cache Creek
Hortense Lake
811
4,760'
Little Cache Mountain
5,340'
500
To 20
MOUNT
old
1.6
burn
Jan Lake
area
WASHINGTON
1.1
Cache Creek
5,550'
WILDERNESS
Mount Washington
7,794'
6,762'
6,444'
0
0.5
1 mile

Highlights

The steep eastern face of Mount Washington is familiar to countless thousands of drivers who have admired the mountain from the popular viewpoint on US 20 above Suttle Lake. Almost none of those camera-toting tourists, however, have attempted to get a closer look at the peak. This is understandable, as no official trail reaches the scenic, sloping meadows beneath the mountain's eastern cliffs. But adventuresome hikers who are willing to seek out a sketchy climber's trail can access this area and be rewarded with a night in one of the most impressive locations in central Oregon. Make this trip early in the summer, however, since Cache Creek (the only source of water) may dry up by late summer.

NOTE This trail has not been maintained in years, so expect to encounter significant blowdown and other trail obstacles.

Getting There

Just west of Santiam Pass on US 20, turn right (south) on Forest Service Road 2690 (Big Lake Road), the turnoff to Hoodoo Ski Area. After 3 miles, take a sharp left onto Old Santiam Wagon Road (FS 811), and continue east for another 3 miles; the signed trailhead is on the right, just before a four-way junction with FS 500 and FS 550.

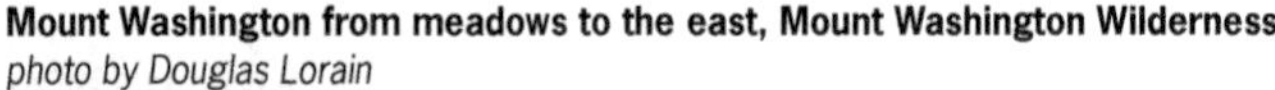
GPS COORDINATES N44° 22.290' W121° 48.408'

Mount Washington from meadows to the east, Mount Washington Wilderness
photo by Douglas Lorain

Hiking It

After obtaining a free permit at the trailhead, hike south on a little-used trail through an open forest of mountain hemlocks, western white pines, and true firs. Unfortunately, the trail soon leaves this shady forest and enters a burn area, where blackened snags despoil the scenery and deadfall often blocks the trail. Expect to make short detours around downed logs or scramble over the deadfall. At 1.6 miles you reenter forest and come to a log crossing of seasonal Cache Creek.

The official trail goes straight, but to find the unmaintained use path up Cache Creek, backtrack about 25 yards and pick up an unsigned trail that goes upstream. This trail has a few old cut logs to help keep you on course, but it is still faint and has some deadfall. Fortunately, the winding path is always just a short distance from Cache Creek, making the tread easy to relocate if lost. The trail is steep at times but is always enjoyable as it follows the cascading little creek.

After a little over 0.7 mile, the country opens up, the trail peters out, and you pass a couple of excellent possible campsites under the shade of some large mountain hemlock trees. More possible campsites are found about 0.4 mile upstream.

To find the best photo spots, keep going west-southwest (uphill) and wander around the trailless terrain north of the creek, passing through several sloping, pumice-covered meadows that provide views of the massive east face of Mount Washington. The rewards for this effort are considerable, with numerous great spots to sit, eat lunch, and enjoy the scenery. Just southeast of the mountain's main summit is a sharp, colorfully striated, unnamed pinnacle that adds to the scenery. Solitude is another bonus, as typically the only other users of this unofficial trail are the few climbers who tackle the difficult east face of Mount Washington.

APPENDIX A

More Short Backpacking Options

Southeastern Olympic Mountains

MILDRED LAKES

Round-trip: 11 miles; 3,000'

Fairly popular but very steep and rough, this boot-beaten path leads to a series of scenic subalpine lakes with fine views of rugged Sawtooth Ridge. The trail is not officially maintained and thus unsuitable for children. Access is from the end of Forest Service Road 25 along the Hamma Hamma River.

Note: For this and all hikes in the Olympics, always call ahead to check road conditions before setting out: 360-565-3131. Also, bear canisters or bear wires for food storage are required in some parts of Olympic National Park; again, check with rangers in advance.

GPS COORDINATES N47° 34.518' W123° 15.672'

EAST FORK LENA CREEK

Round-trip from the Lena Lake Trailhead: 13 miles; 2,400'

An old climbers route (now a maintained trail) branches off from the north end of Lena Lake and ascends a deep valley to scenic camps beneath The Brothers. There are several creek crossings along the way.

GPS COORDINATES N47° 35.982' W123° 09.072'

FLAPJACK LAKES

Round-trip: 15.6 miles; 3,100'

A rather steep trail leads to two pretty and extremely popular lakes in the high country beneath rugged Sawtooth Ridge and Mount Lincoln, with access to the lovely high country around Gladys Divide. Start from Staircase Ranger Station at the north end of Lake Cushman; it is accessed via WA 119, which leaves US 101 at the town of Hoodsport. (A number of excellent trails start from here; ask for recommendations at the ranger station.) A limited-access permit is required from Olympic National Park. Reservations are strongly advised.

GPS COORDINATES N47° 30.950' W123° 19.863'

NORTH FORK SKOKOMISH RIVER TRAIL

Round-trip to the campsite at Nine Stream: 19.2 miles; 1,300' (with shorter and longer options)

This gentle valley walk follows a well-maintained trail through beautiful old-growth forests. The route is fairly crowded and has no views but is pleasant and open for most of the year. The trail also provides access for longer trips to the beautiful alpine meadow at Home Sweet Home and beyond. Start from Staircase Ranger Station at the north end of Lake Cushman; it is accessed via WA 119, which leaves US 101 at the town of Hoodsport. An Olympic National Park permit is required.

GPS COORDINATES N47° 30.950' W123° 19.863'

SOUTH FORK SKOKOMISH RIVER TRAIL

Round-trip to Sundown Lake: 14.2 miles; 3,200' (with many shorter options along the river)

A good trail that traverses magnificent old-growth forest along a pretty stream and past pleasant, kid-friendly camps eventually turns into a rough, steep boot path into the high country. From Shelton, drive 7 miles north on US 101, and then turn left (west) on Skokomish Valley Road, which eventually becomes gravel Forest Service Road 23. After 18 miles veer right on FS 2361 and follow this 5.5 miles to its end. An Olympic National Park permit is required if you go as far as the camp at tiny Sundown Lake.

GPS COORDINATES N47° 28.764' W123° 27.126'

Southern Mount Rainier and the Goat Rocks

BERTHA MAY AND GRANITE LAKES

Round-trip to Granite Lake: 3.3 miles; 750'

The attractions here are two very scenic lakes with fine camps and views of the impressive cliffs on the north side of Sawtooth Ridge. The trail also provides access to a longer trip into Cora Lake. Be prepared to encounter motorcycles, as this entire area is overrun with them. Take WA 706 about 10.1 miles east of its junction with WA 7 in Elbe, then turn south onto paved Forest Service Road 52. After 4.7 miles turn right (south) on gravel FS 84, go 1.5 miles, and then turn right on FS 8410 and drive 3.9 miles to the Tealy Creek Trailhead. Note that you'll need a high-clearance vehicle; the last few miles aren't suitable for passenger cars.

GPS COORDINATES N46° 42.414' W121° 56.220'

KLAPATCHE PARK

Round-trip: 18.5 miles; 3,600'

This famous and breathtakingly beautiful site is located near tiny Aurora Lake in the alpine landscape on Mount Rainier's west face. The trail is prone to washouts, and obtaining a permit for one of the two available campsites is tricky, but the scenery is worth it. The trail starts from the end of the washed-out and permanently closed West Side Road, off WA 7 almost 15 miles east of the junction of WA 7 and WA 706 in Elbe, in the southwest part of Mount Rainier National Park. Hike along the closed road 3 miles, then turn east on the South Puyallup River Trail past the Colonnades, an impressive basalt formation, to a junction with the Wonderland Trail. Turn left (north) and climb past pretty Saint Andrews Lake to Klapatche Park. A Mount Rainier National Park permit is required, and reservations are strongly recommended.

GPS COORDINATES N46° 44.558' W121° 53.960'

CAMP MUIR

Round-trip: 10.5 miles; 4,700'

Perched at 10,100 feet on the south side of Mount Rainier, this climbers camp is exposed to the weather, crowded, and very smelly, but the views seem to extend forever. Considerable snow travel is required (the whole trail is usually under snow until August). Start at famous Paradise Lodge, off Stevens Canyon Road about 20 miles west of WA 123, amid crowds of tourists and acres of flowers before climbing high into the land of rocks and ice. A Mount Rainier National Park permit is required, and reservations are helpful.

GPS COORDINATES N46° 47.160' W121° 44.100'

SNOW LAKE

Round-trip: 2.2 miles; 250'

This small lake in a deep canyon below the pointed summit of Unicorn Peak has no view of the park's namesake attraction, but the gentle access trail passes wildflower meadows and Bench Lake, which features grand reflections of Mount Rainier. A Mount Rainier National Park permit is required, and reservations are recommended. The trail starts off the Stevens Canyon Road about 1.5 miles east of Reflection Lake.

GPS COORDINATES N46° 46.068' W121° 42.456'

JUG AND FRYINGPAN LAKES

Round-trip to Fryingpan Lake: 9.8 miles; 1,600'

These two fairly large and very pretty lakes in the southwestern William O. Douglas Wilderness are very popular with equestrians. Jug Lake is rimmed by a forest, while shallow Fryingpan Lake is in a large meadow. The trail provides access to the PCT and miles of excellent meadow walking, with a possible loop that returns via Penoyer Creek. Expect clouds of mosquitoes in July. From Packwood, go 8.8 miles northeast on US 12, turn left on gravel Forest Service Road 4510, and drive 5 miles to its end at the Soda Springs Campground and Trailhead.

GPS COORDINATES N46° 42.257' W121° 28.914'

BLUE LAKE

Round-trip: 5.2 miles; 1,800'

A steep, hiker-only path follows a creek up a narrow gorge past rock formations and viewpoints to a large and quite scenic lake in an unprotected roadless area south of Mount Rainier. Unfortunately, the lake is also accessible via a separate motorcycle trail, so expect noisy machines at the destination. From Randle, go south on FS 131, drive 1 mile, and then turn left on paved FS 23 (Cispus Road) for 15.2 miles to the trailhead on the left.

GPS COORDINATES N46° 24.450' W121° 44.0350'

MCCALL BASIN VIA THE PACIFIC CREST TRAIL

Round-trip to McCall Basin: 26.8 miles; 4,300'

A very long but scenic high-elevation section of the Pacific Crest Trail south from White Pass leads past meadow-rimmed Shoe Lake to forested Tieton Pass and on to the excellent camps in McCall Basin. The best scenery is another 0.5 mile south along an unofficial trail into spectacular Glacier Basin. This hike is often done as part of a longer point-to-point trip along the PCT through the Goat Rocks Wilderness. Start from the PCT trailhead just east of White Pass along US 12.

GPS COORDINATES N46° 38.8612' W121° 22.730'

Mount Rainier behind Bench Lake on the Snow Lake Trail. *photo by Douglas Lorain*

GLACIER LAKE

Round-trip: 4 miles; 750'

A fairly large lake in the western Goat Rocks Wilderness that is backed by a long, forested ridge is the destination for this nicely shaded hike. The lake is uncrowded and offers good fishing, but the water level tends to recede significantly by midsummer, making it less attractive. Drive 62 miles east on US 12 from I-5, then turn right (south) on good gravel Forest Service Road 21. Go 5.1 miles, then turn left on FS 2110 and drive 0.5 mile on this steep and rocky road to the trailhead on the right.

GPS COORDINATES N46° 32.742' W121° 37.332'

NANNIE RIDGE LOOP

Round-trip for loop: 14.2 miles; 2,000'

This hike in the southern Goat Rocks Wilderness has excellent views and fine wildflower displays. It goes up rugged Nannie Ridge to a junction with the PCT and possible campsites at tiny Sheep Lake. A nice side trip goes north to spectacular Cispus Pass, but the main loop goes south and then returns on a trail down Walupt Creek. Drive 62 miles east on US 12 from I-5, then turn right (south) on good gravel Forest Service Road 21. Go 16 miles, then turn left (east) on one-lane, paved FS 2160 and proceed 4.5 miles to the trailhead beside large and popular Walupt Lake.

GPS COORDINATES N46° 25.386' W121° 28.278'

Mount St. Helens Area

PLAINS OF ABRAHAM

Round-trip as semiloop to camps at south end of Plains of Abraham: 11.8 miles; 1,200'

A wildly scenic trail leads to a spectacular, desolate plain high on the eastern flank of Mount St. Helens. Much of the route crosses the area devastated by the 1980 eruption, so there is almost no shade and no protection from the wind. Trail closures due to volcanic activity are common. The only legal camping is south of the plain near a seasonal creek just outside the devastated area. The trip is better when done as a semiloop with a portion of the Loowit Trail over rugged Windy Pass. Trail starts from the parking lot on Forest Service Road 99 on Windy Ridge.

GPS COORDINATES N46° 14.934' W122° 08.166'

BUTTE CAMP

Round-trip to camp: 4.2 miles; 1,000'

A lovely trail with great views of the south side of Mount St. Helens climbs to a viewless camp below Butte Camp Dome. The trail provides access to great alpine scenery along the Loowit Trail and a less crowded (but longer) route to the top of the mountain than the popular Monitor Ridge route. A reserved permit is required to climb the mountain, but not to stay at the camp. From I-5, take Exit 21 (Woodland) and go 35 miles east on WA 503 and WA 503 Spur to a junction about 6.6 miles past Cougar. Turn left on paved Forest Service Road 83, go 3.1 miles, and then turn left on Forest Service Road 81. Drive 1.4 miles to the trailhead at Redrock Pass. The final mile of the access road is subject to frequent washouts, so check conditions before your visit.

GPS COORDINATES N46° 08.610' W122° 14.106'

SOUTH FORK TOUTLE RIVER

Round-trip by most direct route: 10.4 miles; 2,100'

Permanent road washouts have turned what used to be an easy day hike on the west side of Mount St. Helens into a longer backpacking trip with excellent views along the edge of the devastated area. Drive as to Butte Camp above, but continue past Redrock Pass another 2.3 miles to the junction with Forest Service Road 8123, which is now closed. Walk up the road 1.7 miles, then follow Blue Lake Trail to a campsite on a clear creek a little before you reach the stark canyon of silt-laden South Fork Toutle River. The trip can also be done as a long, rugged loop trip from Butte Camp using a portion of the Loowit Trail to complete the loop.

GPS COORDINATES
N46° 08.850' W122° 16.546'

Find a creekside camp along the trail to South Fork Toutle River. *photo by Paul Gerald*

JUNE LAKE

Round-trip: 2.8 miles; 450'

This popular and easy hike on the forested south side of Mount St. Helens takes you to an interesting lake created by a mudflow, with a scenic waterfall that drops almost directly into the lake. From I-5, take Exit 21 (Woodland), and go 35 miles east on WA 503 and WA 503 Spur to a junction about 6.6 miles past Cougar. Turn left on paved Forest Service Road 83 and proceed about 7 miles to the signed trailhead.

GPS COORDINATES N46° 08.238' W122° 09.414'

BADGER LAKE

Round-trip to lake: 8.8 miles; 1,000'

Tiny but pretty Badger Lake sits in a meadowy basin along the Boundary Trail east of Mount St. Helens. From the lake, a side trail leads 0.9 mile to outstanding views from the old lookout site atop Badger Peak. Sadly, the trails here are a playground for noisy, erosion-causing motorcycles, so be prepared to put up with machines. From the Pine Creek Information Center in Northwoods, go north on 21.4 miles on Forest Service Road 25 to the signed trailhead at Elk Pass.

GPS COORDINATES N46° 17.358' W121° 58.109'

Mount Adams and Indian Heaven

LOOKINGGLASS LAKE

Round-trip: 8.2 miles; 1,450'

A pleasant ridge walk leads to a small lake in the southwestern Mount Adams Wilderness with nice camps and a partial view of the peak. Nearby Madcat Meadow features lots of flowers and better mountain views. From Trout Lake, drive north 1.3 miles and veer left onto Forest Service Road 23. Stay on FS 23 for 7.7 miles, then turn right on gravel FS 8031 (which becomes FS 070 after 0.4 mile) and drive 3.5 miles. Turn right on FS 120 and proceed 0.8 mile to the trailhead in an old clear-cut.

GPS COORDINATES N46° 08.424' W121° 35.867'

PLACID LAKE

Round-trip: 1.6 miles; 100'

A short and nearly level trail leads to a tranquil, forest-rimmed lake in the northwestern Indian Heaven Wilderness. The lake is ideal for fishing, swimming, and the quiet contemplation of nature. For more solitude, continue another 0.8 mile to smaller Chenamus Lake. Expect clouds of mosquitoes in July and early August. From Cascade Locks, Oregon, cross the Columbia River on the Bridge of the Gods ($2 toll), and go 6.1 miles east on WA 14. Turn left, toward the town of Carson; proceed 32.4 miles on Wind River Road and paved Forest Service Road 30; and then turn right on gravel FS 420. Drive 1.2 miles to the signed trailhead.

GPS COORDINATES N46° 02.926' W121° 48.561'

INDIAN RACETRACK

Round-trip for loop: 8.2 miles; 1,700'

A typically lovely meadow and pond in the southern Indian Heaven Wilderness has the added attraction of historical interest, as this was the site of annual horse races by Native Americans until the 1920s. The place can be reached by several trails, but the most interesting is a loop from the south along the Pacific Crest Trail (PCT) that returns via Red Mountain Lookout (views!) and rough dirt Forest Service Road 6048.

Drive as in Trip 23 (page 88) to the four-way junction on FS 65, but turn right (east) on gravel FS 60 and go 2 miles to the PCT crossing.

GPS COORDINATES N45° 54.555' W121° 48.152'

TRAPPER CREEK

Round-trip to lower campsite: 6 miles; 900' (although the best waterfalls are farther upstream)

This heavily forested creek canyon with lots of small waterfalls and old-growth forests is protected as wilderness. The trail is ruggedly up and down, but it is open for most of the year and is a good option for a spring or fall hike. From Cascade Locks, Oregon, cross the Columbia River on the Bridge of the Gods ($2 toll), go 6.1 miles east on WA 14, then turn left and drive 0.9 mile to a junction in the town of Carson. Go straight, proceed 13.6 miles on Wind River Road, and then turn left on Mineral Springs Road. After 0.4 mile you turn right on gravel Forest Service Road 5401 and proceed 0.4 mile to the trailhead.

GPS COORDINATES N45° 52.902' W121° 59.016'

A steep path takes you up to scenic Blue Lake. *photo by Douglas Lorain*

Oregon Coast and Coast Range

BLOOM LAKE

Round-trip: 2.7 miles; 450'

This relatively new and very convenient trail leads to a small lake with cutthroat-trout fishing, beaver activity, pretty forests, and scenic skunk cabbage bogs. The trailhead is at a large road pullout near milepost 24.5 on the south side of US 26.

GPS COORDINATES N45° 50.278' W123° 30.828'

CENTRAL GALES CREEK TRAIL

Round-trip to best camping area: 9 miles; 500'

Enjoy a lovely and uncrowded creekside ramble along the upper reaches of Gales Creek amid lush Coast Range forest. The trail passes a couple of small waterfalls on side streams and offers the chance to see elk. Only mediocre camps are available, so you have to improvise a bit. Start from Gales Creek Campground just off OR 6 near milepost 35.

GPS COORDINATES N45° 38.577' W123° 21.590'

Columbia River Gorge

PACIFIC COAST TRAIL SOUTH PAST TABLE MOUNTAIN

One-way: 16.4 miles; 1,500' (with lots of downhill)

Best done as a point-to-point, mostly downhill adventure, this route starts at the remote Three-Corner Rock Trailhead and follows the Pacific Crest Trail (PCT) along a magnificently scenic ridgeline (with one wildly scenic campsite) before descending to the Columbia River. The only water on the ridge is from a small spring that stops flowing around midsummer. May and June offer the best flower show. The lower (southwest) end of the trail was closed for logging as of this writing. To reach the upper trailhead, start from Washougal along WA 14 east of Vancouver, and go 17.8 miles north and east on paved Washougal River Road. Turn right on gravel Forest Service Road W2000 and drive 10.6 miles to a junction at Rock Creek Pass; take the second right and go 0.3 mile on a rocky road to the PCT crossing.

GPS COORDINATES N45° 44.956' W122° 02.595'

GILLETTE LAKE

Round-trip: 5 miles; 450'

A low-elevation section of the PCT travels over a mostly forested, up-and-down landscape to an unspectacular but pleasant lake that is accessible nearly all year. You can continue the hike another 1.3 miles to a nice viewpoint at Greenleaf Overlook. The well-signed trailhead is about 2 miles east of the town of North Bonneville along WA 14.

GPS COORDINATES N45° 39.030' W121° 55.986'

MULTNOMAH BASIN LOOP

Round-trip for loop: 11.3 miles; 2,950'

A scenic area of old-growth forest with a lovely meadow is found in the old glacial cirque on the north side of Larch Mountain. The most scenic approach is from Multnomah Falls on I-84, 3.3 miles east of Bridal Veil, Oregon, with a hike past a string of waterfalls on Multnomah Creek. The trip is better if done as a loop with the view-packed Franklin Ridge Trail.

GPS COORDINATES N45° 34.657' W122° 07.020'

BENSON PLATEAU

Round-trip to best campsite at the headwaters of Ruckel Creek: 16 miles; 4,150'

The goal is a remarkably flat forested plateau with lots of exploring and fine views of the peaks and canyons of the Columbia River Gorge. Getting there, unfortunately, requires a long, tough climb by any of several trails. The gentlest approach is via the Pacific Crest Trail from the north, which includes one excellent viewpoint along the way. The trail starts from the well-marked Herman Creek Trailhead off I-84, 2.5 miles east of Cascade Locks.

GPS COORDINATES N45° 40.968' W121° 50.549'

Mount Hood Area

DEVILS PEAK LOOKOUT

Round-trip: 8 miles; 3,200'

A long, tough, woodsy climb eventually leads to a grand viewpoint of Mount Hood and an old lookout building that is available for overnight use on a first-come, first-serve basis. A nearby spring provides water. Drive US 26 1.4 miles east of Zigzag, turn right on paved Still Creek Road, and right again after 0.3 mile at a confusing fork. Continue on pavement and good gravel another 3.1 miles to the obscure Cool Creek Trailhead.

GPS COORDINATES N45° 17.834' W121° 53.009'

You can also reach the lookout via a much shorter trail from Kinzel Lake, but the access road is atrocious.

MIRROR LAKE

Round-trip: 3.2 miles; 700'

With a lovely lake with postcard-perfect views of Mount Hood as its destination, this trail is extremely popular, so be prepared for plenty of company. It starts from a pullout off US 26 near milepost 52, just west of Government Camp.

GPS COORDINATES N45° 18.156' W121° 46.620'

WIND LAKE

Round-trip: 6.4 miles; 1,400'

Wind Lake is a shallow, forest-rimmed, and uncrowded lake on the south side of Tom Dick Mountain south of Mount Hood. To reach it, start from the huge Ski Bowl West parking lot of US 26 just west of Government Camp, follow rocky jeep

The biggest challenge at Mirror Lake is finding a parking spot at the trailhead.
photo by Paul Gerald

roads and unsigned trails to the ridge at the top of the ski runs, and then hike west to the lake. Fishing is poor due to the shallowness of the lake.

GPS COORDINATES N45° 18.167' W121° 46.634'

Clackamas River Country

CLACKAMAS RIVER TRAIL

Round-trip to the best campsite: 9.4 miles; 300' (with shorter and longer options)

Pass spectacular Pup Creek Falls on this lovely hike along the clear Clackamas River. The trail is open nearly all year but is immediately across the river from a highway, so the hike is not secluded. Drive 15 miles southeast of Estacada on OR 224, turn right on Forest Service Road 4620 (signs to Indian Henry Campground), and soon reach the developed trailhead on the other side of a large bridge.

GPS COORDINATES N45° 06.544' W122° 04.569'

SKOOKUM LAKE

Round-trip: 6.2 miles; 1,600'

Once popular but now rarely visited after floods permanently closed the nearest roads, this tiny, forest-rimmed lake features a fine campsite, solitude, and very good fishing. It is now accessed by a scenic but hard-to-find trail that climbs over the shoulder of Thunder Mountain (good views) then switchbacks down to the lake. From Estacada go southeast 29.5 miles on OR 224; turn right on Forest Service Road 63. Drive 3.4 miles, then turn right on FS 6320. Go 0.8 mile, then turn sharply right on gravel FS 6322. Drive 6 miles, then go straight on FS 4620. Drive 3.1 miles to the unsigned trailhead on the right.

GPS COORDINATES N44° 59.354' W122° 09.327'

SILVER KING LAKE

Round-trip: 10.8 miles; 1,900'

You'll find a pretty little woodsy lake at the end of this scenic hike along Whetstone Ridge in the western Bull of the Woods Wilderness. The ridge features some nice vistas, although the lake is viewless. From Estacada go southeast 29.5 miles on OR 224, and turn right on Forest Service Road 63. Drive 3.6 miles, then turn right on FS 70. Drive 9 miles, then fork right onto gravel FS 7030. Drive 5.2 miles, then turn right on a spur road to the trailhead.

GPS COORDINATES N44° 52.526' W122° 12.148'

WELCOME LAKES

Round-trip: 9 miles; 1,900'

A gentle woods walk passes a waterfall on Elk Lake Creek, then makes a tough climb up to two small lakes in the Bull of the Woods Wilderness. The lower lake is prettier, but the upper lake has better campsites. Follow directions for Trip 49 (page 171), but instead of turning on Forest Service Road 6340, go straight to stay on FS 63 for 6.8 miles past several intersections to a fork at the end of the pavement. Go right on FS 6380 and drive 0.4 miles to the Elk Lake Creek Trailhead.

GPS COORDINATES N44° 53.580' W122° 00.445'

BUTTE LAKES

Round-trip: 1.8 miles; 200'

A short and easy trail in the Santiam State Forest southeast of Silverton provides access to a group of small but attractive lakes. The gravel and dirt access road is long, complicated, and unsigned, so few people make the effort. The lakes provide pretty scenery and nice swimming. Start from Scotts Mills on OR 213 with a good map (the best is *Salem District—Eastside* by the Bureau of Land Management) and a sense of adventure, then head southeast on Crooked Finger Road. It's about 25 miles to the blocked road at the unsigned trailhead on the right; you can get a trail map online or from the Santiam State Forest office (503-859-2151).

GPS COORDINATES N44° 53.537' W122° 23.335'

Mount Jefferson and Vicinity

OPAL CREEK

Round-trip to camps at Cedar Flats: 10 miles; 550'

Magnificent old-growth forest and a wonderfully clear stream highlight this relatively easy hike in the Cascade Mountains east of Salem. Other noteworthy features include Jawbone Flats, an old mining settlement now used as a nature learning center, and several waterfalls. The trail follows a jeep road into Jawbone

Flats, and then an up-and-down trail south along gorgeous Opal Creek. From Salem, drive 22 miles east on OR 22 to Mehama, then turn left on Little North Fork Road (which eventually becomes Forest Service Road 2207) and go 15.5 miles to the end of the pavement. Continue on bumpy gravel FS 2209 for 5.6 miles to the trailhead, where the road is gated.

GPS COORDINATES N44° 51.582' W122° 15.940'

OPAL LAKE

Round-trip: 1.2 miles; 350'

Discover a deep, meadow-and-forest-rimmed lake at the end of a downhill trail in a remote area north of Detroit Reservoir. The lake has no views, and the access trail can be steep and muddy, but there is plenty of solitude and nice fishing for brook trout. From Salem, drive 50 miles east on OR 22 to a junction just before the bridge near Detroit. Turn left (north) here on one-lane, paved French Creek Road (Forest Service Road 2233), go 4.2 miles, and then turn right on gravel FS 2207. Follow this narrow road 5.9 miles to the trailhead.

GPS COORDINATES N44° 47.368' W122° 13.640'

MARION LAKE

Round-trip: 6 miles; 800'

A gentle, uphill trail in the southern Mount Jefferson Wilderness past lovely Lake Ann and a pretty waterfall takes you up to huge Marion Lake. The trip has been a favorite for generations of outdoors lovers. Sadly, this area was badly burned in the 2003 B&B Complex fire, and one side of the lake is still mostly a shadeless sea of blackened snags, though green undergrowth and wildflowers are thriving. Expect lots of mosquitoes in July. From Salem, drive 65 miles east on OR 22 to Marion Forks, turn left (east) on Marion Creek Road (Forest Service Road 2255), and go 5.5 miles to the road-end trailhead.

GPS COORDINATES N44° 34.612' W121° 53.659'

PARISH LAKE

Round-trip: 1 mile; 250'

An easy hike into a small, forest-rimmed lake in the Western Cascades offers decent views of the nearby Three Pyramids. The lake is rarely crowded and has good fishing for brook trout. From Salem, drive 76 miles east on OR 22, turn right (west) on initially paved then gravel Forest Service Road 2266, and continue 5 miles to the trailhead.

GPS COORDINATES N44° 32.084' W122° 04.401'

GORDON LAKES

Round-trip: 0.8 mile; 175'

A short and easy downhill stroll takes you to a pair of scenic little lakes beneath the impressive cliffs of Soapgrass Mountain in the Western Cascades. The area is little known and rarely visited. The nearby meadows are great for wildflowers from late June through mid-July, while the lakes offer fine swimming and decent fishing for cutthroat trout. From Salem, take I-5 south to Exit 233 (Albany), and then take US 20 east to a junction 28 miles past Sweet Home. At a sign for House Rock Campground, turn right (south) on gravel Forest Service Road 2044. Drive 5.5 miles, turn right on FS 230, and drive 2.6 miles to the road-end trailhead.

GPS COORDINATES N44° 21.339' W122° 15.612'

PATJENS LAKES

Round-trip for loop: 6.1 miles; 450'

This very popular loop trail passes a string of pretty lakes in the northern Mount Washington Wilderness. Campsites are only mediocre, but the views of Mount Washington, especially over Middle Patjens Lake, are excellent. Expect lots of day hikers, mosquitoes in July, and thousands of frogs. From Salem, drive 89 miles east on OR 22 and US 20 to a junction just before Santiam Pass. Turn south on Big Lake Road and drive 4 miles, staying on the main paved road, past Hoodoo Ski Area and Big Lake Campground, to the trailhead on the right.

GPS COORDINATES N44° 22.647' W121° 52.842'

ROCKPILE LAKE

Round-trip: 11.8 miles; 1,400'

This pretty but fishless little lake sits along the Pacific Crest Trail (PCT) north of Three Fingered Jack. The basin immediately around it was not damaged in the 2003 B&B Complex fire, but much of the access trail was badly scorched. The lake can be reached either by a little-traveled loop trail from the east (**GPS COORDINATES N43° 29.013 W122° 10.611'**) or along the PCT past Wasco Lake from the south. The southern approach has better views of Three Fingered Jack and somewhat less fire damage. For the southern approach, start from Santiam Pass, go east 7.6 miles on US 20, then turn left on paved Jack Lake Road (Forest Service Road 12). Follow this road 4.4 miles, turn left on FS 1230, and go 1.8 miles. Turn left on gravel FS 1234 and proceed 5 miles to the Jack Lake Trailhead.

GPS COORDINATES N44° 29.590' W121° 47.648'

The hike to Marion Lake shows a forest recovering from wildfire.

APPENDIX B

Recommended Reading

Even the briefest glance at the outdoors section of any local bookstore shows that there is a lot of interest from the reading public in the Pacific Northwest. It is also clear that owning all of the available volumes would be overkill. Here are some of the authors' favorites to help you build your own outdoors library.

This book is designed for those seeking shorter, one-night backpacking trips. If you prefer day hiking, two of the best guides for the Portland area are *60 Hikes Within 60 Miles: Portland* (Menasha Ridge Press, 2018), which covers many of the best hiking trails within about an hour's drive of the city, and *100 Hikes in Northwest Oregon* by William L. Sullivan (Navillus Press, 2013), which includes hand-drawn maps of many fine trails within a 2-hour drive of the city.

Once you have moved beyond the weekend trip and want to tackle a longer backpacking adventure, pick up *Backpacking Oregon* (2019), *Backpacking Washington* (2020), and *Backpacking Idaho* (2015; all Wilderness Press), which detail the best 3- to 10-day backpacking vacations in every corner of their respective states.

For proof that the benefits of taking your kids hiking considerably outweigh the extra time and effort involved, read *Last Child in the Woods: Saving Our Children from Nature-Deficit Disorder* by Richard Louv (Algonquin Books, 2008). It should be required reading for every American parent. For more on the how-to side of things for outdoor travel with children, two good resources are *50 Hikes with Kids: Oregon and Washington* by Wendy Gorton (Timber Press, 2018) and *Hiking and Backpacking with Kids* from *Backpacker* magazine (Falcon Guides, 2012). You might also consider picking up a copy of a fun little book designed for evening entertainment titled *Spooky Campfire Tales* by S. E. Schlosser (Globe Pequot Press, 2007).

Some of the better books on the various aspects of backpacking are *Backpacker* magazine's *Everyday Wisdom* series, which covers a wide range of topics with hundreds of useful tips from outdoors experts. *Leave No Trace: A Guide to New Wilderness Etiquette* (Mountaineers Books, 2003) is particularly useful. An excellent single-volume guide for the sport of backpacking is *The Backpacker's Field Manual: A Comprehensive Guide to Mastering Backcountry Skills* by Rick Curtis (Three Rivers Press, 2005).

Two classic tomes that cover the topic even more thoroughly are *The Complete Walker IV* by Colin Fletcher and Chip Rawlins (Alfred A. Knopf, 2002) and *Mountaineering: The Freedom of the Hills* (Mountaineers Books, 2017).

Three other good books you might consider are *The Ultralight Backpacker* by Ryel Kestenbaum (McGraw-Hill Professional, 2001), which goes a bit overboard, in my opinion, on the ultralight craze but still has lots of good ideas; *Basic Essentials: Wilderness First Aid* by William Forgey, MD (Falcon, 2007); and *Mountain Weather: Backcountry Forecasting and Weather Safety for Hikers, Campers, Climbers, Skiers, and Snowboarders* by Jeff Renner (Mountaineers Books, 2005).

There are a number of excellent books for hikers interested in the natural history of the Pacific Northwest. The best local wildflower guide for amateurs

The Clackamas River Trail makes its leisurely way through old-growth forest.

is *Wildflowers of the Pacific Northwest* by Mark Turner and Phyllis Gustafson (Timber Press, 2006). If you are interested in birds, the best general guide is The National Geographic Society's *Field Guide to the Birds of North America* (National Geographic, 2017). A particularly fun and interesting little book on our avian friends is *Why Don't Woodpeckers Get Headaches?: And Other Bird Questions You Know You Want to Ask* by Mike O'Conner (Beacon Press, 2007). Two useful (if ancient) books for those interested in edible plants are *Field Guide to Edible Wild Plants* by Bradford Angier (Stackpole Books, 1974) and *Northwest Foraging* by Doug Benoliel (Signpost Books, 1974). The best one-volume general natural history guide to our area, which covers all of the most common trees, shrubs, mammals, amphibians, and reptiles, is *The Audubon Society Nature Guide: Western Forests* (Alfred A. Knopf, 1990). Lastly, for hikers interested in the geology of the Cascade Mountains, a copy of *Fire & Ice: The Cascade Volcanoes* by Stephen L. Harris (Harcourt, 1987) is a must.

For general entertainment on the trail, every hiker should read *A Walk in the Woods* by Bill Bryson (Broadway, 1999). Not reading this book is a disservice to your funny bone.

APPENDIX C

Conservation Organizations and Outdoors Clubs

FRIENDS OF THE COLUMBIA GORGE
gorgefriends.org
503-241-3762

THE MAZAMAS
mazamas.org
503-227-2345

OREGON CHAPTER SIERRA CLUB
oregon.sierraclub.org
503-238-0442

THE NATURE CONSERVANCY OF OREGON
tinyurl.com/thenatureconservancyoregon
503-802-8100

PORTLAND AUDUBON SOCIETY
audubonportland.org
503-292-6855

TRAILS CLUB OF OREGON
trailsclub.org

APPENDIX D

Land Agencies and Information Sources

BUREAU OF LAND MANAGEMENT SALEM DISTRICT
blm.gov/office/northwest-oregon-district-office
1717 Fabry Road SE
Salem, OR 97306; 503-375-5646

CLATSOP STATE FOREST
oregon.gov/odf
92219 OR 202
Astoria, OR 97103; 503-325-5451

COLUMBIA RIVER GORGE NATIONAL SCENIC AREA
fs.usda.gov/crgnsa

Oregon Department of Forestry
902 Wasco Ave., Ste. 200
Hood River, OR 97031
541-308-1700

DESCHUTES NATIONAL FOREST
fs.usda.gov/deschutes
63095 Deschutes Market Road
Bend, OR 97701; 541-383-5300

DESCHUTES RIVER STATE RECREATION AREA
oregonstateparks.org
Biggs–Rufus Hwy.
Wasco, OR 97065; 541-739-2322

ECOLA STATE PARK AND OSWALD WEST STATE PARK
Both managed by Nehalem Bay S.P.
oregonstateparks.org
34600 Gary St.
Nehalem, OR 97131; 503-368-5154

GIFFORD PINCHOT NATIONAL FOREST
fs.usda.gov/giffordpinchot

Cowlitz Valley Ranger District
10024 US 12
Randle, WA 98377; 360-497-1100

Mount Adams Ranger District
2455 WA 141
Trout Lake, WA 98650
509-395-3400

MOUNT HOOD NATIONAL FOREST
fs.usda.gov/mthood

Barlow Ranger District
780 NE Court St.
Dufur, OR 97021; 541-467-2291

Clackamas River Ranger District
595 NW Industrial Way
Estacada, OR 97023
503-630-6861

Hood River Ranger District
6780 OR 35
Parkdale, OR 97041
541-352-6002

Zigzag Ranger District
70220 E. OR 26
Zigzag, OR 97049; 503-622-3191

MOUNT RAINIER NATIONAL PARK WILDERNESS INFORMATION CENTER
nps.gov/mora
55210 238th Ave. E.
Ashford, WA 98304; 360-569-2211

MOUNT ST. HELENS NATIONAL VOLCANIC MONUMENT
fs.usda.gov/giffordpinchot
42218 NE Yale Bridge Road
Amboy, WA 98601
360-449-7800

OKANOGAN-WENATCHEE NATIONAL FOREST
fs.usda.gov/okawen

Naches Ranger District
10237 WA 12
Naches, WA 98937
509-653-1401

OLYMPIC NATIONAL FOREST
fs.usda.gov/olympic

Hood Canal Ranger District
295142 WA 101 S.
Quilcene, WA 98376
360-765-2200

OLYMPIC NATIONAL PARK
nps.gov/olym
Visitor Center
3002 Mount Angeles Road
Port Angeles, WA 98362
360-565-3130

OREGON STATE PARKS
oregonstateparks.org
725 Summer St. NE, Ste. C
Salem, OR 97301;800-551-6949

TILLAMOOK STATE FOREST, FOREST GROVE DISTRICT OFFICE
oregon.gov
801 Gales Creek Road
Forest Grove, OR 97116
503-357-2191

WILLAMETTE NATIONAL FOREST
fs.usda.gov/willamette

Detroit Ranger District
44125 N. Santiam Hwy. SE
Detroit, OR 97342
503-854-3366

McKenzie River Ranger District
57600 McKenzie Hwy.
McKenzie Bridge, OR 97413
541-822-3381

YAKAMA NATION
yakamanation-nsn.gov
Department of Natural Resources
PO Box 151
Toppenish, WA 98948
509-865-5121, ext. 4648

Index

D

E

F

G

H

U

V

W

Y

Z

About the Authors

BECKY OHLSEN has lived and hiked in the Pacific Northwest since 1995. She's the author of *Walking Portland* and the coauthor of *Backpacking Oregon* and *Best Tent Camping: Oregon*. She also writes travel guides for Lonely Planet, covering Scandinavia and the Pacific Northwest. Becky likes discovering mountain lakes and wandering along riverside trails, but alpine meadows are her favorite.

Photo by Becky Lovejoy

DOUGLAS LORAIN's family moved to the Pacific Northwest in 1969, and he has been obsessively hitting the trails of his home region ever since. With the good fortune to grow up in an outdoor-oriented family, he has vivid memories of countless camping, biking, bird-watching, and other trips in every corner of this spectacular area. He calculates that over the years he has logged well over 30,000 trail miles in this corner of the continent, and despite a history that includes being bitten by a rattlesnake, shot at by a hunter, charged by grizzly bears (twice!), and donating countless gallons of blood to "invertebrate vampires," he happily sees no end in sight.

Douglas is a photographer and recipient of the National Outdoor Book Award. His books cover only the best trips from the thousands of hikes and backpacking trips he has taken throughout Oregon, Washington, and Idaho. His photographs have been featured in numerous magazines, calendars, and books, and his other guidebook titles include *100 Classic Hikes in Oregon, Backpacking Idaho, Backpacking Oregon, Backpacking Washington,* and *Afoot & Afield Portland/Vancouver.*

Although he considers his real home to be on the trail, those few days he is forced to spend indoors, he now lives in Hamilton, Montana, with his wife, Becky Lovejoy.